The Young Entrepreneur's Edge

THE PRINCETON REVIEW

The Young Entrepreneur's Edge

Using Your Ambition, Independence, and Youth to Launch a Successful Business

Jennifer Kushell

Young Entrepreneurs Network

www.yenetwork.com

Random House, Inc.

New York, 1999

www.youngandsuccessful.com

Princeton Review Publishing, L.L.C.
2315 Broadway
New York, NY 10024

The **Young Entrepreneur's Edge** is a revised edition of a book published in 1997 under the title **No Experience Necessary.**

The material in Chapter 6 has been summarized with the permission of the Adizes Institute in Los Angeles, CA. The writing and teachings of Dr. Ichak Adizes can be found in **Corporate Lifecycles: How and Why Corporations Grow and Die and What To Do About It.**

Library of Congress Cataloging-in-Publication Data

Kushell, Jennifer.
  The young entrepreneur's edge : using your ambition,
  independence, and youth to launch a successful business /
  Jennifer Kushell.—1st ed.
      p.   cm.
  At head of title: The Princeton review.
  Includes bibliographical references and index.
  ISBN 0-375-75349-4 pb
  1. New business enterprises—United States.
  2. Entrepreneurship. 3. Generation X—Employment—United
  States.   4. College graduates—Employment—United States.
  5. College students—Employment—United States. I. Princeton
  Review (Firm) II. Title.
  HD62.5.K877   1999
  658.1'141—dc21   99-11523
                                      CIP

Editor: Bonnie Szymanski
Designer: Beth Oberholtzer
Production Coordinator: Vicky Dawes
Pagination: Anne DeLozier

9 8 7 6 5 4 3

This book is dedicated to:

The Franchise Consulting Group
Trademark & Technology
Joan Hansen & Company
Kushell Associates
Franchise Search

and their founders:

Dad
Mom
Aunt Joan, Cousin Scott, Nana & Uncle Rick
Uncle Bob & Aunt Natalie
Cousin Doug (Karen & little Zach, too!)

Thank you for letting your little girl play house
in your companies so she could one day grow
up to build her very own.

Acknowledgments

Before I acknowledge anyone else, I have to offer my heart, my soul, and all my love to the person who makes me the happiest I've ever been. Scott—I don't know where you came from, or how we found each other, but every day I am so thankful for your being in my life. Because of you I finally found that balance and what lies beyond work. You have made me a better person, and a much stronger entrepreneur. Thank you.

To my family, particularly my father and mother, for being my biggest fans and inspiration. To my little brother David, who has grown into such an impressive man over the past few years. To my favorite cousins Doug and Scott for being just like brothers, in addition to being my closest friends. To my grandmother (and of course, Ricky) for telling everyone with such pride that her granddaughter is an author. And to my Uncle Bob, who taught me everything I know (wink wink). You and Natalie (and the rest of your side) have always anchored me, and I'll never forget it.

To my mentors and dear friends who have been there for me and my business(es) from the beginning—John Katzman, Steve Mariotti, and Rieva Lesonsky. Your support, encouragement, advice, and guidance have been invaluable to me. Kathy Allen and Ken Gronbach—you've more recently helped me to make some of the toughest decisions of my life, and I couldn't be happier today because of them. Thank you.

To Julie Joncas, my friend of many years, my vice president, my "boss," my anchor, and my daily reality check. Being an entrepreneur wouldn't be as rewarding without you. I hope everyone reading this can find someone like you to share the experience with. And I still firmly believe that Harvard Business School is lucky to have *you*. I certainly have been.

From Boston University, my alma mater (finally), I must thank Candy Brush for being there for me and this book project, from the very first twelve-page draft I did as a junior to the final manuscript over two years later. Special thanks also go to Wendy Greenfield, Rajiv Dant, Bob Cohn, and Jules Schwartz for more reasons than I could ever begin to account for.

From the very early days of IDYE and on through today: Thank you to Ben Kyan for never *really* letting go. And to David Meadows—thanks for thinking of me. To Jolina, Vic, and Elisabeth for sticking it out as my first interns out in the "Allston office," i.e., "International Headquarters" to everyone else. To Danny Essner for managing some of our most critical projects so beautifully. Thank you to Jaynell Greyson and Kathleen Jeanty for always being there. And everyone on our staff today (and in the future) for believing in The Young Entrepreneurs Network and our mission.

To the Isaacsons and Kaufmans for being my second families.

And just because, I'd like to thank Ray Sozzi, Jennifer Iannolo, Eddie Soleymani, Larry Angrisani, Jacqui Brandwynne, Ted "Austin" Tyson, Margaret Dunn, everyone at NFTE, my brother David, and Lee Isaacson, who's been my best friend even when I haven't deserved one. To Alan Ezier and Curtis Estes for teaching me everything I ever needed to know about networking. And many, many thanks to Sheri Sigler for her friendship, continuous support, and help in getting a few different balls rolling . . . including this one!

Lastly, my most sincere thanks go to Rob Kaplan, probably the greatest editor a writer could dream of working with. I can't tell you how much of a pleasure it has been working with someone who *truly* understands what this book means. To everyone at Random House: Peter DeGiglio and Kathy Schneider for the revival and for putting so much into this release; Tom Russell for being there whenever I needed absolutely anything; Jeanne Krier for all the great clips and even better chats; Mary Beth Roche and Will Weiser for their enthusiasm (can't wait to work a lot more with you!); and to Fernando Guillano and Joy Ravin for always trying to make me look my best.

To Daniel Greenberg, my literary agent, for his perfect timing and charisma. And to John and his friend Greer for helping me find you.

To John Katzman, who made this book possible in the first place by starting The Princeton Review himself when he was in college, for recognizing how important it was to publish a book like this, and for entrusting me to write it. Thank you for being my inspiration.

And to all of the young entrepreneurs out there dreaming, building, and succeeding in their own businesses. You're not alone anymore.

Contents

Acknowledgments   vii

Foreword   xv

Preface   xvii

PART ONE   **Introduction to Entrepreneurship**   1

Chapter 1   The Entrepreneurial Decision   3

                Why Take the Entrepreneurial Route?   5

                The Young Entrepreneur's Advantage . . .   9

                . . . And Disadvantages   12

                Combating the Generation X Stigma   21

                Breeding a New Generation of Entrepreneurs   23

                Taking a Personal Inventory and Assessing Your Current Resources   26

PART TWO   **Planning: The Key to Success**   29

Chapter 2   Your "Big Idea"   31

                Separating the Good from the Bad Ideas   32

                The Hottest Businesses for Young Entrepreneurs   34

                Selecting the Right Business Idea   36

                Are You and Your Business Compatible?   43

	Goal Setting and Strategic Planning	44
	Marketing Research	44
	How to Find Industry Information	46
	Resources	49
Chapter 3	**The Big Bad Business Plan**	51
	Do You Really Need One?	51
	The Business Plan	55
	Finishing Touches	63
	Resources	63

PART THREE   Launching Your Business   **65**

Chapter 4	**The Basics of Opening a New Company**	67
	Legally Establishing Your Company	67
	Professional Advisers	73
	Business Credit	75
	Doing Everything by the Book	78
Chapter 5	**The Partnership Decision**	83
	Reasons to Consider Partnership	83
	Reasons to Avoid Partnership	84
	Options to Partnership	85
	The Decision	86
	Tying the Knot	89
Chapter 6	**Building a Team**	91
	The Perfect Management Team	92
Chapter 7	**Staffing**	99
	Interns	101
	Independent Contractors	108
	Real Employees	109
Chapter 8	**Raising Money**	111
	Some Basic Rules	112
	How Much Do You Really Need?	114
	Equity or Debt?	116
	Where to Get the Money	117
Chapter 9	**Building Business Relationships**	123
	Organizations and Associations	126
	How to Meet Important People	129
	Mentors and Advisers	133

PART FOUR | **Creating A Professional Image** | **143**

Chapter 10 | The Entrepreneurial Image | 145
Personal Presentation | 146
Physical Appearance | 152
How Old Are You? | 156
Your Image on Paper | 159

Chapter 11 | Publicity, Advertising, and the Internet | 163
Publicity | 165
Advertising | 172
Marketing on the Internet | 176

Chapter 12 | Your Office | 183
Opening Up Shop | 184
Weighing the Pros and Cons | 185
Equipment and Supplies | 189
Telephone Systems | 191
Technology and the Virtual Office | 194
A Few Cheap and Creative Equipment Solutions | 197

PART FIVE | **Insider Information (Tales from the Trenches)** | **199**

Chapter 13 | Coping with Life as an Entrepreneur | 201
Welcome to the Entrepreneurial Life | 202
Dealing with Those Who Don't Support You | 207
Balancing Your Life (AKA: How to Have One) | 210

Conclusion | 219
Resource Guide | 223
Index | 241
About the Author | 249

Foreword

What an honor it is to be asked to write the preface to one of the best books I ever read on entrepreneurship.

The Young Entrepreneur's Edge is, quite simply, a brilliant and fun discussion of the insights and skills necessary to become a successful young entrepreneur. This book should be read by anyone interested in the subject, as the author's unique insights into the marketplace and the exciting world of self-employment are groundbreaking. Her prose is elegant and such an easy read that one feels the transfer of knowledge almost effortlessly.

I first met Jennifer Kushell in 1994, at a young entrepreneur's conference in New York City. She was putting on a presentation for young entrepreneurs about her company, The Young Entrepreneurs Network, which has since become the leading membership organization in the world for young businesspeople (and a must membership for anybody who is anybody in the young entrepreneur community).

I was impressed with Jennifer's presentation style, her personal charisma, and her unique way of explaining the nuances of small business to those who were just starting out. Since that time, she has become a national spokesperson for the young entrepreneurs in America while maintaining a full schedule at Boston University, where she graduated in May 1996. Jennifer Kushell has received numerous awards and recognition, including the Individual Young Entrepreneur Award from the US Association of Business and Entrepreneurship, the Young Entrepreneur of the Year Award from the National Federation of Independent Business, and a $25,000 research grant from the International Franchise Association.

The Young Entrepreneur's Edge, as well as The Young Entrepreneurs Network, are an outgrowth of more than a ten-year career in entrepreneurial activities. Jennifer has extraordinary background insights, as she has been raised by the most entrepreneurial family one can imagine. In her immediate family, five businesses have flourished, with her father and aunt becoming leading experts in the world on franchising and trademark licensing, respectively.

Jennifer had started four businesses of her own even before starting at Boston University and in so many ways personifies the love of business creation that her generation has become known for. This book, with its unique emphasis on the personal skills needed to be successful as an entrepreneur, as well as the unique problems that young entrepreneurs face (relationships with their families, personal appearance, financing, record keeping, networking, mentoring), are treated with enormous insight.

U.S. News & World Report has called Jennifer Kushell the Guru of Generation X's entrepreneurship movement. Not only does she take an active role in her own entrepreneurial efforts and help countless others get their businesses started, she has become a spokesperson for the world of philanthropy as well. As a member of the National Foundation for Teaching Entrepreneurship's Advisory Board, and as a NFTE Certified Teacher, Jennifer has advocated that her peers should not only make money, but also become involved in charitable activities. Previous generations have usually focused on creating wealth but not giving back philanthropically until late in life. So, many opportunities for personal satisfaction and for using business expertise to solve social problems were missed. Part of Jennifer's leadership role is to change this by encouraging philanthropy by Generation X entrepreneurs.

I read this book in three hours and found myself compulsively taking notes on a wide variety of ideas on my own business career and philanthropic endeavors. I think *The Young Entrepreneur's Edge* will make its mark in the important business publications of this decade. I am proud to know Jennifer Kushell and proud to be associated with this book.

Steve Mariotti
President & Founder
National Foundation for Teaching Entrepreneurship

Preface

"You're too young." "Wait until you graduate." "Why don't you just enjoy being your age?" "Don't be in a rush to grow up." "Go spend some time in a major corporation." "What do you know about running a business?" "Who would invest?" "How would you survive?" "Why don't you just get a *real* job?" "You don't have enough experience anyway."

The Young Entrepreneur's Edge started as a backlash to all of those skeptics who said people our age couldn't run a business. Personally, I had heard enough of it, as I was already on my fourth business by the age of 19. So I went around encouraging as many other people as I knew to start their own ventures as well. Rebellion, ambition, and independence—that's what twentysomethings are good at. I would just build my own businesses to show the rest of them how wrong they were. Then the Generation X thing appeared. Slackers, they called us. Misdirected. The blood began to boil then. How could anyone tell us what we were and were not capable of doing? I began to realize that my anger was just part of the problem.

The more I studied about business and entrepreneurial companies, the more I realized that entrepreneurs were not the greedy capitalists that everyone thought they were, but were agents of change. I was amazed at the notion that you could take almost anything that you loved doing, or were good at, and build a business around it. Evidence of this was everywhere. And for people in their teens or twenties, what more could you ask for than to spend your free time doing something that you love and make money at the same time.

From that point I set out on a mission to learn everything and meet every entrepreneur I could. I attended conferences, seminars, read books and magazines, and devoured everything I got my hands on about small business. I met "The (thirtysomething) Lei Man," who imported and sold floral leis from Tahiti; the twenty-four-year-old creator of Safe-T-Man, the 180 lb. dummy; a twenty-one-year-old women's snow boarding apparel manufacturer; a thirteen-year-old computer programmer and retailer; a twenty-three-year-old importer of fish from Fiji; a nineteen-year-old basket weaver in Jamaica; a twenty-seven-year-old music promoter from South Africa; and so on, and so on. Everywhere I turned I seemed to meet more young entrepreneurs. And even those who didn't have their own business yet were certainly thinking about it.

For someone so young, I had had my share of ventures. Starting at thirteen with the very normal string of little side businesses, I had amassed quite a bit of experience. From hand-painted T-shirts, to gift baskets, safety seminars for women, and even video-taped college tours, I searched long and hard to find the right business. Then in college it hit me—my entrepreneurial awakening! I had started events, seminars, and even an organization or two for entrepreneurs on campus when I realized that there had to be something even bigger.

The opportunity presented itself after a conference for college-age entrepreneurs. We were all amazed at how many people like us had shown up and desperately wanted to find a way to maintain regular contact with each other. Then I was approached by two friends about starting a directory for young entrepreneurs, and we were off and running. The business seemed to take forever to get off the ground, and frustration about the pace and lack of revenue caused both of my partners to eventually pursue other ventures. So there I was on my own, struggling to keep a business afloat that I was convinced had enormous potential.

I ran the first Los Angeles office as Marketing Director from my bedroom at my parents' house, then moved to Boston for college, or "to expand the business" (as far as all of my business contacts were concerned). The new Boston office was in the oversized hallway of my first apartment. I set up a desk, a computer, and the fax machine that my father scolded me for buying when I was eighteen. Piles of business magazines lined the walls, and my one filing cabinet began to overflow. The bedroom proved great for extra storage space and my dining room table became a workstation. When I finally convinced people at school to start interning for me, we used my dining room table as the "mail room" and my living room as a conference room for "staff meetings." Thank god I lived alone because at times I thought even the cat would move out from all of the clutter and stress. Poor Jolina, Vic, and Elisabeth were the first to work part-time out of my apartment. Half the time they would come in the morning to find me still in a bathrobe, trying desperately to wake up after working until 4 A.M. *at the office.*

And school? Oh, yeah, I did that full time too. Well I went to classes . . . most of the time, and really did do the best I could to balance both my business and school obligations. If my business associates ever figured out my student status, I just told them that I was taking a few classes at Boston University. Most others viewed my business as a "hobby," although one professor of mine said, "The business was her job and school just a hobby." My parents often wondered (quite vocally) why they were spending so much money for me to go to school when it was gradually, and obviously, becoming less of a priority to me. I spent a lot of time explaining myself to them, and others, but to me it made all the sense in the world.

On any given morning, at 7 A.M. I would run off to the Venturepreneurs Network breakfast meetings, charitable fund raisers, a Boston Globe community business breakfast, or any of a dozen different functions. And I'd usually wind up sitting next to a vice president from Ernst & Young, an executive from a major airline, a magazine editor, and, occasionally, even a bank president. We would have great conversations. Then I would look at my watch. Twenty-five minutes until Corporate Finance starts. Damn! Again the prioritizing thing. Was I going to be a business person or a college student today? I won't tell you that I ran off to class every time. Usually, but I weighed the opportunities very carefully. If I could spend 15 minutes talking to the head of marketing from Microsoft, I'd just have to let my school attendance suffer. At that point I was willing to risk another percentage of my GPA for the advancement of my business career. And look at the people I was meeting!

Within a year or so I had built up a database of hundreds of business contacts and was being invited to more business functions than college events. Professionally, I was in ecstasy. My own mental Disneyland, I call it. Yeah, I was finally going places . . . kind of. I was always going somewhere, meeting someone, and my calendar was just packed with things to do and places to be. My life seemed to always be in chaos—but more like a tornado rapidly moving forward than a storm that just wrecks everything and dies (the latter could be applied to the condition of my office). I did my best to keep everything in perspective but didn't really even know what that meant anymore. Life was certainly exciting but no bed of roses. I lost many friends. I got sick from stress and physical neglect. Depression got pretty bad and I did come close to starving a few times (or so I thought). But with each of the plagues that fell upon me in trying to build my business, my mission became clearer. I was in business to help people just like me. I felt like an underdog trying to battle the forces that kept entrepreneurship out of reach to so many others. Delirium. I'm sure that had something to do with my romanticizing the whole thing. But, hey, it worked.

When John at The Princeton Review first asked me to write this book, I didn't think I had the experience required for the job. A year passed. We met again, and there was the offer . . . again. Who was I to write a book for other young entrepreneurs? I was barely out of college myself. But there was that mission popping up again. This was an amazing opportunity, and though at first I had no idea how I would do this, I took on the challenge. So if you'd like to know what this book is about, I'll tell you this: It's not so much a "how to start a business book" as it is a "how-to-cope-with-life-while-starting-and-succeeding-in-your-own-business" book. All I can say is that this is the real deal, the real story.

What you will read here is what really happens to you and what you really need to know when you start a company and decide to make entrepreneurship your life. In writing this book I tried to include as many personal stories, and others from fellow young entrepreneurs and business experts, as I could. From what I've seen, no other book has ever taught a young entrepreneur how not to starve when he or she is broke, how to launch a family PR campaign, how to meet important people, how not to get carded while entertaining clients, and other very important, yet seemingly trivial, information about dealing with your life as a business owner. But we know better.

I sincerely hope that this book helps you as much as I'm sure it would have helped me, even if just for the moral support of knowing that there are others like you, living like you, and pursuing their dreams through entrepreneurship . . . just like you.

So enjoy. And keep building and dreaming and teaching others what you learn along the way. There are many others who need you as much as you need them. So as far as the experience requirement goes, no one ever said you can't fill your quota with a little wisdom from others—particularly from your immediate peers.

PART ONE

Introduction to Entrepreneurship

CHAPTER 1

The Entrepreneurial Decision

YOU'VE NEVER BEEN QUITE LIKE THE REST OF YOUR FRIENDS. YOU WERE ALWAYS the dreamer, the inventor, the doer. You were probably the first to open a neighborhood business selling lemonade, your little brother's action figures, or your family pets. Somewhere along the way, you realized that something inside of you was pushing you to do more. Your friends and immediate environment stopped influencing what you did, and some other force kicked into gear. You knew that you were different, and so did everyone else. Your mind worked in ways that exhausted those around you. You obsessed over finding new and better ways to build, sell, or market a product or idea. People said that you tired them out—still do in fact, with your "overactive imagination."

Do you wake up in the middle of the night with earth-shattering ideas? Do new business concepts intrigue you? Does the word entrepreneur excite you? If you can't throw away your three-year-old pile of business magazines because you are convinced that you'll need their start-up, business management, or employee benefits articles someday soon, stop dreaming and start doing something about it.

Maybe you've already started a small business. Or just wish you had. Well listen, you're not getting any younger.

Despite the type of invention, services, or venture, you've always been the enterprising sort, knowing that one day it would lead to something big. Whether people told you that you were crazy or destined for greatness, you've kept dreaming your entrepreneurial dreams. Until now. Now you're debating taking those dreams a step further—establishing or committing to grow a legitimate, legally sound, hopefully successful business.

Call this book your bible, your only supportive friend; it will be there for you from the inception of your brilliant idea to the sound establishment of your business entity. The goal of this book is twofold: (1) to give you the practical and personal insight from a young entrepreneur's point of view to help you get through your first years in business, and (2) to teach you the tricks of the trade that you will rely on to compete successfully in a business world with people twice your age and companies God-knows-how-many-times as big.

You might be hesitant to venture out on your own. And with good reason. The business world can be a jungle for those who are unfamiliar with it. But you *can* do it. Whether you want to start a small, local business or land on the cover of *Forbes* one day, your options are wide open. Easier read than done? Maybe. But it happens every day. When was the last time you went to a newsstand and didn't see someone under 35 on the cover of at least one business or technology magazine? So whatever your personal circumstances are, there are a lot of stellar entrepreneurs out there who started with no more money or experience than you have right now. Here are just a few to keep in mind:

- Michael Dell (Dell Computers) used his college dorm room as a storage shed while selling computer disks to fellow students.

- Frank Carney started Pizza Hut out of a little shack on Wichita State University's campus because no one else would give him a lease.

- Dineh Mohajer's Hard Candy nail polish line (a $25 million dollar company) only took off because a couple of movie stars bought (and wore out on the town) the pale blue nail polish she whipped up to match a dress she owned.

- Paul Orfalea started Kinko's right out of college in an old building in Santa Barbara that was so small he had to roll the copier out on the sidewalk to fit customers in the store.

- Kathy Taggaris got the license to produce Wolfgang Puck's Gourmet Pizza only after *living* at her new plant for the first five weeks.

- Seventeen-year-old Fred DeLuca ended his lifelong dream of going to medical school to start a small submarine sandwich shop—now known as Subway.

You wonder if people called them crazy? You can bet on it. But something made these people succeed in business when everyone told them that their dreams were impossible: Determination, perseverance, and trial and error. You supply the first two, and I'll tell you about some other young entrepreneurs whose experiences can help you avoid the errors. So if you *really* want to build your own business now, and accomplish more than even you can imagine, keep reading.

Why Take the Entrepreneurial Route?

If you have that entrepreneurial flame burning or even flickering somewhere deep inside you, the chances of its being extinguished are pretty slim. And really, if you are ever going to take risks exploring your career options, this is the absolute best time to do it. Why wait until you have a semi-stable corporate job and major financial obligations to discover that you hate your career and need to make a big change? If you think I'm being melodramatic, think again.

Don Seitz was a college student who decided to listen to the advice of his family and friends and become a lawyer. After three grueling years of law school, Don earned his J.D. degree, passed the bar exam, and started working for a prestigious law firm. Remember that entrepreneurial flame? Guess how long Don lasted as a lawyer. Two weeks.

As his parents recovered from the shock of their son's decision, Don was busy starting a company—Sock and Roll. That's right. Don abandoned a career in law to become a novelty sock and T-shirt manufacturer. Many of you have probably seen his apparel. Don's first line of T-shirts featured a big flower on unbleached cotton. In stores, they were displayed in flower pots, rolled up tightly, flower facing outward, and tied with a straw bow. His second line featured an array of oversized sweatshirts with matching socks. Each top had the body of an animal printed on it, and the socks had the animal's feet. You could buy a dog, a pig, a cow, a horse, or even a cat (I still have the socks with the gray cat feet). Another one of his creations was a T-shirt featuring great artists in history—each as happy faces. On each shirt, you had Picasso with his pinpoint eyes and smile rearranged, Seurat in dots, and Van Gogh with one ear.

Today, Sock and Roll does sales of $5 million annually, distributes its products to over 300 retail locations, and is run by an owner who absolutely loves his life. Since the day I first met him, I have yet to see Don without a smile on his face.

Contemplating the Corporate Path

If you ask entrepreneurs how happy they are in their own business, odds are there's nothing else they'd rather be doing. How many people do you know who can say that about their career? Not many I know. Of course there are pros and cons to being your own boss, but in my opinion, the tradeoffs are more than worth it.

If you can manage to figure out early whether you're the corporate raider or small-business type, you'll save yourself a lot of confusion and frustration down the road. Yes, working for a major corporation can be an amazing experience—particularly if it teaches you that working for a corporation is exactly what you don't want to do.

Countless entrepreneurs started their professional careers in the corporate world, and for good reason. It was the *right* thing to do. Who could go wrong? If one was expected to land a stable job, working for a multimillion or billion dollar company was a good way to do it.

That is, it was until the early 1990s, when the bubble burst and corporations started laying off employees by the tens of thousands. But the job market is an unpredictable place, and as the economy has gotten better, so too has the job market.

Today, people in their twenties are being offered astronomical salaries and signing bonuses worth the average person's yearly wages to join Corporate America. The funniest thing about it is that usually after two or three years, most younger people with entrepre-

From: Richard Kirshenbaum— Kirshenbaum & Bond

I started my company when I was 26 years old and people always tell me that I must have been brave to do it at that age. One of the things that I realize is that the older a person gets, the more risk adverse they become. Starting your own business at an earlier age is actually easier. You are more flexible, more resilient, and have less on the line to lose. Therefore I would encourage anyone, if they have a great idea, to start their business as early as they can. Don't delay. Should you fail, you can easily bounce back; get another job or start again. If you wait until you are older and more settled, you may never have the true courage to do it and that, my friends, is true bravery.

neurial tendencies tend to want to jump ship and set out on their own. Obviously, the lure of great salaries and benefits isn't enough for many of today's entrepreneurs. They want freedom and the control to create their own opportunities and capitalize on their own hard-earned skills.

Many people who work for larger corporations (particularly older, better-known companies) find the hierarchical structure quite discomforting. The bigger the company, the greater the competition for the same jobs; and the less of an impact you, one person, can make. That's it in a nutshell. Think of it in terms of film credits. In the making of a movie, hundreds of people come together to work ridiculously long hours for a relatively short period of time. When the credits roll, there's a noticeable separation between directors, producers, and actors and the crew (lighters, electricians, assistants, set designers, etc.). The people "above the line" are the ones who receive most of the recognition for a successful film. In the big scheme of things, they are the ones who "matter the most." The same goes for most major corporations. If you don't sit on the board or have an office on the executive floor, odds are few at the top will consider you to be very important in the scheme of things either. I know this is a pretty bleak picture, but if you really do want to run the show (which I'll assume, if you're contemplating entrepreneurship), getting there in a major corporation could take the next twenty years of your life . . . if you get there at all.

So keep in mind, even if the job market is great, if you don't want to be in it, you probably won't be happy "settling" for it. Even Newton's Law teaches us to know better. What goes up, must come down. Things don't stay the way they are forever, particularly the economy. As valuable a commodity as you may be today, always keep in mind that there are many people right behind you, just as anxious to graduate from a good school, strike out on their own, and take over your job . . . perhaps for less money and with better skills to offer. No one can fire you from a business you own.

Just to round out your view of corporate vs. self-employment, a table of comparison follows. Ultimately, only you can decide whether you'd be better off in a corporation or on your own. Don't let anyone try to convince you otherwise.

While millions of people still work in behemoth companies like Lockheed and IBM, over 95 percent of those employed in the U.S. work for small businesses. But we're not talking about your working *for* a small business; I'm here to teach you how to start one. And as

ISSUE	BEING A CORPORATE EMPLOYEE	BEING YOUR OWN BOSS
Job Stability	Subject to success of company, department, and superiors. Personal success or company loyalty often irrelevant during corporate downsizing and layoffs.	Tied directly to the success of company. Individual success is very important, as smaller businesses rely on fewer employees.
Promotions	Strictly determined by corporate hierarchy. Often position in demand must first be vacated before it can be filled by another. Heavy competition for higher positions.	You're the boss.
Work Hours	Often long, yet predictable. Hours dictated by superiors (either directly or indirectly).	Very long and unpredictable. Hours self determined.
Salary	Set within pre-specified range for department and/or position. Raises usually given after certain (predetermined) periods of time.	Below average in beginning. Often entrepreneurs draw only as little as they need to live on until the business can afford to pay them a salary.
Bonuses	If any, distributed quarterly or at holidays. Based on performance of individual or department. (Though may sometimes be given across the board in larger companies.)	The greater and continued success of your business is its own reward.
Benefits	Major medical, sometimes dental and eye. Paid vacations, personal and sick days. 401(k) plans highly encouraged.	Must provide yourself. Can be expensive to new business owners. Vacations infrequent. Personal days taken at your own discretion, usually only when physically sick.
Expenses	Expense accounts can be substantial for some employees. Out-of-pocket expenses always reimbursed or paid for by company (travel, transportation, meals).	Entrepreneurs often have trouble separating their business expenses from their personal expenses. Until incorporation takes place, separation is not even legally necessary. Expenses are taken care of when businesses have investors (and thus, operating budgets) or are doing well enough to handle day-to-day expenses. Paid for at owner's risk.
Responsibility	Clearly outlined in employee manual or published job description. Responsibility often increases as companies lay off other employees, shrink departments, and cut operating budgets.	Significant. Entrepreneurs must always be prepared to do anything and everything including sweeping the floors, typing letters, and stuffing envelopes.

for major corporations, well, starting one is usually not a conscious decision for those who succeed. Let's face it, we all want to build a multinational corporation at some time in our entrepreneurial lives, but few have admitted to striving for it when they first started. Look at the garage entrepreneurs (those who started businesses at home). Walt Disney, John Hewlett & David Packard (Hewlett Packard), and Steve Jobs & Steve Wozniac (Apple Computers) all started building their empires in their backyards or garages. But according to *Fortune* magazine, they were a lot more concerned with feeding themselves and paying rent than with selling stock options. Do you really think that Walt would have ditched his ambitions and gone to work for a major animation studio if he had the chance? I seriously doubt it. He had bigger dreams.

The Young Entrepreneur's Advantage . . .

If you still can't figure out what you have over older folks other than the freedom to pick up and backpack through Europe for a month or so, you're selling yourself short.

You might be thinking that there couldn't be any more factors stacked *against* you in starting a new venture. But you're wrong. There are several reasons for starting a business while you're young. The fact is, many experts agree that younger entrepreneurs have an edge over their predecessors because we're practically bred to be entrepreneurs by the environment in which we've been raised. (See "Breeding a New Generation of Entrepreneurs" on page 23, later in this chapter.)

You have *a lot* to offer the business world. More than you may realize.

Invulnerability

Although it may be argued whether this is an advantage or not, youth means minimal past exposure to failure. Invulnerability is a natural feeling when you're young. Our exposure to failure has been minimal, thus we feel invincible and willing to take risks. Remember when you were five and a Superman cape or a can of spinach made you feel stronger? How about when you first got your driver's license and thought that you could outsmart a police officer's radar gun if you went above 100 miles an hour? Or that it was okay to stay out partying until 4 A.M. before that huge 9 A.M. midterm, on which your entire GPA hinged?

We take risks until something happens to teach us otherwise. Most people out of college haven't ever tried to start a business before either, so unless you've tried and lost your shirt already, there's nothing to inhibit you now.

Limited Responsibility

While many of us under thirty do spend a lot of time working to pay for our own survival, the level and degree of responsibility held by people our age is still minimal. In most cases, twentysomethings aren't married, don't have children, and don't even own a car, let alone a home. In fact, most of us (students in particular) don't own much more than clothes, some used textbooks, and maybe a stereo, TV, or futon.

If to start a business you have to invest every penny you own, it's probably no great tragedy. Financial loss should not be enough of a reason to fear starting your own business. You don't need that much to live on, if you think about it. You *can* live on macaroni and cheese if you have to—you might even be doing that now. And if you *really* need to, you can probably move back home. Most parents leave the proverbial welcome mat out for their kids, anyway.

For the young entrepreneur, these are not great sacrifices. Kimberly Walsh, past president of the Association of Collegiate Entrepreneurs, once offered some eye-opening encouragement to a financially drained and physically exhausted young entrepreneur I knew in college:

> "Okay, you are out of money, but do you still believe in your business?"
> The girl nodded.
> "Do you eat regularly, despite what it is or where it comes from?"
> She answered yes.
> "Do you have a place to live, whether it's on someone's couch or in your car?"
> Again, she nodded.
> "Do you have people who love and support you, even if they think you are crazy?"
> In tears, she said yes.
> "Well then keep going. You are doing just fine."

The ability to follow through under difficult circumstances has turned countless young entrepreneurs into millionaires.

Physical and Emotional Strength

Talk about living on macaroni and pizza—twenty years from now you'd probably get heartburn just thinking about it. Being an entrepreneur doesn't mean you have to run yourself ragged; but the ability to burn the candle at both ends without burning a hole in your stomach is definitely an edge you should take advantage of. It's just the nature of the beast. In the first six months of opening K.T.'s Kitchen, Kathy Taggeris once spent five weeks straight at her office without seeing daylight or stepping foot in her own house. Kathy claims to have taken turns with two of her most loyal employees sleeping on the couch in the entrance-way and on the industrial carpet in the offices until their new pizza factory was up and running. So what's the moral of this story? You may be thrilled at the prospect of owning your own business, but for a while, your business just might own you. You're going to need all of your youth, college survival skills, and strength—emotionally and physically—to muddle through.

Starting a company is like entering a serious relationship. Unlike a significant other, though, while it won't keep you company at night, or cook for you when you work late, it can be the love of your life. Be prepared for all of the classic milestones of a romantic relationship:

Playing the Field	Researching business options & competition
Courting	Targeted research & due diligence
The Honeymoon Period	Tireless enthusiasm about new venture
First Argument	First pitfall, maybe marketing research was off
Making Up	Readjustment of goals
Rough Times	Bootstrapping & other stresses
Commitment	Writing a business plan
Proposal	Quitting your day job

As with any relationship, starting a business can be physically and emotionally draining. Be prepared for some rough terrain before you reap all the benefits.

Resources

Though you might just be learning the concept of networking, you'd be amazed at how many people are out there just waiting for someone to tap them on the shoulder and ask for help. Where can you find them? Everywhere, really. From local organizations, to your city's business journal, to networking events, to family friends and friends of friends, you'll be amazed once you really start to open your eyes. Your school's Alumni Relations Office can probably help arrange for you to meet or speak with an alum in your field of interest. These are great people to contact because graduates are often sentimental about their college years and love the chance to reminisce, especially with someone who's not asking for a donation. (We'll talk a lot more about this in Chapter 9 "Building Business Relationships.")

You should also take advantage of your "harmless" appearance. When you're young, big companies don't look at you as competition; most will probably be willing to give you an informational interview or just spend a few minutes with you on the phone. Professionals tend to be forthcoming when talking to young, ambitious people. You might gather some valuable information or maybe even valuable contacts.

We also have more access to information than people have ever had before. (Just look at what we can find out about our President's love life!) Today, we can get the scoop on almost anything we desire, and often it's no further than our own computers. If information really is power, then we as entrepreneurs couldn't be in a stronger position.

... And Disadvantages

Disadvantages? There are none. Don't worry about it! Just go out and build your empire.

Well, not so fast. There are some clear disadvantages to being a young entrepreneur, and it's important to look at them closely so that you can prepare yourself.

Thirty-year-old Doug Mellinger, former national director of the Association of Collegiate Entrepreneurs (ACE) and founder of an incredibly successful software development company had this to say in *Small Business Success* magazine: "Young entrepreneurs face five major problems when starting a new business—lack of credibility, immaturity, lack of experience, overeagerness, and isolation and loneliness."

To Doug's list, I'd like to add two more—lack of leadership experience and difficulty in motivating yourself. The good news is these are generally qualities you can work on. Maybe not all of these pitfalls apply to you. But if they do, start working on them now. You have to begin thinking about yourself and your business as a packaged product for sale. The better the package you present, the more seriously people will take you in the business world. So put your ego away and decide truthfully which, if any, might apply to you.

Lack of Credibility

It's one thing for your friends to attest to your credibility, but it's another to convince a potential vendor, customer, or banker that you're a good risk.

There are a couple of ways to gain credibility, and they're really not as difficult as they may seem. According to Mellinger, "If you believe 100 percent in yourself and your product, eventually others will believe in you, too." Having an air of self-confidence (but not the stink of blind conceit) shows others that you are determined to succeed. It's sometimes hard to resist believing someone who is so driven and ambitious. Any successful entrepreneur can offer you multiple examples of this. Your first goal should be to convince others that you're worth taking a chance on.

Your next aim should be to align yourself with people who already have credibility: Mentors, advisers, advisory board members, a major supplier, and so forth. (See "Mentors and Advisers" on page 136.) "Associating yourself with quality people can only enhance your credibility," says Mellinger. People may not know who you are or have a reason to trust you at first, but if you have made contact with or have received advice or other guidance from someone that already has professional respect, you have an added advantage (so go ahead, name drop a little when it counts). Though it is often accepted too simplistically, *who you know* often helps a lot when you are young and just starting out.

At age twenty-three, Ray Sozzi had just quit a great job with Bain & Co., a prestigious consulting firm that hired him right after his graduation from Dartmouth. Ray had an idea to create a national discount program for students similar to the American Association of Retired Persons (AARP), which was the largest association in the country providing discounts and services to retired people. But despite his boundless energy and numerous attempts to convince others that he could command national attention and capture the business of hundreds of thousands of students, he needed help. Who was he to claim that he could command so much attention in the college market? Within a year or so, Ray began negotiating with some major corporations, including Amtrak, American Express, and The Princeton Review, to become national sponsors. With such well-known names behind him, the company exploded with growth and other companies started approaching him. Today, Student Advantage has over 1.5 million students nationwide who carry their discount card, thousands of regional and national sponsors, and with the help of their corporate partners, are now the only ones in the business . . . since they bought out every other competitor in the market.

Your third task is to become someone important in your field of interest. As president of an organization, founder of a small group, or conductor of some relevant or interesting research, you can align yourself with a worthwhile cause or association. But don't waste people's time by pretending to be interested in something you're not. Don't run for a position just for the title. Find a group you do care about (preferably related to your business) and offer as much assistance as you can or start your own. You'd be amazed at the contacts, credibility, and experience being a community or student leader can produce.

Next, know what you are talking about. There's nothing worse than some idiot who proclaims to be an expert on something he or she knows little or nothing about. Don't risk your reputation debating someone who might know much more than you do. No one will expect you to know everything, but *do* do your homework. A little research can go a long way in convincing someone that you're serious about your new venture.

Finally, when you promise to take care of a problem, deliver a high-quality product, or just be there for clients when they need you, DO IT! There's no easier way to lose credibility. Whenever possible, produce the best quality, deliver on time, and be professional about everything. If your office phone doubles as your bedside table phone, be aware that people may call at 8 A.M. Don't yawn when you pick up the phone. If you want to be taken seriously, you have to project a serious image. (I'll get back to this subject in greater detail later.)

Lack of Maturity

If you've been called immature a few more times than you'd like to admit, take a hint. You might be getting into something a little over your head. Do you have trouble admitting your mistakes? Do you fight people who offer advice or suggest that you do things differently? Do you have trouble getting people to take you seriously? Age doesn't have to matter in entrepreneurship, but maturity does.

A lack of maturity in an entrepreneur can cause the untimely death of almost any business. One recent example sticks out in my mind. Two friends of mine, whom I had helped for many years with various business endeavors, decided to start PR consulting . . . with little experience. In almost every respect, these girls were much more mature than their 21-year-old peers and were no strangers to responsibility. Peril struck when a client pulled their first real assignment out from under them and declared that they weren't going to pay. With bills pilling up at home, one of them got so angry with the client that instead of trying to salvage the relationship she told her partner that she wanted nothing else to do with them. If her partner wanted to pursue the project any further on her own, that was fine by her. Not only did she lose the chance to recover the money they were owed, but she couldn't even use them for a reference when they so desperately needed experience under their belt. She also alienated her partner by making her decision independently and by not giving her the chance to talk the sense into her that could have resolved the situation. Last I heard, the partners had spent a lot of time arguing and finally decided to give up the PR side of the business.

The ability to persevere through tough situations is probably one of the most important traits of a successful entrepreneur. If you're still having a problem with immaturity (and others *will* let you know), you should probably start working on yourself before you attempt a business plan.

Mellinger advises, "You have to stop thinking of yourself as a young person and start thinking of yourself as a business person. You must conduct yourself in a professional manner." (Creating an effective personal image is covered in "The Entrepreneurial Image" on page 145.)

Lack of Experience

Problem number one, credibility, can often be a direct result of lack of experience. Whether you're twelve, eighteen, or twenty-four, prepare to spend much of your time proving yourself and your skills to others. Particularly when you're young, people will often assume that you can't possibly be old enough to know what you're doing.

That should give you sufficient incentive to prove them wrong. But there is a positive side to being unreasonably doubted. It forces you to really know what you are talking about. (Something that even older entrepreneurs often take too lightly.) Some of the best things that you can do to gain valuable experience and credibility are:

- Work for someone else in the field (even if you have to work for free).
- Read everything you can on the subject (See "Understanding Your Industry.").
- Take a class or attend seminars on the subject.
- Join major associations or organizations in the industry (and be active).
- Subscribe to and read any major industry journals, newsletters, or publications.
- Volunteer to work on a related project for a well-known company or organization.
- Spend time with people in the field during business hours (You can even ask anyone you know or admire with a similar business if you can just follow him or her around for a day.).
- Build any related, yet indirect skills (such as graphic design, public speaking, or event management, if you are starting a promotional company).

Lack of experience, then, is one hurdle that you have to be very determined and creative to get over. As I mentioned earlier, becoming an expert on your business or industry is a process that can take several years, but doing so can be easily expedited by some serious research, commitment, and networking. As a rule of thumb, an entrepreneur can typically gain credibility after intensively working in an industry for about three to five years. This is about how long it should take you to gain a solid understanding of most industries and gain the credibility that you need to succeed. (Everyone, based on who they are professionally, will have a different standard by which they judge experts.) Whatever you can do to get experience in your field, you should. Though you may not yet have your own office, secretary, or corporate credit card, you can always sell yourself and your business with your knowledge. Without that you have nothing.

Overeagerness

I'm sure that many people have already told you to "slow down" because "you are still so young and have the rest of your life to start your own business." We'll have none of that. If being overeager pushes you to learn faster and accomplish more, then you have nothing to worry about. Keep going. What does hurt young entrepreneurs is moving faster than they can handle; that is, they cannot possibly finance their businesses, find enough time to run their companies, or learn what they need to in time to complete projects. A few mistakes that overeager young entrepreneurs often make include:

- Hiring people prematurely
- Spending money on the assumption that they will be making it soon
- Getting involved in projects or businesses when they do not yet have the necessary skills, thus damaging their reputations
- Taking on too much responsibility
- Appearing too anxious
- Openly admitting too much about their lack of experience
- Not taking the time to become properly certified or trained
- Not taking the time to plan or properly assess their business needs
- Neglecting to write a business plan
- Ignoring the advice of people who appear to be skeptics (even if they are experts themselves)

Being overeager to get your business off the ground is perfectly understandable. Just be smart about the decisions that you make. Listening to your mentors, family, or friends will give you some idea as to whether you are on the right track. Aggressively pursue success yourself and where your company is concerned, but don't be overanxious. You will turn people off . . . especially if they have doubts about your ability or experience in the first place.

Isolation and Loneliness

In taking the entrepreneurial path you separate yourself from the rest of the working world by stepping outside of the proverbial box and creating your own set of rules. Unfortunately, this kind of freedom comes with a price. In most cases your work will be all-consuming and will affect your family, friends, social life, and personal free time. When you can no longer go out at night to meet friends, date, or even spend time with your loved ones, they can start to give up on you. Most of the time, you won't even realize it until it's too late. When they stop calling, even though you're used to turning their offers down, you start to feel pretty alone.

Now if you are at the very beginning of your entrepreneurial career, you will probably be saying to yourself, "That will never happen to me." We all do. Rest assured though, you will feel lonely and pretty isolated from time to time. Whether it is a daily occurrence or an occasional one is up to you and will depend on how well you maintain some sort of balance in your life. A few words of advice from one who has been down that road:

- Maintain communication with the important people in your life, even if just to say "Hey, can't really talk right now, or for the next few weeks, but just wanted to let you know that I haven't forgotten about you and that I think of you often." (You can even leave this on someone's voice mail if you have to.)

- Be honest with people close to you when you are having a rough time. If you try to avoid the fact that you haven't been in touch and that you've really been depressed, others will just think they are less important to you now that you have a business to run. Telling them the truth will help them to be more understanding and even a little more tolerant about you and your calendar. They might even be able to help you if they know you need it.

- Make sure that you have a solid group of mentors and direct peers (other entrepreneurs) that you can turn to for support. Nothing is more frustrating than being at the end of your rope and finally venting to someone who has no idea what you are doing or why you are doing it. Other entrepreneurs will probably also appreciate the opportunity to open up to someone themselves.

"Entrepreneurship is the loneliest job in the world," Lynton Harris, one of my favorite young entrepreneurs, used to say. As an entrepreneur you are going to have to accept that most people will not understand what you are doing or why. You will feel overwhelmed and alone. So stay in touch with the people you care about and make sure that you add others to that inner circle who know what you are going through.

You can also always turn to The Young Entrepreneurs Network online at www.yenetwork.com to find other young entrepreneurs or any of the thousands of other business clubs and associations popping up in almost every neighborhood. For more information and insight into some of the harder parts about owning your own business, check out Part V, "Coping With Life as an Entrepreneur."

Lack of Leadership Skills

If you are going to start your own company, you are going to have to rely largely on your skills as a leader. Even if you won't be starting off with a staff, you are going to have to be very comfortable with being in charge. Leadership is an amazing trait that some are just born with, while others have to nurture and work at it. As an entrepreneur, your ability to lead people, guide projects, and make decisions is key to your success. Those who neglect this responsibility often pay dearly.

One such example is the story of Steve Jobs. Jobs, along with Steve Wozniak, founded Apple Computers out of a garage when they were in their early twenties. As far as young entrepreneur success stories go, this is a classic . . . but with a bitter ending. Though Steve Jobs was a cofounder of the company, and a brilliant technical mind, once Apple became a public company, Steve was fired. (As a public company, the possibility of being fired was just one of the risks to the founders.) But even if Apple had still been a legal partnership, Steve's inability to properly manage the business and be an effective leader might have lost him his job anyway by bankrupting the company.

If you study how people you admire have become leaders, you'll find that for most, it was totally unplanned. And those who made a conscious decision to be in charge have done the best. So, if you are still questioning whether your leadership ability is strong enough, look around. Speak to some of your friends and family. What situations or experiences have you instinctively taken control of? It might be more often that you think. In any case, pursue leadership as a personal goal. Just as entrepreneurship will give you control of your future, leadership will give you the day-to-day control of your life.

Leadership can be addictive, too. As you'll find with your own company, once you get the thrill of being in charge and making great things happen, anything less bores you. To this day, I have a lot of trouble not taking control of situations. The greatest thing about being a leader is the feeling that you can handle anything. Once you have overcome obstacles and helped others accomplish goals they never would have reached without you, the leader in you can't be stopped. It's too damn exciting.

Difficulty in Motivating Yourself

As motivated as you might be to make your business a success, you will not always have that surge of enthusiasm when you wake up in the morning. Since you don't have a boss to yell at you when you come in late, don't have a regular paycheck that can be docked if you miss work, and certainly can't get fired, on a bad day you won't have that fear factor to motivate you to get going. We all get lazy sometimes, but business owners can put their companies in jeopardy if their slacking off gets out of control.

A few ways to stay on track are:

- Get into a strict routine so that you wake up, work, eat, exercise, and sleep at about the same time every day. If you screw it up one day, just make sure that you get back on track the next.

- Schedule early morning meetings and calls if you have trouble getting started in the morning. It forces you to get moving.

- Pack your schedule with appointments. This will eliminate the need to find motivation to work.

- Do things right away whenever possible. Postponing work always makes motivating yourself harder.

- Take advantage of the times when you are on a roll and full of energy so you don't have to drag yourself to work when you really do need a break.

- Put together your own little reward system, like only paying yourself when you get certain things done, hiring some help if you complete a proposal, or letting yourself go home or stop working early if you finish what you need to on time.

- Have other people who work with or for you "be your boss" for a while, and have them stay on top of you in case you start to lose it.

You should also frequently remind yourself what your mission or purpose is. It may be money, but hopefully there's more to it than that. When I feel myself dragging and can't seem to get any work done, I read my mail. No, not the bills. I look for letters from teachers, grandparents, or other young entrepreneurs who often write us to say thank you for the work we do. Then I put them up on our walls (which now are virtually covered with letters), so that my staff and I are always reminded of why we have to work so hard. All I really need is to see a note from a thirteen-year-old describing her business idea and I'm ramped up for days. Whatever that passion is, keep reminders of it all around you. If none of this works, and you still cannot seem to motivate yourself, you should probably think about another career.

So, these are the "big" disadvantages. When you put a positive spin on them, they're really not so terrible. Keep this in mind as you encounter problems with your new ventures. Knowing the most common pitfalls in advance should give you a leg up.

Combating the Generation X Stigma

In 1991, Douglas Coupland offered the world a way to classify the generation without a name when he penned the fictional twenty-something profile *Generation X*. After all the hype over the "baby boomers" (most of our parents), the world longed to label us. Thus, the Generation X stigma was born. The jury is still out on whether to congratulate Doug for his commercial success or curse him for stereotyping us as "the generation that couldn't care less." I would beg to differ—and apparently so would the *Wall Street Journal*, *Forbes* magazine, and a few hundred other major media players that now call us "the most entrepreneurial generation yet." If you have been called a "Gen Xer" so many times that you've lost count, you're probably about ready to pull an Alec Baldwin and attack the first journalist you see. But rest assured, this label is fast becoming a cliché.

In November 1993, *Success* magazine became one of the first publications to run a cover story on our generation's entrepreneurial movement. Although they reported that there was in fact a strong entrepreneurial movement among young people, they also conceded that, overall, Generation X members were a group of "twenty to thirty-five-year-old social castaways adrift in a sea of despair." According to the magazine's findings, Generation Xers believed that their parents and ancestors destroyed any chances there might have been for a happy and successful future. They held that the environment, the economy, the state of world affairs, and the young people of the world were doomed. Generation Xers believed that they had been dealt a bad hand, and they just didn't want to play anymore.

Unfortunately, the Generation X label became a self-fulfilling prophecy for many of us. After being told by educators, economists, and peers how bleak the future was, many found it easier to just save themselves the time and effort of trying to combat the title and went to work as frozen yogurt dispensing drones or record store cashiers until they turned thirty. So, at the time, young entrepreneurs not only had to face the defeatist attitude that "twentysomethings couldn't start businesses" (God forbid if you were younger) but on top of that had this slacker label to deal with.

But many young entrepreneurs, myself included, took exception to this and decided to do something about it. One of the reasons you might have seen me and The Young Entrepreneurs Network in the press so much is because we just couldn't stand by and watch our generation being criticized so harshly, and so publicly, when so many of us were creating so much change in our communities and country. We were starting more businesses than any generation our age ever has. And just because we were a much smaller generation size-wise didn't mean that we were going to let our lives and our opportunities to do great things slip right by.

So after taking to the streets, my meager staff and I, with very little money and almost no experience in dealing with the media, gathered all of the research we could find, conducted a bit of our own, and started talking to everyone who would listen, until we were blue in the face and almost broke. You wonder why I'm always preaching about expertise, perseverance, and passion? Well, I'm proud to say that we made a little dent in the public's opinion of our future prospects, and particularly our ability to start and grow successful businesses. Our heartfelt thanks goes out to all of the journalists who reported the true story of our generation's entrepreneurs and to all of the young entrepreneurs who finally got to tell their stories to the world. You want to know what you, one little person, can do? We made an estimated 40 million people see things a little differently. Imagine what you could do if you really tried.

Breeding a New Generation of Entrepreneurs

According to a study by the National Federation of Independent Business (one of the few of its kind), people twenty-five and under are starting companies at a higher rate than any other age group, and 47 percent of the companies started in 1995 were started by people under thirty-five. That's not surprising, given the fact that 60 percent of eighteen- to twenty-four-year-olds and 70 percent of high school students want to own their own businesses. But despite these studies (released by the International Directory of Young Entrepreneurs and The Kauffman Foundation, respectively, in 1995), many people have continued to question the significance of young entrepreneurs in today's society and the role we will play in the future.

If you look at the skills and experience that create a solid foundation for entrepreneurship, it is not uncommon to find that younger people are probably the best equipped for self employment. Five key environmental factors contribute to this revolution.

Financial Security

For one thing, many people in their twenties are still being supported by their families and are even living at home. Without the burden of financial independence, those who remain or return to the family nest have the extra opportunity to test their business ideas and still be fed at the end of the day. Even the youngest of aspiring entrepreneurs are more likely to create and experiment with several small businesses while living at home. Each dream, attempted start-up, and failure can teach priceless lessons. Cash flow, pricing, bartering, sales techniques, and personal sacrifice are all skills learned from running a business—regardless of whether it's a lemonade stand or an international trading company.

Technology

Technology is another primary benefit to young entrepreneurs. All those hours of video games and MTV did this generation some good. Twentysomethings today are the most technologically savvy of any other age group. (Just look at the demographics of the computer industry.) Naturally, the explosion of computer hardware and software, most quickly adopted by people our age, has created a generation hunger to explore every piece of technology that we can get our hands on. It also sets us several steps ahead of those in business now who didn't grow up with their pointer fingers furiously punching the missile button on Sega.

Personal Contacts

Building personal networks of friends and business associates has never been easier. Anyone who has ever spent any significant amount of time on an online service or news group knows that when you reach out to meet others, more people usually respond than you know what to do with. The Internet offers many wonderful opportunities, the greatest probably being personal contact with people you may not normally have the opportunity to meet. Now we all laugh when we hear that Rush Limbaugh found his bride online, but what about the millions of people who find business contacts, mentors, or even investors with their computers?

Virtual Companies

Now that virtual reality *is* a reality, the concept of the storefront has taken on new dimensions, beyond those that the proprietors of any "mom and pop" shop could ever have dreamed. With personal computers, faxes, modems, beepers, cellular phones, and voice-mail systems, almost anyone can do business from anywhere—and they do. Working on the road, or from home, is becoming so popular that many advertisers, such as Sharp, IBM, Sky Tel, and Motorola, are specifically addressing the needs of telecommuters.

This new mentality has encouraged over 24 million people to start businesses from their own homes (as reported by Link Resources). Young entrepreneurs, traditionally lacking in the capital necessary to start a business, can now operate with close to zero start-up costs.

Education

If studying economics was the trend of the 1980s, entrepreneurship is the major of choice in the 1990s, and will probably remain so into the new century. In 1995, the Roper Organization discovered that 38 percent of college students felt that owning a business was the best route to a successful career. Overall, our generation's interest in studying entrepreneurship is phenomenal. New courses, organizations, and programs are appearing daily. Most significantly, the number of universities that offer formal entrepreneurial programs has grown from 16 in 1970 to more than 1000 today.

Just as small businesses dominate the economy, smaller educational organizations are making strides as well. Small, informal entrepreneurial clubs, groups, and networks are being created everywhere. I know that we at The Young Entrepreneurs Network receive requests for help from all over the world almost daily from people trying to start local programs and networks.

Hard data on the actual number of youth entrepreneurship initiatives and available resources is still sketchy, but the growing trend in entrepreneurial training is apparent—and it's no longer restricted to college students. Just as the Small Business Administration works with older entrepreneurs, significant support is being funneled into training people of all ages. Entrepreneurial programs for elementary, high school, and junior high school students are now as common as those found at the collegiate level. The National Foundation for Teaching Entrepreneurship (NFTE), for example, is the leading organization for teaching young people how to start their own businesses. Steve Mariotti, NFTE's founder, spent almost ten years developing a curriculum before the academic community began to listen. To date, NFTE has trained over 15,000 disadvantaged children in a simplified MBA course in entrepreneurship. Each of the students has written a business plan, created business cards, and opened their own businesses. Now people listen.

About a half-dozen other major organizations also exist for the purpose of teaching entrepreneurship. Junior Achievement, the oldest, has successfully taught hundreds of thousands of elementary and high school students the principles of business ownership through economics programs. An Income of Her Own teaches teenage girls the virtues of economic self-sufficiency, while Inventors Workshop International helps young inventors turn their creations into money-making ventures. KIDZ IN BIZ, Camp Lemonade Stand, One to One, and EDGE/Kids Way are just a few of the other organizations out there sharing the mission of educating young people in entrepreneurship.

Top Five Business Schools for Entrepreneurs

In 1998, *Success* magazine commissioned the College Counsel to survey 130 business schools across the country to determine which were the best for entrepreneurs. The survey focused on five areas: Quality of Curriculum (accounting for 25 percent of the score; Strength of Faculty (25 percent); Support for Students (20 percent); Caliber of Students (15 percent) and Overall Entrepreneurial Muscle (15 percent). Here are the top five graduate entrepreneurial programs in the country:

1. University of Southern California (USC)

2. DePaul University

3. University of Pennsylvania (Wharton School of Business)

4. University of California Los Angeles (UCLA)

5. University of Arizona

Source: *Success* magazine, September 1998

Taking a Personal Inventory and Assessing Your Current Resources

If you're going to go into business for yourself, one of the best things you can do is know what you're getting into and whether you have access to the resources necessary for you to succeed. Entrepreneurs always underestimate what they will need to start their businesses. Honestly, anyone can start a company. But only a small percentage of those who try manage to build successful firms. In one way or another, the reason for failure usually comes down to resources. Businesses that fail most often do so because they lack money, industry expertise, or a viable strategic plan. These are all inputs, or resources, whether they are intellectual capital (knowledge) or monetary capital.

Use the following chart to take a personal inventory of your resources as they apply to starting your company. If you do not yet have your business concept solidified, use the chart to identify how well equipped you are to be in business in general. (For example, under "knowledge" assume that you will need to know how to manage money, create financial statements, have some management or entrepreneurial experience, understand a particular industry, have a better-than-average skill that you will use, and so forth.) As soon as you have nailed down your business idea, recreate this chart and do it again. You might even want to keep it around while you're in the planning stages, updating it until you feel confident that you have the key resources that you will need to begin.

Feel free to add more resource categories and, if possible, in the description/specifics column, order according to importance, giving each item its own line. Then simply check off the appropriate boxes, identifying how accessible each resource is to you *right now*. It is important that this list reflect your present situation so that you don't neglect something that you need to learn or obtain.

Study the completed chart carefully and update it regularly. You may want to recreate it on a piece of paper, draw it on an erasable board, or put it on a computer spread sheet so that you can more easily edit it. It can be of enormous help to you in starting your company the right way, the smart way.

Personal Inventory Chart

RESOURCE	DESCRIPTION (SPECIFICS)	HAVE	CAN GET	MAYBE	DON'T HAVE
Knowledge					
Contacts					
Equipment					
Funding					

PART TWO

Planning: The Key to Success

Your "Big Idea"

HEN IT COMES TO ENTREPRENEURIAL VENTURES, THERE ARE TWO CLASSIC startup scenarios: An entrepreneur who finds an idea and turns it into a business, or a business idea that turns someone into an entrepreneur. Which should come first? Every situation is different. Some people just get lucky. They could be sitting in a bar, riding on a train, lying in bed, or doing one of a million different routine things when the idea hits.

Then there are the others. Those who are dying to do something on their own but have no clue what that something is. So they hunt, and they hunt. They read about other entrepreneurs, talk to friends, attend trade shows, and search for opportunities every-where they go. Some people even get pretty obsessed with the whole thing. (Obsession can be pretty valuable to an entrepreneur when launching a business. Don't let anyone tell you otherwise.)

If you already have your "big idea" it might seem like the greatest opportunity ever. You'll be thinking, "Why didn't anyone else think of this? It's unbeatable! I'm a genius!" But there will be many more brilliant ideas, big and small. Most entrepreneurs, particularly the newer, younger ones, tend to have a new business notion every time you talk to them. Once you get into the entrepreneurial mind-set, everything is fodder for a new business venture. It's just one of those uncontrollable subconscious urges that nudges us to analyze, investigate, reengineer and improve every business opportunity that catches our eye.

As virtual infants to the business world, we sometimes mistake our enthusiasm about entrepreneurship (our own mental Disneyland) for enthusiasm over our business-idea-of-the-moment—in other words, we lose focus. It's important to have that inexhaustible enthusiasm about your great entrepreneurial idea, but sometimes the actual business concepts that will turn that idea into a reality lose their priority in all of the hoopla.

It's easy enough to run around calling yourself an entrepreneur, but you've got to find the right business and get it off the ground before you really are one. Starting a business when you first decide to be an entrepreneur is like getting married before you've ever dated anyone—you should investigate all of your ideas first, then try to commit to one. Where does the demand lie? How much will the startup cost you? Do you have the resources? Is it interesting enough to hold your complete and undivided attention all day, every day?

If age brings any great professional wisdom, it's (sadly enough) skepticism. No longer does every idea that pops into your head make it out of your mouth. You'll learn to control your unbridled enthusiasm, to comply with the reality of your surroundings. In time, you'll learn to better evaluate new ideas, instantly determining the feasible from the ludicrous, the intelligent from the emotional.

Separating the Good from the Bad Ideas

To help you get an edge, here are a few suggestions for weeding out the bad ideas and concentrating on the good.

Determine What You Bring to the Table

Orville Reddenbacher was a farmer who figured out a better way to grow the corn that makes popcorn, and he believed people would pay more for an improved version. From his early teens, Bill Gates was the classic computer nerd who knew he could never wear a suit every day, much less conform to his conservative father's corporate vision for him. And from the time she was five years old, Mary Kay loved repainting her dolls' faces.

There is a compelling reason why you want to become an entrepreneur. There needs to be an even stronger reason for your choice of business. Think about what you're good at, what you really know, and most of all, what you truly love doing.

Eliminate Anything That Smart People Would Do for Free

Looking to start an ice-cream testing facility? To develop an organization that screens and advises potential *Playboy* models? Perhaps you think that a worldwide Resort Certification Program should be established? Nice try. Think again. Find *work* that you love, not fantasy.

Look for "Unsexy" Business Opportunities

Sure, the Internet is cool. Yeah, magazines are glossy and eye catching. But the competition is fierce. Too fierce if you don't have one incredibly stupendous idea. Part of what makes a good entrepreneur is originality, not the ability to catch a ride on somebody else's coattails. Look at "unglamorous" areas for new business ideas. You never know which seaweed encrusted clam will have a big ol' pearl inside.

Determine If What You Want to Do Is Do-able?

The mistake I see young entrepreneurs make most often has to do with *vision.* They are so preoccupied with getting a company started that they don't plan for the next stage in the company's development. Once you get past the initial setup period, one of two things will happen. Either your business will grow really fast or it will grow really slow. You have to be prepared for both possibilities.

Take the proverbial cure for cancer as an example. Let's say you had in your hand the scientific knowledge to manufacture a pill that cured all cancers. Do you have what it would take to deal with the worldwide rush to your door to purchase such a pill? Or would you be a basket case in a year trying to fulfill the need for this product?

People erroneously think that the hardest time in the company's development is the startup. That's like saying the hardest part of raising a child is childbirth. The startup of a new company is physically and emotionally draining, but the harder part is helping the baby grow into adulthood. The successful entrepreneur is overseeing the present while planning two stages ahead.

Decide If You Can Raise the Capital Needed Now and in the Future for This Business

If your business requires tremendous capitalization as it grows, you better have a plan to raise it each step of the way. How well your business grows depends on it. Ted Turner and his cable business may be the ultimate example of a "big" idea that needed enormous capitalization to start up and even greater infusions of cash to keep going in the initial stages. Are you up to the task?

The Hottest Businesses for Young Entrepreneurs

What kind of a book would this be if we didn't have a section on trends? Below, you'll get a peek at the industries that the rest of your peers are swarming to. Obviously, some of these fields are more mature (saturated) than others, so keep in mind the concept of industry life cycles. Trends do not last forever (there's probably evidence of that in your own wardrobe). Before you get into any business or industry, do your homework. If growth rates are slowing, take note, and proceed accordingly. Just because these are the hottest businesses now does not mean that they will maintain their speed of growth in five years. Keep that in mind as you check out the list of today's biggest trends. Foresight is the key. Who knows, you might just start a new trend yourself.

Who's the Trendiest One of All?

Though the dreams of young entrepreneurs have given birth to a multitude of different businesses, identifiable trends do exist. Currently, young entrepreneurs are flocking to five distinct industries: High technology, entertainment, apparel, multilevel marketing and international trade.

HIGH TECHNOLOGY

Software development, community building, networking, on-line publishing, and graphic design are just a few of the high-tech businesses spawned by young entrepreneurs, to whom programming is second nature. The business world can't avoid the information superhighway anymore—so who's left with microchip power? The young and the computer literate. It's not uncommon in the startup period of these ventures for a dorm room or apartment to serve as an office, with monthly parental allowances for food and books going to pay phone bills and on-line charges.

ENTERTAINMENT

Entertainment-focused businesses include promotional companies, music production and publishing, event ticket resellers, moviemaking, and special-event planning. These projects are often developed by students as social boosters but often become lucrative, lifestyle businesses. Promoting and starting clubs and being in or managing a band are probably the most common ventures of this kind. Promotional companies allow you to make money while spending time doing what's, well, really fun. Popularity also soars for those who promote local bars, restaurants, or clubs. It's generally a superficial business, but financially rewarding and socially unbeatable.

APPAREL

The apparel industry creates a whole other spectrum of lifestyle-related businesses that appeal strongly to the hipper-than-thou of our generation. The T-shirt business is the "lemonade stand" of the 1990s—young entrepreneurs paint, design, screen print, market and sell the T-shirts door-to-door, particularly in college. Entrepreneurs in their mid-twenties are more likely to take their apparel interests a bit further and explore importing or exporting a favorite product, creating their own brand or licensing an existing one to manufacture and distribute.

TK MAB (Two Kids Making A Buck) was started by two brothers, Michael and Jonathan Eisenberg, and their college buddy Larry Dear. Originally a T-shirt printer, by the time the founders were in their late twenties, TK MAB had taken the license to design and manufacturer Harley Davidson bathing suits. In the first year, the company did $4 million in sales. Similar to the computer industry, apparel is fueled by young entrepreneurs: Benetton, Cross Colors, HYP, and even Ralph Lauren offer just a few of the many examples of young entrepreneur clothing success stories.

MULTILEVEL MARKETING

Commonly referred to as pyramids or distribution companies, MLMs thrive off aspiring entrepreneurs who can sell. The multilevel concept is essentially this: Think of a pyramid with one person at the top who takes a product and sells it to three friends. They like the product so much that the first person convinces them to sell the product themselves on commission. The first person then receives commission on everything those three sell. To increase their revenue, the three recruit others to sell the product as well. This is called building a downline. The more people you have in your downline, or selling under you, the more money you can make.

Since being successful in this field means recruiting people to work for you, the concept is an exciting one for young people used to friendship cliques, fraternities and sororities, sports teams, and a barrage of social situations. Regardless of what is being sold (skin care, vitamins, makeup, telephone cards), multilevel companies offer intensive training and support, the glamour of business ownership, and dazzling "this-can-happen-to-you-too" success stories.

INTERNATIONAL TRADE

A career once reserved for the more experienced businessmen has become a golden opportunity for today's younger generation. From handwoven baskets, to blue jeans, to wholesale fish, and cellular phones, young people like us from all over the world are instigating and influencing international trade from their bedrooms, dorms, apartments, and high-rise offices. Successful young entrepreneurs in import/export realize that products and services we take for granted in the U.S. don't always exist in other countries, find the need where it exists, and fill it.

Another reason for import/export's popularity is that these businesses can be easily run while working at another job or while still in school, thanks to the ease of modern technology. Instant, real-time communication is readily available via telephone lines, on-line chat lines, and even video teleconferencing. If you have a few seconds to spare, you can fax or e-mail anywhere in the world within a minute or so. And as for shipping packages, who doesn't offer overnight delivery these days? Whereas generations before us had limited contact with people from other countries, for us, maintaining relationships with individuals or companies in other nations is as easy as pressing the send button on our PCs.

Selecting the Right Business Idea

So what's the best way to find the right business idea? Let's assume that you have no idea, no starting point. While the following decision-making process is fairly new, it has worked successfully for several people that I know who were contemplating entrepreneurship.

Adam Guild was a twenty-four-year-old economics analyst in the project finance group at a major international bank when he realized that being a corporate player was not giving him the satisfaction of doing the things he loved. In a professional capacity, Adam knew that he was best at managing people, organizing systems, and marketing new products. His current job was totally wrong for him. Adam then did something that most people his age would never think about: He went to the Johnson O'Conner Research Center (referred to as a "human engineering laboratory") to undergo aptitude testing. The goal of these tests was to determine which jobs he was best equipped and motivated to be doing. To no great surprise, Adam was pulled aside by the psychologist conducting the tests and told that he was in the wrong field.

Meanwhile, Adam had a friend from college who was an entrepreneurial computer genius. For several months, Adam had been seriously contemplating quitting his job and going into business with his friend. Four critical questions arose immediately for Adam:

- Was he ready to take the entrepreneurial plunge—working long hours, taking on enormous responsibility and risk, sacrificing adequate compensation, and dedicating most of his waking hours to a new business?

- Would a small business environment be a comfortable one after spending a few years in the corporate world?

- Since his friend's business was brand new, employed no one, and had not yet been funded by investors, was it smart to take the risk of leaving a secure job for one that was seemingly so precarious?

- Did he love the business, or at least the company, enough to make it his life?

Ask yourself these questions. Then, at the very least, if you are really serious, you'll know that you're making a solid, intelligent decision about entering or starting an entrepreneurial venture.

As you take each of these steps, the main goal should be to narrow your search. Once you have given up on the corporate scenario, start wiping away industries and categories from your mind that do not strike a chord with you. Most will not. Don't feel as if you are limiting your options, because actually this will help you see the real possibilities much more clearly. Oh, and if you're still wondering what happened to Adam, he did follow this advice and reevaluated his situation. Going to work with his friend's startup turned out to be less appealing than he had originally thought. Adam found a fairly small, entrepreneurial video teleconferencing company instead. Involving himself here allowed him to test the waters without the risk.

Step One: Decide If the Entrepreneurial Life Is for You

The best way to find out if you are an entrepreneur is to surround yourself with entrepreneurs, to get a taste of their world. Meet as many of them as you can, read everything you can, ask any questions that pop into your head, and constantly fine-tune your focus. Entrepreneurs are a different breed of people. If you are not one deep down yourself, maybe you feel the need to work with one like Adam did so that you can still live the entrepreneurial life but not actually have to take on all the risk. Figuring this out is priority one. If you are still not sure if the entrepreneurial life is for you, imagine this scenario:

Tomorrow you are going to go to work at your new company. Over the phone, your partner begins to rattle off the task list for the next day, which sparks off a dozen other things you remind yourself to do. Contemplate each item as if you really had to organize, manage, solve, and analyze what was being dumped on you. Think about how you would complete the list and how you would organize your day.

- Your business cards need to be reordered because the printer made a mistake and she wants you to pay for the error.
- The phone company sent you a disconnect notice.
- You still need a FedEx account number.
- The trade journals that you ordered are still being delivered to your neighbor.
- A new intern starts tomorrow, and you don't have anything planned for him.
- The local paper needs a biography from you and your partner for a story.
- The ATM machine won't even give you $20 from your account, your credit card is maxed, and you're meeting clients for drinks later.
- The landlord is asking for your workers' compensation papers again, and you still have no idea where to go to get them.
- A big prospect is asking for company literature and it won't be ready for another two weeks. You told them originally that it would be there a week ago.
- Someone just informed you that you need to be paying your business taxes quarterly.

- Three irate customers called to complain about something. You need to call them back and straighten everything out.

- The new version of Quickbooks was just released. You spilled a Frappachino on disk number 3 as you pulled it out of the package three weeks ago and decided just to wait for the new version to come out before you take a shot at exchanging it. Anyone see the receipt?

- The bank wants the new draft of your business plan by the end of the week.

- Two computers are frozen and your printer will only print in blue ink.

- Your car insurance is due.

- If you can put an ad together by tomorrow, a friend of yours will slip it into a new magazine she is starting that hits your target market.

- Your father just called to find out if you've reconsidered getting a "real job."

How do you feel? Exhausted? Do you have a headache? Are you getting nervous? Or are you excited? When you read through this list, how you feel is a good indication of how you might feel in real life. Real entrepreneurs start thinking a million miles a minute, shuffling and prioritizing tasks in their head. When one item is remembered, four more things to do come to mind. Yes, it does get exhausting for us too; but flying by the seat of your pants, stress, overwhelming situations, and general chaos are just part of the game. If you can't image how people cope with this *every day,* you'll probably regret leaving the safe haven of your old life.

But maybe the idea of accomplishing everything on that long, daunting list and having such an unstructured daily schedule makes your blood pump a little faster. If the good feeling of owning your own business completely overshadows all of the on-the-edge, oh-no-what-am-I-gonna-do situations presented above, then you're definitely on the right bus.

For an entrepreneur, something as menial as cleaning your office windows gives you a sense of satisfaction because they're *in your own office.* You are so happy just to be there—to actually have four walls that represent your business—that it's almost a pleasure. When you run out of envelopes in the middle of a big mailing, pulling out your own Staples credit card almost makes the hassle not seem like such a big deal. After you've struggled the way younger entrepreneurs must to succeed, your office, your windows, and your corporate cards all become symbolic of your progress and professional accomplishment. Yes, these little thrills fade with time, but new ones always seem to pop up in their place. An entrepreneur finds bliss in these little events.

Step Two: Find What You Love

The perfect entrepreneurial venture is one in which you'd work for free (You'll probably have to at first anyway!). If you are not absolutely in love with your concept, it will be very hard to motivate others (like clients and employees), let alone yourself. The best salespeople are the ones who truly believe in what they are selling. If you don't love your business and what you offer to customers, it will be obvious. But odds are there is a related business venture that is perfect for you.

Without thinking about any specific business opportunities, spend some time thinking about the things that you love to do. Write down your hobbies, passions, and interests. Next, create a list of things that you are good at, have special skills in, or have a degree or certification in. Study the two lists very carefully. Then work on a third list for related opportunities. Don't try to be too practical or let yourself be critical. Just write down everything you can think of in which your skills and hobbies would be useful in a business capacity. Show the list to some close friends, and ask for their opinions. There is a very good chance that someone else might recognize your entrepreneurial calling before even you can figure it out. Start to get a sense of potential business ventures that fit your lifestyle, interests, and talents.

An enormously helpful thing to do is to go out and buy a bunch of small business magazines and journals. Definitely pick up copies of *Entrepreneur, Inc.,* and *Success* magazines, the top three for entrepreneurs. Then grab a copy of your city's business journal. You might even take a look at the latest issue of the *Wall Street Journal, Business Week,* or *Forbes.* Give yourself two or three days to a week to read, skim, and scan these publications. Dog-ear the corners of magazine pages that catch you eye. Read anything that appeals to you, and skip anything that doesn't. Just make sure that you look at every page. You never know what you might miss with a too quick glance. When you are finished with all of the reading, take note of the subjects that appealed to you the most. Create a list with the subjects on all the pages you marked. Are there any similarities, repetition, or patterns? Try to identify what types of businesses and opportunities appealed to you the most.

Again, you may want to write this all down on a piece of paper. Many business experts agree that people who write down their goals are more likely to achieve them. One of the main reasons writing things down is so effective is because it allows us to brainstorm ideas then refer back to them later—something we are incapable of doing off the top of our heads. Another reason is that your initial ideas might sound better to you later on, after you've had time to mull them over and build on the initial concept or run them by others.

Step Three: Conduct Your Own Industry Study

Once you have settled on an industry or concept, the best thing to do is to create your own textbook—one that is totally customized to your industry and interests. To create a textbook, you need to spend a good amount of time and energy in researching the industry you have selected and business opportunities within that field.

Start by going to the library or using your home computer to run a search for articles that have been written about your area of interest. Lexis/Nexus is one of the leading on-line databases that allows you to search through millions of articles that are published all over the world. (The Lexis/Nexus system is available at most major university libraries. Public libraries often have a comparable system, but they tend to have fewer computers dedicated to running such searches.) Find out who the industry experts are and run a search for articles on them. Then ask a librarian for any reference books in which you can find demographic information on your field. They should be able to give you sources that would have statistics about the market size, annual industry revenues, and customer profiles. Look for charts and graphs to make your book more interesting and your knowledge of the subject more credible.

Once you have located a variety of industry articles that appeal to you, print them out so you can have your own copies. Then, run a search on the web. Use one of the major Internet search engines like Yahoo or Webcrawler to find any websites relating to your industry. Print out copies of those too. If you read about any associations or organizations for your industry, call them and request literature. Take all of the articles, newsletters, information packages, and case studies that you can get copies of and put them in a big binder. (You may even want to get the whole thing professionally bound at a print shop or copy store for about $3.00.)

Take your personal textbook everywhere you go. Highlight important ideas, information, and statistics. Read an article or page every time you have a few free moments. This is by far one of the best ways to research and get a good feel for an industry. Another great benefit is that you can keep the book for future reference. Odds are that if you went through all of the time and trouble to do this much research on an industry, even if you chose to go into another, this one will come up again at some point. So hold on to these. Published articles never lose their value because when they are not teaching us about the current trends they are teaching us about the history of the subject.

Toward the end of step three, you should be looking more closely at a few select opportunities in your industry. Remember, you must constantly refine your focus if you are going to select the right business to zoom in on.

Step Four: Become an Expert on Your Business

Even if you haven't officially started, or committed to your business idea, take the one in which you are most interested and zero in on it. Repeat as much of Step Three as you can, using your best business concept as the subject of research. Then, look around for competitors. Request information from every competing firm that you can find. Start collecting articles, information and literature. Create a supplement to your original textbook. Seek out information on any classes, expos, or events that relate to your business and attend them if you can. These experiences can be invaluable, as they are taught by experts, you will meet other enthusiasts, and the overall result is that you learn more about your business. Hop on-line and look for any newsgroups or chat lines that relate to your business.

Speak to as many people as possible about your idea. People who are already in the field will always be the best ones to advise you on whether your business idea has potential or not—if they are honest with you. If you talk to people who could be direct competitors, some might actually try to discourage you and maybe even use your idea themselves. Find other young entrepreneurs in the field. They are more likely to share their startup experience with you because most young entrepreneurs love to help others in the same situation when they can. And *everyone* likes to talk about their own business. If you can find people who at one time had a business like yours but failed or walked away, you've struck a golden information source. People who were once in a field, particularly if they were business owners, often have strong opinions and vivid memories of their former entrepreneurial haunts. If they ended on bad terms, you'll get even more valuable information on what leads to failure and/or about what you need to be concerned and aware. In this case, bad news can help you avoid making a frustrating, time-consuming, expensive, and all-around bad decision.

If you follow these steps, researching, learning about, and narrowing your focus along the way, the business you eventually decide to commit to will have a significantly greater chance of success.

Are You and Your Business Compatible?

Now this should be pretty obvious to you if you are serious about opening a business. Will your business enhance or destroy your lifestyle? Will your business require you to do things that you hate to do on a regular basis? Though we all have duties we despise performing—like administrative work and filing for instance—it's just part of the price you have to pay to build your own company. Look at the big picture. If you are in a service business, for example, you'd better *love* dealing with people. If you're in the pet-grooming business, you'd better have warm, fuzzy feelings for furry little creatures. *Use your common sense.* Don't enter into anything if at the very heart of the work lies your most dreaded task.

Michelle Barsamian, a sixteen-year-old student, was enrolled in an after-school entrepreneurship class I taught. One day she came to class announcing that her father had given her another business idea. The idea was to sell Las Vegas paraphernalia in Boston from kiosks in local malls. Her father figured that if Vegas was such a popular vacation spot, East Coasters would love the chance to buy Vegas-wear at home. Michelle wasn't sure if she should take her father's advice or not. After hashing the idea out, she realized that she 1) wasn't thrilled about the idea of standing at a kiosk in a mall all day long, 2) probably wouldn't have related well to prospective customers, and 3) hated Vegas paraphernalia. Wrong business. Clearly.

If you know what you like to do and understand the type of person that you are, listen to those clues. Ideally, your business should be something that you're in love with, or at least interested in enough to dedicate most of your time to.

Goal Setting and Strategic Planning

Imagine that you could be happier than you've ever dreamed, living the perfect life, arriving at the end of your ideal career path, and surrounding yourself with people you admire and respect. Take a minute, close your eyes, and paint for yourself a picture of your ideal life. Now without giving weight to any roadblocks you might encounter, or any personal handicaps, construct a plan to get where you want to go.

Steven Covey, author of *The Seven Habits of Highly Effective People*, says that in order to do this you must begin with an end in mind. To make your dreams into reality, you must first have a clear picture of where you want to be. Some of the most successful people in history later attributed much of their success to having a clear picture in their heads to guide them along. If you are trying to reach a cliff with a beautiful view of the ocean, you don't focus on the obstacles you must overcome to reach your destination. You think about why you're out there in the first place—you are there to see the ocean.

Where are you in your life? Are you a student, a young business owner, someone's employee? Why are you where you are now? What are the most important reasons for what you are doing with your life? Are you in the position you are in now because someone else wants you to be there? Or are you following a dream that is yours?

If you are not passionate and dedicated to striving toward your goals, to being your personal best, why are you wasting your time?

Envision your ocean view: your goals, your dreams, your future. Use your business to make them come true.

Marketing Research

When you are young, you tend to think you know everything. The truth is, the more you learn, the more you realize how little you actually do know. My favorite phrase when I was a teenager was "trust me." If any one taught me that I wasn't as "all knowing" as I thought I was, it was my father. Though I often thought he was just trying to burst my bubble, he actually was teaching me to recognize my own intellectual boundaries—not so I could merely accept them, but so I could recognize what I really didn't know and learn what I needed to.

Even today, the more I learn about a subject—even my own industry—the more I realize that I still have so much to learn. Though there are a million benefits to building your own intelligence, funneling that energy into a business of your own can be among the most fulfilling. It also doesn't hurt to keep in mind that the younger you are the more people will question your ability to run a successful business.

In "Selecting the Right Business Idea," we outlined four of the best steps to determining your ultimate business venture. If you actually followed the steps, most of the questions raised in this section will have been answered. This section is meant to help you prepare yourself for your new business by ensuring that you know what other people will assume you know.

History

Regardless of what industry you are in, it has a history. Find out how your industry began and evolved, and any major events that affected its progress. Who was the first to offer your product or service? If it was a major corporation or the concept failed at first, find out why. If anyone ever approaches you for background information on your business, you'll sound like much more of an expert if you know what the field was like before you got there.

Technical Knowledge

Technical know-how is crucial and can't be compromised. If you are interested enough to start a business in a particular field, you must surely know about the technical skills that are required for your success. Reading trade journals and speaking to experts should enlighten you about the latest advances and techniques with which you should become familiar.

Trends

Keep on top of trends in your industry. If certain skills are required to keep up with the trends, learn them. There's nothing worse than an accountant who doesn't know how to use an electronic spreadsheet program, or a twenty-four-hour repair man without a pager. If you are a graphic artist, know the top software programs. If your company is in the communications industry, make sure that you have an e-mail account.

Industry Experts

Often the leading industry experts are your competitors. Don't be shy. Seek out and talk to your competition. If they are experts in your field, you should attend the same events, expos and conferences that they do. Make yourself known in your industry by getting to know the established experts. If you can create a good rapport with them, incredible advice, insight, and often even referrals will follow. What's even better is that when someone asks you about a well-known industry insider, you can say that not only do you know of them but you actually know them personally.

Competition

The value of information cannot be stressed enough. Understanding your competition is important for many reasons:

- You should always have a good idea as to your position in the marketplace.
- Without knowing about your competition, you can easily underestimate their power to take away your clients or market share.
- Next to innovation, imitation can be an excellent route to success (if clean and legal).
- You might find that you can share business. If your busy season forces you to turn customers away, referring them to a competitor shows goodwill and concern for customer satisfaction. Making the gesture will often solicit a similar response from your competition. It also shows that you have respect for them and their work.

How to Find Industry Information

With all of the ways to find information these days, you shouldn't have a problem learning about your industry. Remember, knowledge is power. Young entrepreneurs wind up having to prove themselves over and over in the business world. Knowledge about your field is your first line of defense. From the easiest to the more complex and time-consuming investigation techniques, try to be diligent about the points that follow.

Compile a List of Competitors

Creating your own list of competitors will force you to find out what you're up against in your business. Not only can you get a better understanding of who they are, but a list may help you identify some hidden trends or the need to gather even more information.

Plain old observation is usually a good way to start building this list. Drive around your neighborhood. Talk to people who might be potential customers. Where do they go for service? You might also want to check with your local Chamber of Commerce or even the Yellow Pages to see who might be a competitor.

If your search needs to be a national or international one, hop on the web. Run a keyword search under your service or product. Look through industry trade journals. Find the trade associations or organizations. If you go to a library, the reference desk has two great books called *The Directory of Associations* and *The Directory of Directories*. If your industry is an established one, someone has probably started an association for it, or compiled a directory of firms within it. These can be a gold mine of information on your competitors. Ask a librarian for other reference books. You may have to go to a business library, but it is well worth the trip. You never know what kind of information you can find.

Become a Customer of Your Competitors

Becoming a customer of your competitors can be the easiest way in the world to learn about them. Many think that learning about your competition involves Mission-Impossible spy trips to their facilities at 3 A.M., but let's be realistic. How would we get into their buildings anyway?

Becoming a customer to your competition allows you to learn about, observe, and gather all of the following juicy information with very little effort:

- Literature/marketing brochures
- Sales pitch
- Customer relations
- Knowledge of the business
- Size of operation
- Feelings about their competition (you)
- Competitive advantage

In most cases, all you have to do is walk into their store, send away for information, or purchase something and observe.

When you run a company, your number-one objective is to please the customer. Whether you have to give them special attention, answer their questions, or hold their hands while they try to understand your service or product, you do it. Now, imagine this being your competitor, and you being the consumer. Pretty easy work, this learning about your competition, huh? However, the bigger and more diversified the company, the harder it is going to be to get a complete idea of how they operate and make money, but do your homework accordingly and you should be able to find out most of the information you need to create competition, or even better, an original business concept.

If this sounds like dirty work, that's because it can be. How far you decide to take this is ultimately up to you, but I recommend you keep it aboveboard. If you don't play fairly in business, people will find out . . . and return the favor. You *can* create a very successful company honestly, ethically, and still manage to have the respect of your competitors—the greatest feat.

Scour Industry Publications and Articles

If anything is going to give you detailed information on your industry and competitors, it's going to be a publication or article dedicated to it. Reading trade journals will do a lot to build your knowledge of your own field, and most importantly, give you an excellent indication of how you and your business size up.

Read Relevant Case Studies

If you've gone to business school, you've probably read more case studies that you can stomach, but don't give up on them yet. Case studies, for those who are unfamiliar with them, are reports or documents that tell the story of a company or organization. Most will offer background information, industry demographics, personal stories from key executives and staff, and detailed financial statements. While several business schools publish their own case studies, Harvard Business School Press is not only the most prestigious, but the most successful at this type of publishing. If you can get a catalog of their case studies and find one on a related business or direct competitor for about $5–10, you will often be sent one of the most comprehensive documents on your industry publicly available.

Survey People in Your Target Market

An amazing yet largely underutilized practice, surveying people in your target market is one of the best ways to find out if your product or service actually *has* a market. Far too many people stake their reputation on something that they believe is wonderful, believe everyone will like, yet have no reason to believe so other than their own pre-monition. Don't waste your time and money on a business unless you are sure that a market exists for it. Create a survey that is objective and doesn't persuade or lead people to answer in favor of your product.

Then go to a place where people in your target market might gather, like a shopping center, a gym, a college campus, or even on an on-line bulletin board. Politely ask people to fill out your survey (which incidentally shouldn't take more than five minutes). Tell them that you are looking to introduce a new product or service to the market and that you'd really appreciate just a minute of two of their time for their input. Don't expect everyone to stop what they are doing to help you. If you are very courteous, smile, and are sincerely interested in their opinion, people will be more likely to help. Thank everyone, regardless of whether they fill out a survey. Also, get a good sample size. Depending on how large your customer base will need to be or how specialized your service is, a good start is to collect at least fifty surveys.

Tabulate the results and write a summary of your findings. This information will be very useful to you personally, as well as to any staff, prospective customers, and investors, should you put together a business plan. Armed with this type of information, you are in an incredible position to satisfy your market's needs.

Work for Your Competition

There really is no better way to learn about a business than to work in one. If you can hold out long enough to get some feeling for your trade "on someone else's dime," all the better. Depending on your industry, some companies may ask you to fill out a "non-compete form," which basically says that you legally give up the right to go into a competitive business. These are more common in high-tech, finance, service businesses, and companies with proprietary information to protect. If you sign one, you waive your right to start or work for a competing business. Don't take this agreement lightly. You don't want to be sued, and you probably don't want to make arch enemies of your competition either.

Resources

Here are a few great, basic resources for finding information on other businesses that will come in handy when you're doing your research:

Pacific Bell 1-800-848-8000

Pacific Bell publishes some of the best resource books for business owners available anywhere. Most are updated annually and will help you find more resources for your individual needs than you could ever imagine. One book that I have come to rely on almost daily is *The National Directory of Addresses and Phone Numbers.* Call the company for a list of other available titles (and prices), including *The National Shopper's Guide* and *Small Business Success.*

NYNEX 1-800-34-NYNEX (346-9639)

NYNEX's *Business to Business Directory* is another great resource book that covers specific regions of the country. Inside you can find many business support networks, state-supported organizations, resource centers, convention centers, meeting facilities, classified sections, and the like.

AT&T 1-800-426-8686

AT&T's Smart Resource Center offers a variety of great resources for small business owners. There are a couple that I would recommend to any entrepreneur, but definitely call to find out about other great reference books for you. The *Business Buyer's Guide* is a great place to find thousands of business-to-business listings with 800 numbers for vendors, manufacturers, and wholesalers all over the country. AT&T also offers a workbook for new entrepreneurs called "Smart Steps to Small Business Success."

CHAPTER 3

The Big Bad Business Plan

OMEONE ONCE TOLD ME THAT IN ORDER TO WRITE AN EFFECTIVE BUSINESS plan, I'D have to lock myself in a room for sixteen hours straight and just hammer it out. I didn't believe it at first, but five months into the writing of my last one, the advice started to make a lot of sense.

Of all the tests of discipline in your life, prepare for this to be one of the biggest. It's a little scary to write a business plan. In fact, it can seem like a nightmare, but consider it a master's thesis for your business. Many more people take on the project than finish it. But those who do are rewarded. Your reward as an entrepreneur is the validation of your business idea. If you can finish your business plan, and the numbers and analysis in it makes sense, then you can march ahead with confidence rather than fear or uncertainty.

Do You Really Need One?

I'm going to give you a big firm YES! You should write a business plan not because other people want you to, but because you want your business to have the greatest chance at success that it can. Unless you plan on financing your business by yourself, no investor will look at your company without a business plan. So whether just for yourself, or as a sales tool, you do need a business plan. Let's see how serious it needs to be now.

How Complex Should It Be?

When in doubt, look to your environment for clues. The industry, type of business, and size of investment required will largely determine how complex your business plan should be. Also, you must consider for whom you are writing the plan. Are you using it to convince your aunt to give you a loan, to help you get a better idea of what you need to do, or to get a line of credit from your bank? Each situation calls for slightly different information and levels of complexity. If you are still unsure of what your business plan must convey, come right out and ask the people you are submitting it to. Do they want five years of financial forecasts, by month? Personal income statements? Extensive market analysis? Maybe they just want a really strong executive summary, for now. Having this insight *before* you dive into a business plan project can save you so much time and energy that it might just salvage your sanity.

Show Me the Money

I'm sure that you've read about those high-tech companies that raise a few million dollars in venture capital in their first six months in business. Well, if this sounds like a realistic possibility for you and your company, then your business plan had better be worth a million dollars. To raise a few million, you are probably going to have to spend some money to get your business plan up to standard. There are a lot of great books out on business plans that can walk even the most inexperienced entrepreneur through the process. (For a list of recommendations, check out the resource section at the end of this chapter.)

See if you can get your hands on some other plans that have succeeded in receiving similar financing. Talk to venture capitalists and to business professors who teach business plan writing or have come across quite a few plans in their time. Investment bankers have their own version of a business plan called an "offering circular." Used mostly to raise money by selling shares of a corporation, some young entrepreneurs have used offering circulars to quickly woo investors. If your business plan needs go far beyond your own capabilities, talk to some MBA students about writing a plan for you, or attend a local venture network meeting. Every major city has them and their usual overflow of service providers, lawyers, and yes, business plan writers. Venture networks are also the place for you to raise the investment capital once you are ready. So you could feasibly kill two birds with one stone by getting involved in one.

Okay, a million dollars would be nice, but it's way more than what you need for your business. Maybe $50,000, maybe a few hundred thousand, or even $1,000 would do for you. What kind of information do you need to convey about your business to prove that it, and you, have the potential to be successful? Again, who are your investors? They will dictate which information they are most concerned with getting from you. Do this business plan yourself. At this level of investment, you should be able to create a plan solid enough to do the job on your own. Be diligent, covering all of the major issues outlined below. This plan may be easier to write, but it should not be a walk in the park.

Let's assume that you really don't need to raise any money for your business. Do you still need a business plan? What did I tell you before? The more time and energy you put into planning, the more likely you are to launch a successful venture. Do it for yourself. Having your business fail is a gut-wrenching experience, but a good one for any entrepreneur. Why? Because failing teaches you the hardest lessons. Your business plan forces you to look at potential problems objectively and plan for them accordingly.

Create the outline for yourself, then go through and lay out your plan for each section. Ask yourself all the questions that you would expect others to ask. What will you be doing to market your product? How do you know that people will buy from you? Are you sure that you should be pricing your product at $69 instead of $59? Are all of your costs covered with the selling price? Have you considered all of the legal and tax issues? When will you break even? If you can answer questions like these and feel comfortable with this type of interrogation, then you've probably done the research you need to. Putting it all on paper not only strengthens your knowledge of your business but allows you to reevaluate and update your strategy periodically. When you are running a business, you can hide a lot of things—particularly from yourself. A business plan pulls everything out into the open, airing problems that must be resolved for the business plan to have any value. So there are your options: to write a plan or to wing it with your business. Think of your business plan as an insurance policy. Though you may not have too much to lose, you have everything to gain with one.

Getting Started

Before you do anything, gather together all of the articles, books, literature, and information that you have on your business and industry (now that "textbook" I told you about in Chapter 2 is really going to come in handy). You are going to need a lot of facts, figures, and statistics that you may never have used before, so it is best to have them with you when you begin to create an outline for your plan. Without an outline, you can make a mess of your business plan quickly. Because there is so much information to organize, the more you are consciously aware of at first, the easier it will be to find a place for it all and make it all flow in the end. Start with the order of the major sections. Then begin noting places where various information can be added. As you do this, you may want to keep a list of things to do. Many bits and pieces of information will be missing along the way. The more diligent you are about keeping track of the necessary steps, the faster you will finish your plan.

A Guiding Outline

What follows is a general outline to help you lay out your final business plan. Use this information to spark your own creativity. Some sections will require that you add to this information provided here, while other sections may be irrelevant and thus should be discarded. Start by creating your own outline. Determine what information and questions must be addressed, then begin by filing in the outline with bullet points of important topics or by plugging in information that you have already compiled. Keep in mind the following points as you go along:

- Be as professional as possible.
- Write your plan in the third-person perspective.
- Be honest.
- Have at least one or two business people proofread your plan.
- Make sure to include ALL relevant information on your business.
- Explain everything clearly and concisely.
- Use a computer and laser printer (color, if possible).
- Use visuals in exhibits (pictures of product, graphs, charts).
- Have the final copy bound in some form.
- Use one-and-a-half-inch spacing and at least one-inch margins.

Unless you can find a more useful model, follow this outline. Now you're armed and ready to start writing your business plan. Again, there are many different ways to compose such a document. This is one of the many effective ways for you to communicate your concept to investors.

The Business Plan

I. Executive Summary

The Executive Summary should be a brief overview of your business plan. In one or two pages (but no more!), this should enable someone to understand the essence of your business. This is not the place for details. This is simply a preview of what's to come inside. This is your chance to convince someone to read the rest.

Although it's one of the most important parts of your plan and should appear first (after your title page), the

> **From: Devin Schain— On Campus Mktg**
>
> When I started my business in college 10 years ago, I took a course at The Wharton School called Entrepreneurial Management. I did a business plan about the company I started a year earlier called, Campus Carpets. My professor used the old saying, "Cut your projections in half." Well I would like to modify that saying as a result of personal experience. I exceeded my sales goals by 125 percent in 1986, however my bottom line (net income) was almost 75 percent lower than my original projections. I did not know who these guys FICA and FEUDA, etc., were. The moral of my lesson is that you may have the vision and sales to achieve numbers, however costs are always higher than you anticipate. There are many hidden costs that you will not encounter until you run a small business and have to pay real taxes and deal with state and national governments.

Executive Summary should be *written last*—and for good reason. You can't give an accurate synopsis until after you've worked out all the details yourself, which most entrepreneurs don't really do until they write their business plan. This summary should, however, give readers an idea of what they will find in each of the major sections—The Product/Service, Market Description, Management Plan, Operations, Marketing & Advertising, Sales & Distribution, and Financials. Use this section as a teaser. Most people will read the Executive Summary first, and often it will be the only thing that they will read. This first section allows people an opportunity to quickly preview your business plan and get a feel for how well written they can expect the document to be.

II. Business Description

A. *Introduction.* A personal introduction statement is like a one-minute speech you would give to introduce yourself to a group. Use your personal introduction statement to get the main concept of your business across quickly and concisely. In writing your business plan, you must be even more careful than you are with your verbal presentation because you are putting it on paper. Start by describing what you do, what you make and/or what service you provide. Illustrate your service/product's attributes. Why is it different? Who are your ideal customers? (Be brief here. You will have an opportunity to go into depth about your target market in the Marketing & Sales section.) What benefits do you provide to customers?

B. *Business Background.* In a paragraph or so, explain where the idea for your company originated. Did an experience help you recognize a market need? Did you find that you could provide a product or service better than other businesses in the market? Don't be shy about your reasoning. This is an opportunity to show off your intuition and business savvy.

C. *Product/Service Description.* If you have several different packages, models, or products, clearly separate each, then describe the differences in detail. Be specific and very clear about what your customers will receive from your company. Indicate how much customers will pay for each item or service and whether tax will be included in the price, or added to it. (This is not mandatory information, but it is good to include if you can. If you have any questions about requirements for your business, call your local IRS office or department of taxation.) Make sure that anyone completely unfamiliar with your business will have a good understanding of what you propose to do after they are finished reading your business description.

D. *Legal Structure.* Describe the legal status of your company. For example: "The XYZ Company is legally structured as a sole proprietorship and is registered in the city of Boston, MA."

III. Market Description

This market description should clearly and specifically describe who your target market is, as well as highlight the need you will be filling. Add the market research you conducted and feature your market surveys. (See the section on Market Research on pp. 48–49.) Break each of these into different sections and make sure to show how much work you have done. This gives you an excellent opportunity to prove how well you understand your market and customers.

In this section, you might want to add a "market segmentation" grid. A market segmentation grid is a chart that identifies potential customers for a company. Breaking prospective customers down into different groups will allow you to then identify different characteristics about them, such as how many of each group exists, where they can be found, the best way to market to them, and so forth.

Keep in mind that the column headings can be adapted to represent any major concerns or issues that you need to address when starting your company. Other possible headings could include group goals/concerns, contact person, typical events, legal considerations, potential trips desired, and so forth. Keep in mind that this chart is not a boilerplate and should be unique and customized for your business venture.

A market segmentation grid can be easily incorporated into your plan to impress investors with your understanding of your market. Clearly show who your target customers are and why; identify who your competitors are; if possible, show what your target market's share is, what it's estimated to be, and what you project your market share could be. The following is an example of a market segmentation grid for a travel agency that specializes in group packages. Use this as a frame of reference to suit your own needs.

IV. Management Plan

This section should describe your background, how your experience is relevant to what your company does, who will be in charge of what functions, and how employees (including yourself) will be compensated. Indicate here who will be paid on commissions and who, if anyone, will be on salary. If more than one person will be running the company, clearly separate each person and biography. This could be formatted in the following way:

Jessica Hunter—President

Jessica has been a recognized community leader since her graduation from high school in 1994. As an all-league softball player, Jessica gained an intimate knowledge of the needs of younger athletes. To help fulfill a need that she herself recognized early in her career, Jessica joined The Softball Services Company to assist young athletes like herself . . . etc.

Jason Marcus—Vice President

Jason began his entrepreneurial career at the age of fifteen, when he started a T-shirt company selling preprinted shirts to spectators at high school football games. The company stayed in business for one year, then was closed as Jason entered his junior year . . . etc.

Market Segmentation Grid

GROUPS	GROUP SIZE	HOW TO REACH	AVAILABLE INCOME	FREQUENCY OF TRAVEL
University groups/clubs (fraternities, student government, cultural groups)	Varies, usually 20–50 people	Direct mail, present at group meetings, school papers	Limited on an individual basis, yet group activity funds for trips may exist	Up to five times/year, including major holidays and vacations
Professional groups (chambers of commerce, marketing associations, industry organizations with local chapters)	Varies, from 50–200 members	Direct mail, present at group meetings, advertise in city business journals & newspapers, meet with membership directors	Stable cash flow due to more permanent jobs, tend to have money saved, willing to spend reasonable amount to have great trip	Once, maybe two or three times per year, subject to vacation time from work
Local companies	Usually between 20–100 employees	Varies depending on type and size of company; sometimes coordinate trips and offer to share costs with employees	Presentation to owner of company or director of human resources; advertising in city business journals & local newspapers	Probably one to three times per year, depending on company

List the different positions people will hold in your company and explain clearly what each position will entail. (Remember to keep your formatting consistent. The style used above can be easily adapted here as well.) You also might consider combining this section with the one above if you already have specific people placed in positions.

President—Compensation: 10% commission on all sales

The president will be in charge of overseeing the other managers and sales people and maintaining the company's finances. All bookkeeping functions will be handled by the president. The president will also be in charge of representing the company to the media as well as other community leaders.

Remember to keep as many costs variable as possible. The best way to start this is to pay everyone on commission. A good rule of thumb is to offer salespeople (check with an accountant to see if you can consider them independent contractors) 10–20 percent of the sales price of goods/services. Though this is a good range, keep in mind that your situation may require that you pay slightly more or less depending on your circumstances. If you are having trouble deciding on a suitable percentage, study your income statement to review your costs and profits. Do not allocate more for commissions than you can reasonably afford to pay and still profit yourself.

If you are concerned that your business background is a bit weak, insert the information about your background after the description of management positions to downplay any lack of experience. Though everything in your plan must be factual, you can enhance sections with some eloquent descriptions. One way to strengthen this section is to identify two or three mature experienced business people who will act as unpaid advisors to the company.

V. Operations Plan

This area can be handled in different ways. Use it to explain the processes that will be followed to manufacture, service, and deliver your products to customers. Try to create a flowchart of operations to show that you have carefully planned the manufacturing and delivery of your product and service. Detail what steps will be taken from the time a customer places an order to when you will deliver the final service and receive payment.

VI. Marketing and Advertising Plan

How will prospective customers learn about your company? What marketing or advertising methods will you use to get the word out? Identify, in order of descending importance, your most reliable marketing channels. Then briefly describe each. Be specific, mentioning any secured contracts or established relationships that you might have with anyone to market your business. Also identify how many customers you can expect to reach through each channel. If you can barter for ad space or cross-promote your product/service with another, this is an excellent place to show your resourcefulness.

VII. Sales and Distribution

How will your goods be sold? Will you sell through an organization, local stores, at school or via mail order? Again, if you have previous arrangements or agreements with local vendors, explain them here. How will you collect payments? When will you collect payments—in advance, at point-of-sale, through billing?

VIII. Financials

Begin with a brief description of what the cost of establishing and capitalizing the business will be and how you plan to make money. What are your revenues and costs? Why are certain ones greater than others?

This section should have the following critical financial information: per unit costs, cost of goods sold, income statements, historical data, balance sheets, and a breakeven analysis. But before you start to pull your hair out, do some research on your business and talk to some advisors about what you really need. If you are going for a bank loan or for venture capital, there are very strict guidelines that you will have to follow. The information I'm offering here, is VERY simplistic. It is meant only to give you a taste for what you are going to need to do. I highly recommend buying a book dedicated to business plan writing, or taking a class on the subject if you are about to seriously attack one.

For those of you who need some help with the bare bones basics, let's review them with the most basic financial document that any business plan must include—the income statement. The income statement involves a few elements that you might not know about. Next to financial forecasts, your income statement is the first thing that most people will want to see in this section, and often in the whole plan.

What an income statement does is tell someone how much your company has made in a specific period of time (usually a year, or a month). An income statement is essentially a statement identifying how much money you have made, how much you have spent, and what you have left over at the end. This is a factual statement and cannot be "doctored" to make it look more attractive. Consequently, this is the best indication of a company's financial stability. If you haven't realized any revenue yet, you'll want to create a *pro forma income statement,* which estimates how much money you will spend and earn over a period of time. Make it a point to spend some time on your own learning about the various types of financial statements, because you will come to rely on them as your company grows and seeks outside funding.

Before I show you the format, let's just review some quick definitions:

Sales: Any inflow of money that you have received from the purchase of your service or product. Also referred to as *revenues*.

COGS: Costs of goods sold is simply the cost of your raw materials, whether purchased (usually at a wholesale price) or produced, or how much it costs you to provide your service. COGS are the hard costs or *direct* costs of your goods and are directly related to your sales price. Do not include your rent, office expenses, or other *indirect* costs here.

Gross Profit: This indicates the money you have left after you are paid for a sale, minus the direct cost of that item or service (COGS). Gross Profit = Sales – COGS.

Variable Costs: Variable costs are expenses that change each month (the opposite of fixed costs). A variable cost might be the purchase of software, commissions paid, setup fees, consulting fees, travel, or other sporadic expenses associated with, but not directly tied to, producing your product (as opposed to COGS).

Fixed Costs: Fixed costs are those that stay constant over time. Your rent, insurance payments, salaries (not commissions), and any interest payments are considered fixed costs. Fixed Costs are also commonly referred to as *overhead expenses* and are very important, as many businesses tend to have higher overhead expenses than necessary; and this can cause problems.

EBIT: Earnings before income tax can also be called *profit before tax* or *pretax profit*. It means how much you have left over after you've paid all of your expenses. Unfortunately, though, this is not the amount we take home, but rather the number that the government uses to determine how much it "takes home." EBIT = Gross Profit – Variable Costs – Fixed Costs.

Taxes: Depending on how much you make, the IRS and your state department of taxation and finance will require that you pay a certain percentage of your EBIT in taxes. This is a percentage that you must get from the IRS or your accountant and should range from 15 to 40 percent.

Net Profit: Your *net profit* is your real profit, or what you can take home or reinvest at the end of the day. This number is also referred to as your *bottom line*. Sometimes you may hear people talking about being "in the black" or "in the red." This refers to your net profit and whether it is positive (black) or negative (red), depicting losses.

Follow this format to create your own Income Statement:

Sales	10,000
COGS	3,000
Gross Profit	7,000
Variable Costs	1,000
Fixed Costs	2,000
EBIT	4,000
Taxes (25%)	1,000
Net Profit	$3,000

Don't forget about your other statements. Since it is very difficult to predict what specific needs the thousands of different people reading this book will have, I'm going to have to make this a research assignment for you. After all, you don't want to spend your time crunching numbers for documents you don't need, and you certainly don't want to leave something out that is essential. To help you out in your fact finding, here are some questions to keep in mind:

- Which documents are essential to your investor?

- How many years of each document do you need? (For example, how many years/quarters of past balance sheets do they want? Or how many years of income projections?)

- How should they be broken down time-wise? Some investors like to see financial documents on a monthly, quarterly or yearly basis.

- Do you need to have your financial statements audited by an accountant?

The more specific you can be about these requirements, the less time you will waste and the stronger your plan will be. And one last word of advice, always have someone you trust, who understands business financials, review your documents to avoid errors and omissions. (See the end of this chapter for some great business plan books and guides, which will go into much greater detail on your financial statements.)

IX. Appendices

Use the appendices for exhibits providing additional information for your readers. Such exhibits can include media articles, charts and graphs, brochures, pictures, contracts, legal documents, and other exhibits. All you have to remember in using exhibits is (1) make sure that you reference them with numbers in the text of the plan (e.g., See Exhibit 5), (2) clearly label each exhibit, (3) place them in the back in the same order in which they appear in the plan, and (4) separate the Appendices section the same way you would any other section of the plan.

Finishing Touches

As with everything you do in business, pay close attention to your image. Your business plan is no exception. For a document that will represent you and your business, make it an impressive one. Here are a few quick last minute tips:

- Add a table of contents to the beginning.
- Start each new section with a new page.
- Cite all research.
- Include charts and graphs to illustrate points.
- Print with a high-quality laser printer.
- Use high-quality printing paper.
- Spell check everything twice.
- Put your logo and contact information on the cover.
- Bind the document so it appears professional.
- Use at least one-inch margins.

Resources

To get really down and dirty with your business plan, you might want to enlist the help of some experts. While they are probably too expensive to bring home with you for guidance, their books should do the trick.

Basic Business Plans

The Young Entrepreneur's Guide to Starting and Running a Business by Steve Mariotti (New York: Random House 1996)

Advanced Business Plans

Launching New Ventures by Kathy Allen (Upstart Publishing, 1997)
The Ernst & Young Business Plan Guide by Eric Siegel, Brian Ford, Jay Bornstein, and G. Young Ernst (John Wiley & Sons, 1993)

How to Really Create a Successful Business Plan: Featuring the Business Plans of Pizza Hut, Software Publishing Corp, Celestial Seasonings, Ben & Jerry's by David Gumpert (Inc. Publishing, 1996)

Business Plans That Win Dollars by Stanley R. Rich and David Gumpert (Harper & Row, 1987)

"The Business Plan—Your Roadmap to Success," video by the Small Business Administration. Includes workbook and resource book for Small Business Management. Order at 1-800-827-5722

The Complete Book of Business Plans: Simple Steps to Writing a Powerful Business Plan by Joseph Cavello and Brian Hazelgren (Sourcebooks Trade, 1994)

Raising Money

Entrepreneur Magazine's Guide to Raising Money by Entrepreneur Media (John Wiley & Sons, 1998)

The Ernst & Young Guide to Taking Your Company Public by Stephen Blowers, Gregory Ericksen, and Thomas Milan (John Wiley & Sons, 1995)

PART THREE

Launching Your Business

CHAPTER 4

The Basics of Opening a New Company

EFORE YOU RUN OFF AND START YOUR COMPANY, THERE ARE A FEW ADDITIONAL pieces of business that we really must address. As tedious as these issues are, ignoring them and hoping that they go away can either land you in a lot of trouble, or even, if you're really lucky, in jail.

What was your business address again? Are you a sole proprietor or a Sub-Chapter S? And how good did you say your credit was? Do you have a record of that last payment you made to the phone company? What about proof that that weekend trip to New York really was a "business trip"? You know your client may also ask you to back up that expense report with receipts, right?

If you are like most new business owners, many of these questions, which I assure you won't remain novel for long, are bound to come up. And you'd better be ready with some answers.

Legally Establishing Your Company

First things first. Where are you going to operate your business from? Home, an office, a deserted shack, Suite 412 (often Box 412 in disguise at the local Mail Boxes Etc.)? Wherever you eventually end up, you are going to have to let a lot of people, particularly your friendly neighborhood government agencies, know your official company address.

To legally register your business, your journey will begin at the City Clerk's office, usually located in your town's city hall building. There you will fill out a very brief form called a DBA Statement (with your name, address, company name, etc.), fork over $20, $50, or some other relatively small fee to the clerk (varies by state), and you will officially be recognized as a business by your state. The DBA Statement is short for "Doing Business As," meaning, the piece of paper that you walk out of the City Clerk's office with will be your legal proof that you are "doing business as" your company name.

Now why do we need proof of this anyway? Imagine that I wanted to make a withdrawal from my company account at the bank, or discuss my tax returns with the IRS. How are they to know that I am really the owner of my company? Your DBA Statement proves to any banker, government official, or even potential landlord that you do in fact have the right to view and make amends to legal documents pertaining to your company.

Legal Structures

When you first open a business, you must decide how that company will be legally structured. This will affect the way you originally form your business, manage your business affairs, pay your taxes, and assume certain liabilities. The legal form of your business also determines who receives profits from the business, who has voting rights, and what your funding options are. Deciding on the legal structure of your business is a serious issue that should not be taken lightly. As you will see below, your decision will affect your rights and freedom as a business owner, so proceed with caution.

There are four major types of legal structures for a business: *sole proprietorship, partnership, corporation,* and *nonprofit.* (There are also four different types of corporations, which we'll look at later on.) Odds are your first businesses will be sole proprietorships or partnerships.

SOLE PROPRIETORSHIP

In a *sole proprietorship,* a single person owns the company fully and assumes full liability for it. A DBA (doing business as) statement means that you, Jane Doe, are doing business as your company name, Doe Enterprises. So, the company, in a sense, is the same as its owner. If your company makes money, you make money. If your company gets sued, you can be sued personally because of your unlimited liability.

Most people starting out opt to register their businesses as sole proprietorships because it is the simplest form of enterprise, requires the least amount of paperwork, the taxes are the lowest, and full control of the company remains with the owner. The main disadvantage is that funding a sole proprietorship can be difficult. Because the owner assumes all risk, the owner must be responsible for paying off investors at some point or another. If the individual entrepreneur does not have the financial means to make good on this promise, then it is risky for someone else to invest in the business. (This is another reason why you sometimes hear the phrase, "Investors invest in you, not your business.")

PARTNERSHIP

A *partnership* is very similar to a sole proprietorship, but with a few exceptions, the first being that the company is owned by two or more people. A partnership can be divided up and structured in any way that the owners see fit. This understanding is spelled out in a partnership agreement, which is a standard document created when two or more people go into business together. Some partnerships are 50-50, i.e., people split all of the labor and profits and own an equal share of the company. Then there are those partnerships where one partner might do all of the labor or administrative work while the other partner just contributes money to the business. (This is essentially a silent partnership, in which one person runs the business and the other funds the business but does not take part in day to day decision making.)

The biggest benefit to a partnership is that the responsibilities and liabilities are shared. This means that the business is perceived as stronger by creditors, bankers, vendors, and sometimes even customers. The problem with partnerships is that there must be an enormous amount of trust, communication, and compatibility among the owners. See Chapter 5 for a more detailed rundown of partnerships and risk in undertaking this sort of venture.

CORPORATIONS

An entrepreneur typically incorporates his or her business for several reasons, the biggest usually being personal liability. Forming a *corporation* is like creating a person. Where a person would need a birth certificate, a corporation needs documentation called "articles of incorporation." And where young people typically have parents to take responsibility for them in the early years and guide them as they grow, a corporation has a board of directors that acts as parents might in managing the company, and shareholders who fund the company in exchange for equity or ownership.

As a legal entity, the corporation can typically be sued without putting the owner's assets at risk. The main reason that corporations are considered as people, or living entities, is that they are taxed as people are and can be sued or held responsible for any wrong doing. Many entrepreneurs favor doing business as a corporation because they have limited liability, or responsibility, should something go wrong, unlike with a sole proprietorship.

A corporation limits the liability of its owners because it, in a sense, assumes responsibility for itself (as you did when you turned eighteen). The owners may also give up significant amounts of equity or ownership in order to raise money. That is why the real owners of a corporation are the shareholders, and not necessarily the entrepreneur(s) who founded it. Ownership of a corporation is determined by who holds the largest amount of shares. So, by selling equity or shares to raise money, the entrepreneur gives up part of the ownership of his or her company.

The four different types of corporations are:

- *C-Corporations*
- *S-Corporations*
- *Limited Liability Companies*
- *Non-Profits*

Each were created to meet the needs of different entrepreneurs and their businesses. As would be expected, there are pros and cons to each.

A C-Corp is the most common type of incorporation for major corporations because they are the ones who most often need to raise very significant amounts of capital at different times throughout their growth. (These different stages of fundraising are called *rounds of financing*. If you are just taking your first major investment, you are in your first round.) A C-Corp is the legal structure that is most conducive to raising capital, because the number of shareholders you can have is unlimited. The downside is that the company is subject to double taxation, which means that the company must pay its own taxes on what it makes, and then the shareholders are again taxed on the dividends they receive. This is very discouraging to many entrepreneurs because their businesses, in this form, end up paying very substantial amounts, up to 40 percent or so of revenues, in taxes.

An S-Corp is very similar to a C-Corp, with the exception of the double taxation and the number of shareholders permitted. As far as taxes are concerned, a Sub-Chapter S, or S-Corp, offers the same liability protection, while only taxing the personal income of shareholders and not the corporation itself. The number of shareholders is restricted to thirty-five U.S. residents in an S-Corp. Smaller companies typically incorporate as S-Corps because they don't need thousands of shareholders, often do not require foreign investments, and want to limit the taxes they pay.

A Limited Liability Company (LLC) is a new legal structure that was created to help the sole proprietor obtain the protection of a corporation without having to suffer the higher taxes or extensive paperwork involved. LLCs are available in almost every state and have made the corporate legal structure available to many entrepreneurs who could never have managed it before. With an LLC, entrepreneurs still limit their liability, but not as much as they would with a C-Corp. An LLC essentially recognizes a company as a sole proprietorship or partnership, offering it similar tax rates and exemptions, while still protecting it and its owner(s) as a corporate entity.

A non-profit corporation is a business that is committed to serving the community rather than its shareholders. For that reason, a non-profit corporation cannot have any shareholders or owners. While a non-profit does need a board of directors to govern and guide it, its profits cannot be distributed among its board members. One popular misconception is that a non-profit is not a business, while, in fact, it is very much a business. Non-profits must deal with management, operations, budgets, and funding, just like any other business. The biggest difference lies in the way a non-profit must raise money.

Because it cannot sell shares, a non-profit must rely largely on donations from individuals and foundations and the sale of products or services, if it has any to sell. In most cases though, the services it provides are free, and any sales made by non-profits usually go to covering the basic expenses of offering those services. One last point to note is that non-profits are not subject to taxes. But this is not as simple as it seems. Forming and running a non-profit is a difficult and time-consuming task. Because taxes are not being paid, and most of the supporting money comes from donations, there are heavy restrictions on and much scrutiny over the operation of a non-profit.

To give you a quick overview of the different types of legal business structures, the following chart should help you understand which makes the most sense for you.

ASPECTS	SOLE PROPRI- ETORSHIP	PARTNERSHIP	C-CORP	SUB-CHAPTER S-CORP.	NON-PROFIT
Ownership	The proprietor	The partners	The stockholders	The stockholders	No one
Liability	Unlimited	Unlimited	Limited	Limited	Limited
Taxation	Lowest rate	Lowest rate	Double taxation	Lowest rate	None
Distribution of profits	Proprietor receives all	Partners receive profits according to partnership agreement	Earnings paid to stockholders as dividends in proportion to the number of shares owned	Earnings paid to stockholders as dividends in proportion to the number of shares owned	Surplus cannot be distributed
Voting on policy	Not necessary	The partners	Common stockholders	Common stockholders	The board of directors
Life of legal structure	Terminates on death of owner	Terminates on death of partner	Unlimited	Unlimited	Unlimited
Capital- ization	Difficult	Better than sole proprietorship	Excellent because ownership can be sold to raise capital	Good	Difficult because there is no ownership to sell as stock

* Reprinted with permission from The National Foundation for Teaching Entrepreneurship

How to Do It

To form a sole proprietorship, you need not do anything but register your business with the City Clerk's office to obtain your DBA statement. For a partnership, it is usually wise to draw up a legal partnership agreement with the help of a lawyer. And if you are considering a corporation, regardless of which type, see a lawyer for assistance. Though now you can incorporate your business on-line and receive your articles of incorporation within a few days for about $300, most experts—and lawyers, of course—still advise that you seek legal counsel, which will probably run you a good $500 or more. And if you are thinking about starting a non-profit, expect to spend a lot of money up front in legal fees.

The more complex your business, the more you probably need a lawyer and an accountant. While they may cost you some money up front, they can save you countless amounts in the long run. But, as with anyone you must pay by the hour, just make sure that you learn as much as you can before you meet with them. You want to spend your money paying for their work and expertise, not for them to teach you basics that you could have learned on your own.

Professional Advisers

Another important step you are going to have to take in establishing your business is finding a lawyer and accountant. This doesn't mean that you have to put them on retainer right away but rather that you should have some sort of relationship in place, even if it isn't well established yet. The thing about professional advisers is that you never really know when you are going to need their help. And when you really do need them, you tend to need them quickly.

There are a couple of ways to find good professional advisers. If you have no idea where to start, you can always contact your local chamber of commerce or a business organization in your industry. You could also contact an old business professor of yours or one in a local university with a good business or entrepreneurial program. The best source is always going to be through personal referrals. The more small business owners or entrepreneurs in your industry that you know, the better. And while it is always great to have a lawyer or accountant in the family to help you out, you really should find someone who is familiar with the type of situations that you are most likely to encounter. If you have someone like that, you don't even have to have the foggiest idea what lies ahead for you legally— they can and will prepare you for whatever lies ahead. So go for personal referrals from people in similar entrepreneurial situations.

Look for firms that have worked with companies through different growth stages that you expect to follow. When we first talked with our accounting firm, the first thing they told us was that they had worked with dozens of small businesses, often run by young entrepreneurs in the Boston area. They also told us that they had helped many of the start-ups get to their initial public offerings (IPO). From there, their clients usually went on to one of the "Big 6" firms like Ernst & Young, Coopers & Lybrand, or Deloit & Touche. In analyzing this firm we said to ourselves:

- They are comfortable (and really enjoy) working with people in their 20s.
- Most of their clients are small businesses (no question will be too simple).
- They are used to teaching entrepreneurs about basic accounting practices.
- They can even help introduce us to other small businesses in the city.
- If we ever get really big, they will know how to help us.
- They came very highly recommended from friends.

As you can imagine, the decision to hire them was an easy one. Once you've identified the best candidates, sit down and get to know them. (Your first meeting, often called an "initial consultation" will most likely be free . . . but don't get used to it.) Tell them about your situation, questions, concerns, and aspirations. Full disclosure is in order here. I always say there are three people that you never hide anything from, no matter what: your doctor, your lawyer, and your accountant. Besides being bound by law to respect your privacy, they can't help you or anticipate problems for you if they don't know what is going on in your life—yes, personally too. So get used to these people knowing your most intimate secrets and fears. That's what they are there for. That's their job. The better these relationships are, the more comfortable you'll feel tackling anything that comes your way.

Of course, there will be some basic services that they can perform for you, like incorporating your business, obtaining trademarks, setting up your accounting system, preparing your taxes, and so forth. But unexpected situations do pop up, and the earlier you are in your business venture, the less you tend to know about dealing with them.

When my company decided to go out for a business loan once, we must have called our accountant Noreen a dozen times with quick questions that we had no idea how to answer. Then, when we had to suddenly place a value on the company, Noreen set up a meeting for us with the head of the accounting firm. Bill spent an entire afternoon with us teaching us how to do this and sharing his experience and expertise gained from dealing with dozens of other companies in our position. How we would have ever come up with a logical valuation for our business without Gately and Associates, I don't know.

One more quick example I have to share regarding relationships with lawyers. Growing up I always thought that lawyers were supposed to be evil beings who conspired to sue and divorce people all day long. Then I met my lawyer through a friend with another small business. Eleanor Uddo has since become one of my closest advisers in the world and a sincere friend. As you can imagine, I do call her to look over contracts every few weeks, with random questions every week or so in between. She even helped us set up a non-profit organization the other month. But what I didn't expect when I hired her was to get a personal coach out of the deal as well. I can't tell you how many major negotiations and meetings she has now prepped me for, helping me solidify my goals and pumping up my ego when I most needed it. The results have been amazing.

So, even if you are just starting out, don't ever underestimate the value of professional advisers. You never know, but they might just become your closest friends.

Business Credit

Probably one of the most exciting, nonacademic things about being a freshman in college is having credit card companies beg you to carry their plastic. You walk by their tables in the student union trying to look as cool as you can as the salesmen grovel, offering you T-shirts, candy, and cheap airline tickets. You pick up an application and begin fantasizing about what you'll do with your first $500 credit line, or the "free money" that they're giving you.

If you're among the masses of ignorant students, as I was, you take your cards and run as fast as you can to the mall, hitting your limit faster than you can say, "Charge it, please." After they raise your credit limit to a few thousand bucks, you boost your spending habits to match your available credit. Boom! You hit your limit again. Your next statement comes and they want you to pay $70 just to maintain your finance charges. Finance charges! Who said anything about interest? And 21 percent! Do they realize how much money that means? Your parents give you no sympathy, even though you beg them for help and tell them that you haven't even had enough money to eat lately.

Then one day, after you've learned your lesson, paid your overdue accounts, stopped getting those threatening "pay or else" letters, and come to terms with having blemished your credit history for the next seven years, you decide to start a business. All of a sudden you feel like a freshman again. Some big company puts you on their "new business owner" mailing lists and credit card companies and office supply stores start asking you to apply for their credit programs. Your daydreaming turns to financing that great U-shaped desk you've been eyeing, and maybe even a copier or high-quality laser printer. Once you've made out your shopping list and lived in bliss for a few weeks, you get a letter in the mail. You feel around the envelope for the card, then rip it open to find a letter. A thin one, just like those college rejection letters. "We are sorry that we are not able to accept your application at this time." Your heart sinks. "But I was only a freshman!" you cry out loud. No one's there to listen, not even the credit companies. Time to do some big-time damage control.

Recovering from Bad Credit

Okay, if you were one of those credit card angels, you might already have been offered a gold card by now, leaving many people still green with envy over your creditworthiness. So stop reading this section and go spend money recklessly for once in your life! For the rest of us, we need to dig ourselves out of the grave we dug as freshmen or older slackers. What do we do now? Today, you either own a business or are in the process of starting one, and your credit stinks as badly as your refrigerator did that time you forgot the leftover Chinese food in it for a month. You need help. I know, I've been there. So I won't lecture you on what you can't do without credit, because you've probably gotten a good taste of that already. But I will tell you this: There are just a few ways that bad credit will block your path. With "blemished" credit, you can have problems:

- Renting office space, even if it's your apartment
- Leasing anything (a car, postage machine, credit card processor, photocopier)
- Getting more credit (corporate card, corporate accounts for office supplies, car rentals, courier services, or even FedEx accounts)
- Getting a line of credit or loan from the bank
- Finding an investor

Remember, you and your business are the same entity, yet your business will need credit accounts on its own, which, legally, will become your credit accounts. This I learned while trying to buy furniture for an old apartment with my roommate. While she was offered a hefty credit line, I was rejected. Why? I had been paying my bills on time, and five years had lapsed since my freshman year of credit hell. I was even declaring a healthy salary. An investigation about the rejection showed that I had too many inquiries on my personal credit recently, and thus I looked desperate for credit. The problem was the inquiries (my requests with other vendors) had not been personal reasons but rather for my business. I hadn't asked anyone to grant *me* credit lately. But since I was still a sole proprietor, my business inquiries were my personal inquiries. I had also just moved into a new commercial office and had my credit checked for that and a few other new office necessities. So despite the fact that I did pay my bills and was actually accepted for all of the other business credit, the furniture store could not take the risk on me personally.

The moral of the story here is take your credit needs into consideration before forming the legal structure of your business. Another lesson is not to ask for credit on anything that you don't really need. Yes, it might be cool to have a company gas card, or pagers, or even a credit card for an office supply store, but realize that every time you ask, even if you are accepted, the credit bureaus are counting. What else should you do? Let's do another list, just to be perfectly clear:

- Limit the times you request credit.

- Always pay at least the minimum due on your bills, and pay on time.

- If you have to be late on a payment, call the company to let them know.

- Don't rely on credit accounts when you can pay cash.

- Keep track of the credit debts that you accumulate throughout the month.

- Don't let anyone use your credit accounts unless you trust them completely.

- Even if you have a good credit limit, don't use it all—keep as much room free on it as you can (which boosts your available credit or debt-to-equity ratio on your credit rating).

If anything good can come of your nightmarish experience with credit, it should be that you gain a healthy respect for what it can do to and for you. Everything I've said here should be pretty obvious, but we all need to hear things like this from someone other than our parents sometimes for it to really sink in.

Doing Everything by the Book

Record Keeping

There are two simple lessons to be learned here: Keep a record of everything you do and play by the rules. As far as records go, save everything. Keep files with all of your receipts and bills organized chronologically (to save you time and money on taxes). And it's even a good idea to keep track of your meetings, letters, and phone calls. Meetings are easy to keep track of if you keep a calendar or planner, and when you write letters, you should always keep a photocopy, as well as store them on your computer. When e-mailing, always blind copy yourself on anything you write, in addition to saving any business correspondence you've received.

As for phone calls, I've gotten in the habit of recording them in a spiral notebook or writing journal. This might seem tedious, but the effort has proved quite valuable to me on several occasions. (FYI: If you keep track of everything else on your computer, you may want to log phone calls, letters, and even meeting notes with the help of a contact management software program, like Access, from Microsoft, or ACT, from Symmantic.) How many times have you forgotten having spoken to someone, or remembered the conversation but not exactly what was said? How about when you last called someone or when they last called you? Have you ever been in a legal dispute and needed to recall the dates that you met, spoke with, or attempted to contact a certain person or company?

If you had a record of all of this, you'd be able to. My phone record does all of this for me and even helps me remember to follow up on things that I might normally forget. If you typically have problems remembering random "to dos," start writing things down. Not on scraps of paper or Post-It Notes. Buy a notebook, date each page at the top, and start recording your business life. This way, you'll always have a physical record of your actions on a daily basis. Another added benefit: When you feel down about your business venture you can look back through the log and see all that you've accomplished or could still do.

Following the Rules

The second concern you should have is following the rules—not those of tradition, but of the law. Do everything you can by the book. Though certain laws, like taxes, might make no sense to you, it is your obligation as a citizen and as a business owner to abide by the rules that govern society. If the FDA (Food and Drug Administration) says that you cannot make chili from your kitchen to sell at retail outlets, listen. If your friend who also owns a small business is paying unemployment taxes, find out why and whether you need to as well. Ignorance of the law is no excuse. When it comes to the legal issues, be very proactive about learning what you need to know to follow the rules. Operating your business illegally should not even be an option in your mind. Regardless of how much money you can make or how unlikely you think it is that you will be caught, it is *never* worth the risk. Don't wait to learn that lesson yourself. There are plenty of people around with stories about how they suffered because they didn't play by the rules.

Taxes

Without going into too much detail, here is a general overview about taxes and some words of advice to start. When it comes to taxes, be paranoid. People don't compare the IRS with the former Soviet Union's KGB for nothing. The IRS (Internal Revenue Service) can be ruthless in collecting the money that is owed them, and again, not knowing is no excuse. Thousands of businesses and people each year are ruined because they did not comply with the tax rules, however screwed up they may be. (Keep in mind that the tax code is 38,000 pages long and virtually no one understands all of it. It is also very inconsistent and subject to many different interpretations, any one of which can get you into a lot of financial trouble.)

Whatever you do, make sure that you consult an IRS representative or, better yet, an accountant about what you and your business owe to the government. You can speak to an IRS agent for free (there are local offices in every major city), get great information from their website (http://www.irs.gov), or even meet with someone at the SBA (Small Business Administration) should you need to. An accountant will cost you money, though you might be able to get some free advice with an initial consultation through a business organization, or if you can find one who is a friend. And now the dirty work of filing taxes. You are responsible for paying taxes to federal and local government. At the federal level, you must file:

PERSONAL INCOME TAX

If your personal income is more than $5,500 in a year, you are single, and under sixty-five years old, you must file a 1040 Individual Tax Return form with the IRS.

SELF-EMPLOYMENT TAX

If you are a business owner, and make a net profit of $400 or more, you must file a Schedule SE.

PROFIT OR LOSS FROM A BUSINESS

To report whether you have made or lost any money with your business, you must file a Schedule C.

INDEPENDENT CONTRACTORS

If your company has hired independent contractors, you must report any payments made to them with a W-2 Form.

EMPLOYEES

If you have "real" employees (according to the rules of the IRS), you then need to file a 1099 form for each of them.

And at the local level, you have to pay attention to state and local taxes. Form ST-100 is what you need to file quarterly taxes for the state and local government. And yes, that does mean four times a year, or every three months.

If all of this is confusing you, it should reinforce the serious need to consult an accountant. Keep in mind that each state's laws are different and that certain regulations have been known to change almost yearly. Remember, be paranoid about complying with the necessary tax laws and make it your own responsibility to find out what you need to know about taxes. The IRS will not slap you on the wrist and tell you to pay closer attention next time, but they will fine you and have no qualms about shutting your business down from penalties that you cannot afford.

So, to review our business basics:

- Make sure that you chose the right legal structure for your company.
- Protect your credit with your life.
- Surround yourself with the best professional advisers.
- Make sure that you pay your taxes.

- Whatever you do as an entrepreneur, follow the basic legal rules of business.

Don't risk creating a nasty situation out of the best opportunity of your life. Follow this chapter's advice and sleep a lot sounder knowing that you're on the right track and have a great foundation and support system on which to build your business.

CHAPTER 5

The Partnership Decision

O NE OF THE MOST IMPORTANT DECISIONS YOU WILL EVER MAKE WILL BE whether to go into business with a partner or on your own. There are many strong opinions out there on the subject, so take your time, gather as much information as you can, and take this decision very seriously. When partnerships work they're great, but when they don't they're ugly.

Reasons to Consider Partnership

There are a lot of good reasons people take on partners. Some just feel more comfortable knowing that they are not in it by themselves. Some have people in their lives who they always really liked, worked well with, or thought they could. There are also cases where people come up with an idea for a business together and just go straight to work on it. A lot of people also find that in order to go into their own business, they need someone with complimentary skills or resources to successfully take advantage of an opportunity.

If you find yourself seriously lacking the money, expertise, contacts, or experience that you need to start a particular business a partner might be the solution that you are looking for. Remember, there are several ways you can structure a partnership agreement (which we will get to in a minute). Some partners just give you money, take a piece of equity (percentage of ownership), and let you run the business. Others will want to get involved as full partners and work with you on a day-to-day basis. As you can imagine, there are also many different scenarios in between. Take some time to think about what kind of relationship you would most like to have if you were to bring in a partner and what type of relationship you could tolerate if you didn't have your ideal situation.

A Few Other Reasons to Consider a Partner

- You need money that you can't possibly get on your own, and someone out there who has it might find your business interesting and want to get involved.

- You are in school and have very limited time to get everything done.

- This is your first venture.

- Your partner has done this before and it is all new to you.

- One of you is business-oriented and the other has some unique skill that can be packaged and sold to customers (this is very common in high technology).

- You see a great opportunity to combine resources.

- You are starting a business casually, for fun, and not as a career.

- You can identify clear weaknesses in yourself that would preclude you from running a company successfully on your own.

The best partnerships are ones in which the two (or three, or four) people complement each other. This holds true with skills and resources and is especially important with personalities. A very introverted person can have an incredible idea or passion, but without an extroverted sales person, it's hard to get very far. If you feel confident that you can both work together, find different roles in the business that you are comfortable with, and not step on each other's toes all the time, then you might be doing a very smart thing.

Reasons to Avoid Partnership

One of the most common urges that young entrepreneurs have is to start a business with a friend. Seems like a logical thing to do, right? You trust each other, you get along great, why not?

Well, I'll tell you why not. If you're a young entrepreneur starting a new business, you already face enormous odds. Double those odds if you do it with a partner, and triple them if you do it with an equal partner. A partnership can easily turn into a disaster.

Why? Think about it. First of all, taking on an equal partner immediately eliminates one of the prime reasons you had for becoming an entrepreneur. If you wanted to avoid having to answer to another person (like a boss), or if you wanted to sidestep all forms of time-sucking bureaucracy, both incentives just flew out the window. Almost every decision, large and small, must be cleared with a partner, and every decision holds the potential of requiring hours, maybe days of internal discussion.

Second, every equal partner feels that he or she pulls more weight than the other. Ask anyone who has been there. One partner always feels they put in more hours, works harder, compromises more, and is less appreciated. The other—surprise, surprise—feels the same way. Inherently, the potential for resentment in an equal partnership grows fast. If business is not thriving, your partner may begin questioning every penny spent, every minute you're not in the office working, and every non-business phone call you take.

The dynamics of this kind of relationship quickly deteriorate in other ways. Often, it becomes a contest of wills between two partners. If one or both of you are eager/aggressive/competitive types, every issue offers the psychological challenge as to who will give in first. You begin keeping score in ways you can't imagine.

More important, any problems or hostilities between partners affect more than just those two players. Internal operations people are frustrated and confused by having no clear leader. Which boss do they follow? Even clients may find it difficult to determine who is actually in charge. Finally, if you do split up, it is often a deadly blow to the venture. How do you split a company? Who has money to buy the other out? It is an ugly situation, often with no winners.

Options to Partnership

Without question, when starting a new company you will need a key person (and many more) to help you get the venture moving along. The question you, the entrepreneur, need to ask yourself is this: Does he or she have to be a partner? Or would a different post keep the perspective partner deeply, seriously involved without undermining your control of the company? Here are some options:

- *President/Vice President.* Think of this as a pilot and co-pilot situation. Both are vital in making the plane fly, but one has the ultimate decision-making power and responsibility. There is no dishonor in serving as the No. 2 person. The "you as the president and your non-partner as vice president" solution also makes the division of labor easier. If your No. 2 person's contributions are strongly financial, other executive titles, like chief financial officer or treasurer, may be more appropriate.

- *Minority Stockholder.* While I strongly caution people against giving away stock to their company (it's the same as giving away control), in this case, giving some stock offers a non-partner a "voice" in the company without undermining your ultimate rule.

- *Ongoing Consultant.* Say you're setting up shop in Washington, D.C., as a lobbyist for a special interest group. It may be that a full-fledged partner is not what you need as much as someone with a specific area of expertise who can work with you on an ongoing basis for some period of time (not forever). Don't give away half the company and half your control for someone you eventually won't need. Pay more and make him or her a consultant.

- *Independent Contractor.* Suppose your new product involves an element of laser technology, which is not your area of expertise. You will need this expertise to develop a prototype of the product and help in setting up the manufacturing process. Then you may need this kind of help regularly, but in the long run, not full time.

The Decision

By yourself, sit down and create a chart of pros and cons. This may sound rather simplistic, but it really helps you make solid decisions like this. You can even score the importance of different items, like adding more weight to financial responsibilities, for example. Spend a few days on this. Make sure that you take your time and be brutally honest. You might even want to show it to someone you trust (other than your potential partner) to get his or her feedback and to ensure that you are not missing or avoiding anything. That piece of paper should give you a good idea of whether you are on the right track or not.

Before you take on a equal partner, sit down and go through the reasons you think you need a partner. Here are a few more things to consider:

PERCEPTION	REALITY
The work and responsibility can be shared.	Work and responsibility are extremely difficult to measure and impossible to divide 50-50.
There are always two opinions.	There are always two opinions.
A company is stronger with two people running it.	Having two people in charge is confusing and frustrating to your staff and customers.
Most entrepreneurs need help to keep from doing everything themselves.	No one does it the way you would do it.
Ideas can be shared and refined more easily with two people.	Dissenting opinions cause conflict.
Working with a partner can make business more fun.	Working with a partner can ruin a friendship.

Now, if you are looking at this business venture as a short-term deal or as a fun side project, then you don't have to get too paranoid. If you are about to invest a lot of time, energy, and money into your business, follow this section very closely.

Spend some time doing your own due diligence on your partner(s). This means holding your own investigation. Talk to some of their former business partners or colleagues. Talk to mutual friends. You could even find out a lot from talking to their parents. If they are a bit older and more experienced, or have run other companies in the past, you could probably get a financial report on them from Dun & Bradstreet, or even find newspaper clippings about them and other work they have done. Don't be intrusive but make sure that you find out a little more about your partner than what they tell you themselves.

Your next step is to spend some solid time with your intended partner. One thing I've always wished they had for business owners, and especially partners, was something like premarital counseling. After hearing about all of the programs out there for engaged couples that force you to talk about your feelings on everything from sex to kids, in-laws, careers, retirement, and personal goals, I've always wondered how many people "pre-entrepreneurial venture counseling" could help. In the mean time, construct your own list of topics and questions to cover. Think about issues that could pop up on a daily basis and even situations that might

not happen for years. Here are a few areas that you should talk
about:

- Your individual roles
- Authority and decision making
- Money (investment, cash flow, financial management, report-
  ing, goals)
- Hiring employees
- Other potential partners/partnerships
- Personality conflicts
- Growth
- Long term goals (personal and professional)
- Company philosophy and mission
- Motivation for entering partnership/business
- Exit strategies (how and when you leave the business
  someday)

At this time you should be airing all of your deepest darkest concerns and secrets that could later affect your relationship. If you
were ever sued, or kicked out of a business, if you owe money, or
have bad credit, you really should disclose this to your partner. Do
you have any other obligations that could interfere with your being
a good partner? Were you intending on taking a month off in the
summer? Are you planning on getting married or having children
anytime soon? Have you always promised to take your mother into
any business that you start? You are really getting married, in a matter of speaking. That is why you need to really make this decision
carefully. Be your own devil's advocate and try to draw out anything
that could ever become a problem. Figure that anything you neglect
to bring up now, you will have to deal with later, possibly under
much more stressful circumstances.

One last thing: Before you move forward, make sure that you come
to an understanding with your partner about communication. You
should both now understand how a lack of it can impact your company. If you both feel comfortable discussing difficult issues and can
come to each other with any problems or concerns you might have,
you are on the right track. The better you are at openly communicat-
ing, the more successful your partnership (and company) will be.

Tying the Knot

Once you've done all of your due diligence and you feel confident about the decision to make this person a partner in your business and life, there are a few more loose ends to cover.

The Partnership Agreement

A partnership agreement is probably the most important document you will ever draw up. This is basically the written law in your company and is quite similar to a pre-nuptial contract many couples draw up before a marriage. You will learn a lot about your potential partner's flexibility, commitment, and creativity in the process. In actuality, a significant number of "marriages" never take place because the couple is not able to resolve their differences in a pre-nup. You'll find that this is no different.

Essentially, the partnership agreement lays out the specific terms of the partnership: Division of power, responsibility, and most importantly, the terms of a break up should one happen. If the endgame has not been negotiated beforehand, it will be played out in the most excruciating way imaginable. Spare everyone this pain. There are very few friendly divorces.

Here are the basic issues that should be addressed in your agreement:

- Where the money is coming from, and how much
- Interest payments on any loans
- Split of profits and ownership percentages
- Roles and responsibilities
- Adding or removing partners (buyout clause)
- Transferability of ownership
- Procedures for sale of business
- Restrictions on spending money
- Settlement of disputes
- Division of authority

One more thing. The terms of the agreement are as important as the dollar amount. You must address the non-competition clause. This basically says that the leaving partner will not start up or participate in any business that would potentially compete with and take away business from your company for a specified amount of time. If the partnership breaks up, starting a new company alone will be hard enough without having to fight the competition from a former partner. Protect yourself.

A LAWYER

As you can probably guess, you should have a lawyer look at this to offer input and ensure that you have a legally binding agreement when you are all done. Drafting your own outline of the agreement beforehand will also help you save a lot of money in legal fees. Why waste your lawyer's time on things that you should have figured out beforehand? The more you can bring to attorneys when you are ready to finalize the agreement, the less work they have to do, and the more focused your discussions can be.

You might also want to spend some time with your lawyer to discuss any issues that might affect you personally.

BREAKING UP

The question of what will happen to the company if the partnership is dissolved is a hard one to resolve. Generally, the choices are

- fold the company;
- have one partner buy out the other;
- sell the company to a third party and split the profit.

Usually, one partner will buy out the other. In this situation, a fair market price for the company must be established by independent sources. Try to get three outside estimates, and then take the middle price.

What if both partners want the business? Seeing as you probably won't want to flip a coin, you'll have to come to some kind of mutually agreed-upon ending. For instance, one partner chooses whether he pays that price to stay, or receives that price to go. The first partner, of course, has to be prepared to take his or her own offer.

As you can see, getting involved in a partnership is not a decision to be taken lightly. Be responsible, professional, and honest, and you can focus on the really important things, like making your business a smashing success!

CHAPTER 6

Building a Team

LTHOUGH NOT NECESSARILY IN THIS PARTICULAR ORDER, IN THEORY, WHEN you start up a business venture, you legally register, secure the financing, begin selling, and find an office to house it all. As your business begins to grow beyond a one-person operation located in your apartment or parents' basement, you need to begin pulling together your management team. This may be your biggest challenge yet.

A management team is the same thing as a staff, right? Wrong! Your management team will be a small, intimate group that, in addition to the members' own duties within the company, interacts as a unit to help you make decisions that will "grow" the company.

You, the founder, are the heart of the company. Your team (of which you are a member, of course) will be its soul. The heart loves the company, cultivates it, inspires it to greatness. The soul is the structure that gives substance, direction, and courage to guide the company down a path of continued growth. After all, steady, controlled growth is what keeps a company young, vital, and profitable. If your company is not growing, then at best, it's standing still—which is the first step toward an entrepreneurial disaster.

Putting together a good team doesn't happen in a week. According to Peter Drucker, considered by many to be the guru of entrepreneurs, it may take twelve to eighteen months to find the right combination of people for your venture—but, trust me, it'll be worth the effort.

The first step is to think about what you want in a teammate. You probably have a good idea of what kind of experience, educational level, and personality you think you want and what you can afford to pay. The temptation may be to grab whoever you know and put them to work. Resist. This style of management results in what I like to call the Wardrobe Theory: A closet full of clothes that don't match and leave you with nothing to wear. Besides, an eclectic style might work when picking out what you want to wear to that new, trendy club downtown Friday night, but it doesn't cut it for selecting your key management team.

Throw together a team haphazardly and you won't be leading your company to greatness, you'll be refereeing "family" disputes. Then, in six months, you'll get fed up with the whole lot, clean house, and run ads to bring in a whole new group, but with the same results. This is how the "revolving door" syndrome starts. It's an energy suck, a burden on your customers, and does nothing to build your corporate reputation (which, as all young entrepreneurs know, isn't so easy anyway).

Like every other aspect of starting a business, putting together a team requires a plan. There are many theories of how to build a good management team; but there is one in particular that I find really helpful in drawing out the grand scheme. This concept is detailed in *Corporate Lifecycles: How and Why Corporations Grow and Die and What to Do About It* (Prentice Hall, 1988) by Dr. Ichak Adizes, who has studied thousands of companies over the course of thirty years. The ideas are a little ethereal, but they're a strong and proven outline for continued success. What follows is a brief summary, which should give you a clearer idea of who should be on your team and what its function is (although I definitely advise picking up the book at some point).

The Perfect Management Team

As his title implies, Dr. Adizes maintains that all living organisms are subject to a phenomenon called Lifecycles. Plants, animals, people, and, yes, companies travel a similar course in that they are born, grow, age, and die. As they travel over this course, there are predictable patterns of behavior that are established.

From: Peter Kraft, President of Link—The College Magazine

The most important thing I can say about starting a business it to surround yourself with smart people and people you can trust. Do not wear everyone's hat and try to do it all yourself. I know in the beginning, keeping things lean is a key to staying alive, but there's a balance between staying lean and covering the essentials. Good people definitely fall among the essentials. When I started my company, I hired people who knew much more than I did in their respective areas. The reason for doing this is simple. Starting a business (by that, I mean the first three to four years) is extremely trying on the president because he/she encounters so many new experiences that take an unusually long time to execute. I call this the "unknown factor." And what you think you will have time for in the beginning you will soon realize could not possibly have been managed by you alone.

The saying for new businesses is that it takes "twice as long and twice as much money" as you anticipated when you started. This is due to the unknown factor—even with a detailed business plan, you may find yourself moving in directions you never anticipated. And those moves need a lot of thought because they are new to you. More thought means more money (either spent or not-earned), and hence, what you thought would take only 25 percent of your time is consuming 50 percent or more. And we all know, time is money.

Good people are not a luxury, they are an absolute necessity. And by good people, I don't mean your best friend (I made that mistake). I mean people that can come to you with suggestions, people that are self-starters. Do not fall into the trap of hiring your friends simply because you can trust them. If they don't have the experience required for the job, you'll spend an inordinate amount of time babysitting them, which is a lose-lose situation. Good people are those that have proven themselves in your area of need. They may cost more, and in fact, you will probably be forced to pay them more than you pay yourself, but again, the value is apparent. These people are crucial to freeing you, the president and founder of your company, to manage the growth of your business.

HOWEVER (there's always a however), equally important as hiring good people is not letting them set their own agenda and determine their own course for your company. The good ones will teach you, because it makes their relationship with you so much more effective. But be cautious not to allow your three different "good people" to pull your company the way they want it to go. It's up to you to maintain the vision and direction and to make sure your people execute that vision and direction for you. Good people are a great investment.

The cornerstone of Dr. Adizes system is known as PAEI, an acronym for each of the four principal roles in a perfect management team. Naturally, there is dissent as to whether the "perfect" team exists. Even Dr. Adizes, with all his years of study, has yet to witness it, but there are excellent examples of companies that hit three or three-and-a-half of these four functions, achieving enviable results. One of the most dramatic success stories utilizing the Adizes Method is Domino's Pizza, which grew from a $150 million company to a $1.5 billion company in seven years.

You will assume one of the roles, probably the E part, which stands for entrepreneur, in addition to your role as founder and ultimate decision maker. Then, like a director hiring specific characters for a play, you must cast the three other parts . . . even if you can only afford one person to play all three roles in the beginning.

Essentially, what you are looking for in the PAEI system are three surrogate parents who, in addition to yourself, will combine efforts to raise this child, your company. Each "mother" or "father" will focus on a different set of short- and long-term goals that will combine to raise a healthy, happy, successful entity.

Here is a brief description of the PAEI roles:

P—*Performer.* This is the person you count on to put out fires, who has the attitude "Let's get it done today." This individual is a no-nonsense doer. If the office runs out of Xerox paper, P runs right out and gets a box of paper *now.*

A—*Administrator.* This is the organizer and, essentially, a systems person who continuously asks "How can we do this better?" If the office runs out of Xerox paper, A says, "Let's set up a system so we won't run out of paper again."

E—*Entrepreneur.* In this role, two characteristics are mandatory: Creativity and risk-taking. Dr. Adizes defines creative here as being synonymous with planning, or "deciding what to do today in light of what you expect tomorrow." Creativity, he says, is necessary for building scenarios of the future in order to predict the changes that will occur. "The role of the (E)ntrepreneur is not to adapt to the changing environment. Adapting means being reactive, not proactive. We must proact, project what the future is going to be, and then do something about it." Now, let's go back to the office paper problem—E's question is "Why do we need paper at all? Let's develop a system where we don't need paper."

I—*Integrator.* While the whole team works as a unit to parent the corporation, I's role is to "mother" the team. Just as a parent nurtures children, encourages them to play well together and protect each other against the outside world, so does I strive to develop within the company a culture of interdependency and affinity. As Dr. Adizes says, *I*'s role is "to nurture the unique corporate religion in your company." When confronting a shortage of Xerox paper, *I*'s question might be, "Are we sure that no one else in the company has some paper left that we can share?"

In addition to the specific duties P, A, E, and I must perform, it's equally important that all four relate openly with each other. Just as a mother and father interact to make decisions throughout the child's development into adulthood, so will your management team focus on specific goals, some immediate, some long range, for the corporation.

Managing Team Conflict

The way PAEI is set up, each member of the team has a voice in the decision-making process. It is not an equal voice compared to yours because, ultimately, you will make the final decision. But each voice, by virtue of the fact she is a team member, has earned the right to be heard. Until the moment comes for the final decision to be made, your team is a democracy. (Then it becomes a constitutional monarchy, you being the monarch who makes the decision.)

Be prepared, though. The team won't always agree on the correct course of action for the company—nor should they. Dr. Adizes says that anytime there is a complementary team, there will be conflict that stems from the differences in style. Don't be surprised by this. If you've put together a strong PAEI team, there will be conflict because you've deliberately chosen four different styles to work together. Sometimes the conflict may be an ego, other times a power struggle.

As the head of the team, you need to understand three things. First, there will be conflict between the four members of the team. Second, and this may require a leap of faith for some, conflict is not only good, it's healthy. Third, realize, or at least remember when it counts, that you are not always right. Get over thinking, or even wanting, perfect harmony within your team all the time. The magic of the PAEI system is that conflict is built in. If your team goes for weeks without a major disagreement, then at least two members are asleep at the wheel.

However, understand that there's a big difference between constructive conflict and destructive conflict. "Conflict is constructive when it produces the desired change. There is no change without friction and the difference between revolution and evolution is the degree of friction and the form that the friction takes," says Dr.

Adizes. Conflict becomes particularly destructive when the subject moves off business and becomes personal. Avoid this at all cost.

So how do you keep conflicts constructive? Mechanically, it's a two-step process where the key is respect. When there is a conflict (that is not personal), quite often it's because one party has information the other doesn't. The first step, then, is to establish a learning environment where conflicting parties listen and make every attempt to understand a different point of view. If this is done in an atmosphere of mutual respect (which you and teammate *I* have worked to build), then invariably both parties learn something, which leads to an understanding.

A strong, functional management team serves as a form of checks and balances—they inspire or incite healthy discussion that leads to a decision, and then implement the decisions that lead to growth. This is the unit that, when acting together and in the best interest of the company, will help you make and then implement the decisions that will help the company either grow or die.

Defining the Team's Purpose

You have your team in place. You understand their individual roles and how they interact. Have you defined the team's overall purpose?

The answer an amateur would give is "to make money." But ask yourself this: Why do people like Time-Warner Co-Chairman Ted Turner or Ron Pearlman of Revlon, both billionaires with more money than they could ever spend in a lifetime, keep working?

The answer is *the true entrepreneur has an itch that money can't scratch.* For them, money is the result of success, not the goal. Profit is only the scorecard that indicates if you're playing the game well. So what is the object of the game? For a young entrepreneur, it may be moving a company from the Infancy stage to Prime, and once reaching Prime, keeping the corporation delicately balanced between being flexible and controllable. It's that very balance that will keep the company growing.

How Your Team Interacts to Form and Implement Decisions

And you thought a decision was the answer to a "yes" or "no" question. Well, yes and no. "Yes" if the decision is whether or not to have dessert and a Frappachino. "No" if it has anything to do with your business.

To help us understand the mechanics of a corporate decision, Dr. Adizes has dissected it into four parts, or dimensions, each directly corresponding to the four roles of your team. A decision has four dimensions, and they are:

- *What* to do   —(p)
- *How* to do it   —(a)
- *When* (and *Why*) to do it   —(e)
- *Who* should do it   —(i)

Under the Adizes Method, there is also a fifth dimension. The *why*. It is hidden because it is included in the *when*. The timing of a decision is derived from the reason for the decision. *Why* we do something has to be operationalized into *when* it needs to be done. You can't decide *what* is the right timing, unless you know *why* the decision was made. Get it? *Why* is hidden inside the reasoning that leads to the *when*.

The Anatomy of a Decision

Here's an example. John (*E*) strolls back into the office after having lunch with the ambassador from China and tells the team that China is opening up its trade negotiations with the United States and placing a high priority on educational products, which just happen to be what their company produces. If the company can move quickly to put together a deal with the ambassador, it would have the potential of increasing sales twofold, blowing away the competition and furthering the company's presence worldwide.

The question he puts to the team is "Are we able to jump on this opportunity now?" The team debates the *why* of this decision. Why is it a great opportunity? Why is this right for us? And why should we grab it and run? These questions are answered to everyone's satisfaction, but the decision to proceed has not been made.

Step 2 is for the team to look at *when*. John says that in order to be competitive, product must be ready for shipment in 90 days. Can the team make this happen in three months' time? Before that question is answered, Mark (*P*) steps in to ask "What exactly has to be done to meet this deadline?" The group makes up a list of "To Do's," which would have to happen quickly to make the deal a reality. Looking carefully at this list, Bruce (*A*) asks *how* each department can increase its current workload to accommodate the China deal. More discussion. Then Mark points out that there is a worldwide paper shortage and that an average order of this size takes about sixty days. If the company pays a 30 percent rush charge, the time can be cut to forty-five days.

Trouble. Apart from a 30 percent rush charge being financially hurtful, Linda (*I*) points out that the staff really needs a full sixty days to translate product into Chinese. Even with rush charges, this wouldn't provide enough time to meet the ninety-day deadline. Is the deal off?

Bruce (*A*) takes the team back two squares. What if the company insures that the paper can be delivered, without rush charges, in under sixty days and hires a second shift of translators to double the translation effort and finish in thirty days?

Good try, but the cost for a second shift would double the company's costs and, as Linda points out, a second shift of Chinese translators would tip off the competition, something that could cost the company the whole deal.

John says, keep the paper delivery at sixty days with no rush charge, hire two teams of Chinese translators, half in San Francisco and the other half in New York. No overtime and no alerting the competition.

Voila! An important decision is made. All PAEI dimensions were considered, and the decision was complete.

A Round Trip

Good decision making, points out Dr. Adizes, requires continuous back and forth communications to correct mistakes in understanding. If a new decision does not get implemented correctly the first time, it doesn't mean that the people you assigned to the job are incapable or intentionally trying to sabotage your beautiful idea and decision. It just means it's time to go back and fix what broke—with the help and combined efforts of your PAEI.

CHAPTER 7

Staffing

NOW YOU REALLY HAVE NO LIFE. AFTER THREE MONTHS OF NAGGING FROM family, friends, and significant others who never see you anymore, you've accepted it. You need help. Not psychiatric. Not medical. The kind of help that comes in the form of eager employees. Here are the warning signals that you might need to hire yourself a staff.

You don't remember the last time you:

- Went out socially
- Had a full night's sleep
- Got any real exercise
- Saw the sun (from the outside)
- Felt really happy
- Were satisfied with your progress
- Were excited about your business
- Spent time with family and friends
- Took a Sunday off (Saturdays don't count)
- Ate something that didn't come out of a box or wrapper

Sound familiar? If you can say yes to most or all of the above, welcome to the club. Don't worry too much though. As usual, I'm here with options for you. Just because you have to start thinking about bringing other people into your company's little nest doesn't mean you need to bust out the employment contracts and get your lawyer, accountant, and financial advisors on the phone ASAP. You can bring in quite a few people before you have to shell out the big bucks.

Before you do anything, though, the first thing you have to think about is overhead. When you hear people talk about how overhead kills more businesses than anything else, what they mean is that far too many entrepreneurs load themselves up with so many fixed, or monthly expenses, that it becomes almost impossible for them to earn enough money to cover their overhead, let alone end up with a profit at the end of each month.

When it happens in some of the biggest companies in the world, their stock usually plummets as their financial ratios get thrown out of whack. When it happens to small business owners, they usually drag it out as long as they possibly can, give themselves an ulcer trying to fix it, or simply shut the doors and walk away from the business.

So how do entrepreneurs suffocate their businesses with overhead expenses? There are three ways:

- They anticipate that they are going to be making enough money soon enough to take care of their overhead (but don't).
- They get excited about the idea of being in business and spend money recklessly. (All those trips to Staples, Home Depot, and the bookstore add up).
- They employ people when they can't afford to.

As you can imagine, the big killer in the overhead game is employees. Depending on a variety of different factors (your business, industry, setup), each full-time person that you bring into your company can run you a minimum of $20,000 to $30,000 per year, not including all of the related expenses. That assumes that these employees are paid, full-timers.

So before you run out and start hiring a bunch of people, do yourself a big favor. Sit down with your financial statements and/or budgets and honestly decide whether, after you pay your rent, phone bills, marketing expenses, transportation, etc., you can really afford to take on the responsibility of other employees. Remember, as an employer, you're not just responsible for your business and your own personal needs anymore. Your employees now come first, in many more ways than you can imagine.

You do have options, though. There are three types of people you can bring into your business: Full-time employees, independent contractors, and interns. I'll discuss interns first, for the best reason in the world—they're free.

Interns

All right, for starters, I need to admit a bias here. I'm one of the world's greatest advocates of interns because my company probably wouldn't be alive today without them. And while I'd love to just stop and thank all of the people who have worked for me in this capacity right here and now, you'd have to turn several pages to get to the end of the list. You might not believe this, but I recently counted over 70 students who have worked for The Young Entrepreneurs Network. I also figured out that they wound up saving me over $150,000 in labor costs over the years.

So how did interns save my company from premature death? Well, like most other young entrepreneurs in college, we had to bootstrap the start-up of the business, since we didn't have a bank account full of money when we started out. Actually, I probably went through about 20 interns before I could actually afford to hire anyone full time. The greatest thing about it was that my relationships with interns were always "win-win" relationships.

How so? I needed the man power, the image of having employees, the new ideas, the energy, and the motivation to keep going. My interns needed something interesting to do, real business experience, resume builders, great employer recommendations, and some guidance. I was just a few years older than they, too, and it was pretty exciting for them to work for a peer. They also really liked our office environment—chaotic, but casual, flexible, fun, and forgiving. We walked around the office in socks, ordered pizza in for them all the time, laughed constantly, took them on trips, invited them to TV show tapings, and overall, gave students more responsibility and experience than any employer ever had. And yes, that does go for most of them. So, if you're not convinced already, give me another minute or two to prove how great this staffing option is for you.

But first let me respond to the questions that most people have about student interns.

WHY WOULD A STUDENT WORK FOR FREE?

For one very good reason: students have another piece of paper to worry about other than their diploma, and it's called a resume. Though you, as an entrepreneur, may have been working or creating your own companies since you were ten, many of your peers spent all those years at ice-cream parlors and retail shops in the mall. When it finally comes time for these people to enter "the real world," no one is going to be too impressed with their summer grocery-bagging job. Panic strikes thousands of students each year as they realize that they have no practical, hands-on work experience to offer potential employers. The golden word at this point in their lives is *internship*—work for free, get experience, then get a job. It's very simple. It is also a widely respected and expected practice among students. In many cases, they will work for free—if the experience warrants it.

Interns know that you, as an employer, hold some very valuable cards:

- Personal references and recommendations
- Contacts with other prospective employers
- Opportunity for a permanent, paid position
- Amazing chances for real hands-on experience
- Ability to give impressive job titles (great for resumes)
- Knowledge to share with them—the ability to teach and offer career guidance and industry insight
- Prestige of working for a successful, newsworthy, young, or maybe unique company

Essentially, you have the power and ability to make them more marketable by doing little more than treating them like a part of your company.

HOW COMPETENT CAN THEY REALLY BE?

Believe it or not, sometimes interns can be among the most valuable assets to a new company. Not only are they free, but they are determined, driven, and committed to the short-term success of any project that you throw their way. Interns will often work long hours, and do everything in their power to catch on quickly. In many cases, your interns may be business students or communications majors and might know more than you about cost accounting, market research, public relations, or advertising strategy. If your company (or sales pitch) is really impressive, and you're lucky enough to be located in the vicinity of a major university, you can often get the cream-of-the-crop for employees in the following year. Don't underestimate the knowledge of a student. Because of their intensive classroom training, they may even be more up-to-date on industry news and events than you have time for.

WHY SHOULD I BRING IN INTERNS?

There are a lot of great reasons to bring interns into your company. Personally, much of my motivation came from wanting to offer students (particularly from my alma mater) more exciting jobs, and wanting to bring new blood and ideas into our company. Okay . . . and I also kind of liked having all those extra people running around the office. Not only did we look bigger, but it made work a lot more exciting.

Students have the energy and the knowledge to be successful, but many companies will not hire them because they can only work during the summers or part time while they are taking classes, and of course they do not have the "two years experience necessary." These situations, however, can actually be a benefit to an employer. College students are hungry for experience, which is often of more value to the student than the salary.

Hiring interns is also an excellent way to prescreen future employees who will succeed and be a good fit for your company. There is no better way to determine whether a person is qualified for a job than to actually have him or her perform the job. You will have lower employee turnover if you hire interns after they graduate. Because former interns are familiar with your work environment and have proven their abilities, they require minimum supervision. They can handle more responsibility than a new person because they are not starting from ground zero.

By the way, international students can be an amazing resource for your company. Their diverse cultural backgrounds, as well as their knowledge of different languages, can be invaluable to a new company. They provide new perspectives and can be future contacts abroad. Due to their student visas, they often cannot be paid for working but desperately want to utilize what they have learned in the classroom. By hiring an international student as an unpaid intern, you will gain an excellent resource and employee at no cost, and the student will get the job experience he or she needs. It's a win-win situation.

How Do I Find Qualified Interns?

STEP 1: DEFINE THE TASK OR JOBS YOU NEED TO ACCOMPLISH

Create a specific job description that clearly outlines what the internship will involve. The biggest mistake you can make is to be vague. Define measurable goals and expectations. An internship should have two characteristics: real responsibility and the opportunity to learn. Although any internship is going to include some administrative work, the quickest way to discourage an intern is to monopolize his or her time with faxing and filing. A student's main objective is to discover what the work environment is all about. A successful internship is a two-way street.

STEP 2: DETERMINE WHAT PRIOR EXPERIENCE AND QUALIFICATIONS ARE NEEDED FOR THE JOB

Remember, experience can come in many forms. Students might have gained leadership skills from extracurricular activities and computer know-how from class projects. One bright point in hiring someone inexperienced is that you don't have to worry about breaking old habits.

STEP 3: CREATE A FLYER THAT WILL ATTRACT STUDENTS TO YOUR COMPANY

Once you've created the job description, type it up on a piece of your letterhead with the contact information readily apparent. Make sure that you put a big bold heading on it that says something like "Internship Opportunity," or something else to grab attention. Then just get right to the point. State as briefly as possible what you're looking for someone to do, what qualifications they should have, any other important information (like "must have a car" or "be willing to work weekends") and what you're willing to offer. If you're not offering any financial compensation, make sure that you are creative here and talk about all of the other perks. If you can't think of any, figure some out before you go looking for interns. (Try "flexible schedules," "travel opportunities," "work directly with president," or offer a great job title—but only if you really intend to put up.) Lastly, you should give them some instructions for follow-up. Do you want them to send resumes? Something more creative? Should they drop in? Fax you? Call for more info? Just let them know what works best for you.

STEP 4: CONTACT COLLEGES AND HIGH SCHOOLS IN YOUR AREA

Your next step is to see if any local colleges will post the flyer for you. If you live in an area with many colleges nearby, you should select the ones that offer classes related specifically to the job description for your prospective intern. For example, if the internship requires some knowledge of financial planning and analysis, contact schools that provide strong accounting and finance programs. Some colleges have formal internship programs that require students to intern for a semester. In addition, many colleges have career offices that provide job and intern posting services for local businesses. Some schools even have specific centers for each major. Contact colleges in your area for more info.

Do not, however, restrict yourself only to nearby schools. Many students would jump at the opportunity to live in other parts of the country or the world. A summer internship can prove ideal. If you are looking for international students, you may have to focus your search on larger schools that have stronger international appeal.

STEP 5: HOLD INTERVIEWS

Here's another great chance to learn from someone else's mistakes. When I first started hiring people to work for me, this is how I went about it:

A very warm, friendly, smiling me would say hello, give them a quick tour of the office, introduce them to everyone, then sit down for small talk. I'd give them a history of the company, tell them what we were up to lately, let them know what I was looking for, and then ask them if it sounded interesting. If it did, and it usually did, I'd ask a few fluff questions, then ask them if they had any questions. If they seemed like a cool person, and one who could do the job, I'd hire them right there.

After a few mishaps and a few more years in business, I learned how to handle interviews like a real employer. Now this isn't to say that I was no longer sweet and all smiles, but I did learn to stop selling so much and let them sell me a bit. So that would be my first bit of advice for the complete novice at this. You certainly have to sell interns on working for free by making it so exciting for them that they can't resist. But you do have to remember that you're running a business too, and that these people will be representing both you and your company.

With all that in mind, my best advice for holding decent interviews is as follows:

- Have them fax or mail you a resume beforehand so you can check out their efficiency, their style, their professionalism and their credentials.

- Give them a call to thank them for their interest and briefly pre-qualify them on the phone so you don't waste time meeting with someone who clearly is looking for something else, or vice versa.

- Set up a time for them to come to the office for an interview. If there is any background information, or examples of relevant work that they have done, ask them to bring it. Don't say anything much about the attire, even if you wear jeans to work. This is another great way to check out their style and see how well they might fit into your culture. Keep in mind that they will probably overdress to impress you, but that should always be a good sign to you because you'll know if you can put them in front of clients.

- When they come in for the interview, start by having them tell you about themselves. Let them talk for a bit. Ask questions about their background, course of study, professional interests, goals, and so on.

- Let them know about your company, giving a fair amount of attention to the things that would be exciting to a student. You should also be trying to figure out how to modify the job to better fit the interviewee if you like him or her. Selling directly to their interests is another great seducer.

- See what kinds of questions they have.

- Ask them to tell you what they are looking for and how, if at all, they see themselves fitting in to your company.

- If all is still going well, start talking about responsibilities, schedules, and the nitty gritty stuff.

- Then, tell them you'll get back to them in another few days, or hire them on the spot.

- If you do tell them you'll call them back, make sure you do regardless of whether you like them or not, and give them the courtesy of letting them know as soon as possible.

If you follow these quick tips, you'll slide through your first interviews like an old pro. And sooner than you can imagine, you'll develop your own system and style for interviewing people. Just stay calm, don't look too anxious, and realize that you are in control.

STEP 6: BE SELECTIVE!

Because it is often difficult for students to find internships that fit their needs, employers looking for interns often have a large number of very qualified applicants to choose from. Know what to look for. A cover letter is a must. An excellent cover letter is one that is tailored to your specific job description. Look at the writing style. Is it clear and concise? Is it articulate? Communication is an essential skill and one that you must demand for any internship.

A resume goes without saying. Look at the whole picture. Does it communicate ambition? An unlisted GPA is usually not a good sign. However, a 4.0 does not guarantee a good worker, and 2.0 does not always translate to a poor candidate. Is the student involved in extracurricular activities, or does he or she have previous work experience? If so, it can be a good indication of time management and a solid work ethic. Leadership positions suggest that he or she takes initiative and is a self-starter. What it comes down to is this: Does the prospect have transferable skills?

Once You've Hired an Intern

Once you find your ideal candidates, how do you hold onto them? Here are a few tips I've picked up for success—for both you and the intern:

GIVE INTERNS LEGITIMATE TITLES

Believe it or not, a title can do much for employee empowerment. It gives interns the feeling that they are an integral part of your company. An intern is more likely to provide input on projects, strategies, and proposals if she is not merely labeled as "the intern."

MAKE THE JOB AS EXCITING AS POSSIBLE

Have fun at work. Remember, if you are a small company, your company name will not carry as much weight on a resume as the IBMs and P&Gs of the world. In order to get the best interns, you need to differentiate yourself. It must be clear that the experience will be something that they could not gain in a classroom or from any other internship program. Being a small company can work to your advantage. Emphasize that in a smaller work environment there's more opportunity to have responsibilities and make an impact on the business.

GIVE INTERNS RESPONSIBILITY

Make the internship worthwhile for a student. When you assign specific responsibilities, good interns will take the initiative to start projects on their own. Trust must be gained, but interns first need to have the opportunity to gain that trust. Remember, an intern wants to learn.

GIVE INTERNS LOTS OF FEEDBACK

Think of yourself as a coach. How well are they meeting your expectations? How well are you meeting theirs? Communication is extremely important. They need to know when they are excelling, but they also need constructive criticism. Remember that these are students. They are accustomed to constant feedback through exams, projects, and daily class discussions. Interns want feedback sessions that will help them grow professionally.

SPEND TIME WITH YOUR INTERNS

It is often easier and faster to complete a task than to sit down with an intern and get him up to speed. However, think long term. A few minutes now may be worth hours later on. *The American Heritage Dictionary* defines a student as "one who makes a study of something." Students are sponges. They are programmed to absorb knowledge. So go ahead and share some of your knowledge and experience with them.

Independent Contractors

Over the past few years, *independent contractor* has become a very popular—yet misunderstood—label for a part-time or non-salaried employee. To give you a very brief rundown, independent contractors generally do not work only for you. They work on an hourly or a flat rate on a project-to-project basis, as their services are needed. They are considered independent because they should technically be working for other people in the same capacity. You don't have to pay payroll taxes for independent contractors because they are responsible for their own, whereas with staff members, responsibility is shared between the employee and the employer. However, you do need to report wages earned by independent contractors to the IRS, either quarterly or annually. The best thing about independent contractors is that you don't have to make a long-term commitment or incur substantial overhead to hire them.

Check with a certified public accountant (CPA) or call the IRS for guidelines and more information. The penalties for not following the rules could easily put any entrepreneur out of business—so don't hire anyone before you get the facts straight.

Real Employees

By "real," I mean real in the eyes of the IRS—and your wallet. Real employees are great because they are there from nine to five without other commitments. They also have a greater opportunity to get as addicted to your company as you are. Hiring employees involves paying for workers' compensation, insurance, payroll taxes on Social Security, and taxes at the local, state, and federal levels. Once you hire employees, your business overhead and risks as a business owner will increase significantly. Be sure to discuss the full implications of hiring with your advisers and a CPA. Though you might be able to scrape together a salary, you might not be able to handle the other associated costs. Be very careful when hiring people. There are many considerations that you must force yourself to consider before making a smart step forward.

So as not to discourage you unnecessarily, here are a few pros and cons about hiring "real employees" for you to weigh:

PROS

- If they're full-timers, they're all yours 40, 60, 80 hours a week
- They will take more ownership in your business
- They will be more concerned with staying for a while
- You can delegate a lot more, relieving yourself of a lot of responsibility
- They can motivate you and make work more fun

CONS

- You now have the responsibility of someone else's livelihood
- You must pay them, regardless of how your company is doing
- You have to pay taxes for them and offer health benefits
- Your overhead increases
- You might need to pay for more office space
- You might have to offer equity to them

Actually, much of the decision about whether or not to hire salaried employees boils down to how much money you have or are willing to spend. You also have to decide how it will change your business and affect your lifestyle or work style. Once you have come to terms with all of the pros and cons, just take your time. Do your research by talking to other employers and lots of potential employees. Make sure that you really trust the people you hire and can justify the expenses. Be honest with them about your company's situation and encourage them to be honest in sharing their feelings and concerns with you. Keep open lines of communication and you'll be off to a great start. Other than that, you're just going to have to give it a shot and see how it works for you. You never know until you try. Yes, it's a tough decision, but think of it as another milestone in your entrepreneurial career.

CHAPTER 8

Raising Money

W HERE *AM* I GOING TO GET THE MONEY I NEED TO START AND RUN MY OWN business? That, my friends, is the age-old question that entrepreneurs grapple with the most. So if the question sounds all too familiar, don't worry, you're not alone. There are viable solutions to getting the money you need. As usual, we just might have to be a little bit more creative to get it.

As younger entrepreneurs, we've got to face certain realities when it comes to raising money.

- It is very difficult for us to have *a lot* of experience in our industries or as business owners.

- Most investors, and particularly the bigger institutions, perceive us as a big risk.

- We usually don't have houses, cars, stock portfolios, or other things that we can offer as collateral.

- We usually don't have a lot of historical financial data to prove that we can in fact generate money with our businesses.

- We often don't even know how much money we're really going to need, because we haven't been through the experience before.

So why are so many people our age able to build multi-million dollar companies when they don't have that much more than we do? There are a lot of reasons. Basically, if they want it badly enough, successful entrepreneurs find a way to get what they need. Your first task in raising money for your business is deciding how badly you want it. It probably won't be easy. Look at this as one of the first big tests of your ability to succeed in your own business.

Since there are so many things to think about when you decide to finance a business, I'm going to give you a bit of a laundry list to start you thinking in the right direction. Then I'll take you through the various forms of financing and sources.

Some Basic Rules

The Money Is Out There

There are a lot of people out there with a lot of money. Whether you need $5,000, $500,000 or $5 million dollars, there are many more people than you can imagine who have it, can get it, and can be convinced to invest it in a new business.

Everyone Wants to Be an Entrepreneur

Well, not everyone, but most people do, even if they never actually take the big step. What that means is that there are a lot of people out there who would love to be a part of a new venture. When those people have the opportunity to invest in a new business, and often become a partner in it, they get that sense of ownership that they always wanted (even if they are totally inactive in the business), and you get the money you need to run the company.

Investors Invest in People First, Ideas Second

If you really think about it, the greatest business idea in the world wouldn't go anywhere if there wasn't a competent entrepreneur behind it. Conversely, skilled entrepreneurs can often create great successes out of half-baked business concepts. What that means is that you'd better start thinking about why someone would invest their money in you. When you can single-handedly make or break your business, why do you think you're one of those who can make it work?

Know Your Business

If you can't talk intelligibly about your business concept, answer questions, and convey statistics, trends and the insight of an insider, you are going to have a tough time convincing people to put their money on your ability to run a business. The more information you have, the better, because you don't want to be struggling for answers when a potential investor is questioning you.

Do Your Research

With all of the information that is now available out there, you should be able to get some information on how other businesses like yours were financed. (It's also good to find out why others weren't given the money they needed.) Who were the entrepreneurs behind the businesses? What was their background? Who gave them the money? How much? What did they have to give up? You can probably get some sales information, and maybe even profits, if you dig enough. Meeting other industry players will also help you because they are more likely to divulge the kind of financial information that you'll need for investors.

Focus on the Numbers

Start creating and crunching your own financial projections. You might be totally off on your first shot at it, as you might not have any idea how much advertising, rent, signage, and other business basics, are going to cost. Get the numbers out of your head and onto paper. Only then can you embark on the humbling experience of showing them to other people and having them rip your projections apart. (It's painful, but we all have to do it.) The more you work with the numbers, the more familiar you become with them, and the quicker you can start to understand the profit potential in your business. This is what investors are most concerned with: Will this entrepreneur return my money to me with a profit?

Start Talking

Unless there is a serious need for secrecy about your concept, start talking up your business to as many people as you can. If people don't know that you are looking for investors, let alone trying to launch a new concept, how can they even know to offer their help. You never know who you might be dealing with. Your ninth grade teacher might have a millionaire aunt who would just love your business idea. Your best friend's father might just be looking for some new investment opportunity, or might consider it since you've always been like a second son to him. Take a very close look around you. Behind those friendly and familiar faces might be a lot of incredible contacts that you never knew about.

People tend to get so frightened at the prospect of raising money that they forget some of these basic rules. Get comfortable with these and you're ready to move forward.

How Much Do You Really Need?

Determining the actual amount of money that you need to start your business can be pretty tricky, depending on how complicated or advanced your concept is. The biggest thing to avoid is underestimating how much it is really going to cost you. Most entrepreneurs do this in the beginning, either because they simply don't know better, or because they're scared that if they ask for more money they might lose the investor's interest completely.

The best way to start estimating your start-up and operating costs is to take out a piece of paper and a pencil and make a laundry list of products, services, and employees that you will need. Make sure to include the following, even if they are just estimates of the actual costs:

- Rent
- Salaries
- Employee benefits (health care)
- Your living expenses
- Transportation and travel
- Utilities
- Phones
- Insurance
- Office supplies
- Printing
- Postage
- Shipping
- Inventory

Again, your financials will be unique to your business. You may have certain expenses that other businesses don't, and you might not have—or be able to avoid—certain expenses that other companies can. Talking to others in similar businesses will again help you here. Be as conservative as possible and overestimate whenever you're not sure. It is better to be overprepared than underbudgeted. Next, after you've begun to feel comfortable with your basic costs, you'll want to transfer all of this data to a spread sheet so that you can start working on financial statements for your business plan. You've never seen a spread sheet? Then now is the time to do it. There are numerous books on financing for new companies, and virtually all of them include examples of spread sheets. Check them out.

One last thing to keep in mind is to always leave a cushion for yourself in case things don't go exactly as you planned. Always expect that you will not know all of the costs and that other expenses will pop up or will exceed your budget. Also make sure that you have enough operating capital to last you for a few months. There's nothing worse than getting the money you need to start up the business then running out before you have a chance to turn a profit.

Speaking of how much you really need, you never want your business associates or clients to know that you are struggling financially because:

- They will wonder why.
- They might assume that business is bad.
- You could be close to bankruptcy.
- They may decide that you may not be as good as they thought.
- Clients should be proud of doing business with you.
- You might be too focused on financing to attend to their needs.
- Image and size matter.

Growing up with five entrepreneurs in my immediate family, I learned more about this subject than I could fit into another whole book. If I assume that I started comprehending what was happening around me at the age of two, I have a good twenty-four years' experience in looking "larger and more successful" as an entrepreneur. Though few have ever known it, there have been times when my family's businesses have made millions and other times when we could barely afford to feed our dogs. The amazing thing was that no one ever had any idea if we were struggling. They couldn't! Why would a major corporation or emerging company ever want to do business with someone who could be going out of business? But the truth is that most entrepreneurs (young or old) come close to losing it all more often than you'd think. Just don't expect them to tell you that. Entrepreneurs, almost by definition, take risks that could propel them in either direction at any time, and all entrepreneurs have rough times. My family's businesses were no different. And neither is mine. If you don't already have a great collection of "I'm broke and they don't even know it" stories, here's one to chew on for a bit.

I was once at the office of some very successful investment bankers with two other young entrepreneurs. As their friend, I was doing whatever I could to make them look more substantial as they prepared an offering circular (a more complex and expensive business plan) to help them raise about a half-million dollars. The meeting went very well and everyone seemed quite happy. So I packed my briefcase and started to say good-bye. Just then, one of my friends quickly pulled me aside and whispered that he needed a small favor. Neither he nor his partner had the money to grab a taxi back to their hotel. I discreetly pulled out my wallet to save them. It was empty. So the two of us made up some ridiculous excuse for why he, and no one else, needed to escort me downstairs, so we could race off to the nearest cash machine. On the way down in the elevator, we couldn't stop laughing. Here they were trying to raise hundreds of thousands of dollars, and I was brought in as some big business expert, and neither of us could afford to take a bus. With the last $30 in my bank account, we were both able to save face. (And yes, my friends did end up getting their financing.)

Being strapped for cash in the beginning is just part of the territory—you get used to it in the short run so you don't have to settle for poverty in the long run. So hang on to your dreams about growing rich off your business, because you'll need the incentive along the way.

Equity or Debt?

Regardless of what you've read in other books or business magazines, you must realize and accept that not all financing options are going to be right, let alone available, to you. That's just the way it is. As a starting point, bear in mind that when you're thinking about raising money for your company, you have two major decisions to make. The first involves how you would like to raise the money, and the second regards where you get the money from.

Your first choice for a financing strategy might not necessarily be the best or most readily available, so you must learn to be flexible and keep your options open. As a businessman once told me during an offer to invest, "He who holds the gold makes the rules." That may not jibe with your perspective any more than it did with mine, but realize that this is the stance that many investors will take with your business. So be firm and hold your ground, but be reasonable and smart about your decision.

The first decision you have to make is whether you want to give away equity or incur debt to raise money. If you give away equity you are consenting to sell part of your company to an investor in exchange for a specified amount of money. If you go the route of debt financing, though, you borrow money without giving away any ownership and must repay the debt or loan over a set period of time at a pre-specified interest rate. Deciding whether ownership or indebtedness is more important to you is something to which you should give careful thought and consideration. You can even decide not to choose between one or the other. Most companies actually raise money through a combination of debt and equity financing. After all, there is no rule that your money must all come from one place. Actually, it can be much smarter to raise money from more than one source so that you do not become too dependent on one.

Where to Get the Money

The second decision you have to make is determining where you'll raise the money. The following are the most common options.

Angels

Angels is the term used to identify private investors who may be family, friends, or wealthy individuals who believe in you and your business enough to give you money. Angel investment is the most common because it is the easiest to obtain and can be repaid as a loan, offered as a grant, or given in exchange for equity, or a percentage of ownership. The terms of an angel investment are completely negotiable and can essentially be whatever the angel and the entrepreneur(s) agree on. Anyone can be an angel—your grandmother, a professor, a neighbor, or a business associate—so don't rule anyone out.

Banks

This might not be your best option, particularly if the section on business credit left you feeling a little jittery. But just in case you want to consider it, you have two options with a bank, both being debt financing. A straight loan can be made for virtually any amount of money, but you must provide sufficient collateral and assets. Basically, the bank will not lend money unless you have money to back it up. So why would you be asking for money if you already had it to put up as collateral? Good question. Big problem also. The bank can assume only so much risk by giving you money, so be prepared to reveal all of your worldly goods of any value, to pledge them as assets, and to offer a personal guarantee as well. A personal guarantee says that even if you don't have the money to pay back the loan, you accept the personal responsibility to see it paid back, any way that you can.

A second option for bank financing is through a line of credit. A line of credit is a virtual credit card for your business. After putting you and your company through much of the same scrutiny that a financial institution would for a loan application, a bank might offer you a line a credit where an approved amount of money will be placed into your business account as a reserve. So, if your bank account has $3,000 in it, and you are given a line of credit of $15,000, your bank balance will still show $3,000, but you will have the additional $15,000 at your disposal on credit. Any money that you use from the line will be subject to interest payments that you will have to maintain as long as you are borrowing the money. If you happen to keep a fair amount of money in your account but think you might need a good deal more, or are concerned about unexpected expenses, you could be a good candidate for a line of credit.

Your bank's loan officer will be able to supply you with all of the necessary paperwork and give you an idea whether the bank is likely to lend you money or not. Since it's their job to give loans—the way banks make money is through interest payments—they are usually quite willing to tell you what you need to make you eligible. If you haven't already guessed, a business plan will probably be the first item on their list (See Chapter 3).

The Government

The Small Business Administration (SBA), an agency of the U.S. government, was created to help entrepreneurs start, build, and expand their businesses by offering a range of seminars, mentoring programs, published material, resources, and loans. SBA loans are usually more lenient than banks because they recognize the needs, challenges, and importance of small business owners. This is not to say that getting a loan from the SBA is easy, just easier—but there are no guarantees.

The good news is that the SBA has loan programs directed at different groups of people. The most popular these days are their women's and minority business loans, but there are a variety of others to help almost any small business owner raise capital. Again, be prepared to submit a business plan, financial forecasts, current financial records, personal income statements, and even your personal assets in intimate detail. Most SBA loans will also require that you come to the table with assets and put a certain percentage, like one-third of the money requested, up front yourself. So, as you may have guessed, when deciding how much money you really need, you must take into consideration the money you already have and ask for that much more than you originally anticipated.

Venture Capitalists (VCs)

Unless you need to raise a couple of hundred thousand or a few million dollars, forget about venture capital money right now. Everyone seems to think that to raise money for a business you need to deal with venture capitalists, but it's simply not true. Venture capitalists are responsible for funding some of the largest companies in the world, but they're generally not interested in funding companies with relatively low start-up costs.

Typically, a VC firm will spend much of its time looking at new deals and listening to various entrepreneurs explain why their venture is such a good investment. So there is the usual inquisition, where everything about the business and entrepreneur is evaluated, and then a decision is made. If the VC firm decides to invest in a company, they are usually committing a large sum of money for a large share of equity or ownership. When you raise money with venture capitalists you typically expect to be giving away majority— or less, but a still painful amount of—ownership in your business. But again, entrepreneurs turn to venture capitalists because of the large sums of money they can invest.

A great benefit of venture funding is having someone from the firm sit on your board of directors and act as a partner or key adviser. The VC firm's goal in investing is to make your company grow as fast as it can and make as much money as possible so that you can then take the business public. When you go public, you allow the public to buy shares of your company through a stock exchange. When that happens, the venture capitalists cash out (sell their interest in the company) at a solid profit.

Most VC firms have a certain profile of businesses that they invest in. This profile typically includes a certain level of necessary investment and a particular industry, such as high-tech, entertainment or publishing. Before you waste time talking to any VC firm, find out what their typical investment profile is and whether you fit into that category. Also, be very realistic about the kind of money you need and whether you have the potential for exponential growth—a requirement for venture financing. Most venture capitalists will give you a few minutes to pitch your business, but the clock will be ticking and, out of courtesy, you should retreat when they give you the signal. They must examine hundreds of deals before finding one that they are truly interested in. Yours may not be it. Learn to deal with that. You'll save time and possibly pick up a few VC friends along the way.

Organizations

Organizations are another possible source of funding. You should take a close look at some of the industries and associations that are related to your business. Even if the connection is a vague or remote one, look for common goals. Many times, larger organizations will have foundations affiliated with them whose main purpose is education, legislation, or activism. If you can think of a special project that will help you understand your industry better, attract new customers, or entice the media, see how it may fit into the goals of an organization. If it does, then you can approach them about a joint venture in which they provide the funding. Though not a commonly recognized funding source, foundations and organizations can contribute significantly to a company's growth, let alone recognition.

The possibility of funding projects through organizations was an intriguing lesson I learned. Anxious to produce some hard-core information—statistics, data—about young entrepreneurs, get some media attention for the market, and have our company further recognized as the experts, I did some research on an organization I knew of through my family. Though the organization's focus was franchising, they had a special educational foundation devoted to encouraging entrepreneurship through franchising to the next generation. Bingo! Though our company didn't really do much with franchising, we did refer a lot of people to the organization for more information, and as far as the next generation, we were the experts.

So, after a few months of written proposals, I got the chance to speak to the board of trustees at their annual convention in Honolulu. I presented our company as the perfect joint venture partner and offered to do a study on young entrepreneurs, investigating their business interests and attitudes on franchising as a viable entrepreneurial option. (I also mentioned that I had been attending their events with my family since I was five. That didn't hurt either.) By the end of the conference, I had received the largest grant in the organization's history—$25,000—just what I needed to conduct a psychographic research study and the largest PR campaign anyone had ever seen done over research in the field.

Oh, did I mention that I was even offered a job by one of the trustees? Never saw myself in the home decorating business, though.

So that's the story on financing your business. Keep in mind that over 80 percent of businesses started by young entrepreneurs are financed through friends, family, credit cards, and personal savings. The banks and venture capitalists aren't going anywhere, so if you don't make it to them on this round of financing, you'll likely have occasion to call on them again. Just talk to a lot of people, keep your overhead and expenses low, and don't believe that you have any money secured until the papers are signed or the check is in your hands. (My dad taught me that last one, despite having to learn it myself a few times.)

CHAPTER 9

Building Business Relationships

ONE OF THE GREATEST WAYS YOU CAN SPEND YOUR FREE TIME AS AN ENTRE-preneur is by getting out and meeting other people. And as a young entrepreneur, building your business network should be toward the top of your list. Granted, the more involved you are in your business, the less time you will have to do the "networking thing," but don't lose sight of how expanding your personal network can increase your opportunities.

Unfortunately, some people have a terrible fear of speaking to people they don't know. If you're one of those people, you're going to have to learn to get over that fear—it's something you just can't afford. For the rest of us, the ones who can't stop talking, we have an issue called "control" to deal with.

Al Kao, a high school senior with a new direct-mail business, was terrified about starting conversations with adults. With people his own age he was usually outgoing, though clearly lacking in self-confidence. After speaking with him for some time, I found out that Al was scared that he would "mess up" conversations with business people. He was afraid that he might say the wrong things. It took me a while, but I was able to convince him that his fear was not only unnecessary but was paralyzing his ability to meet new people at all.

If you have a similar affliction—fear of speaking to strangers, practice makes perfect. Go out of your way to speak to people you normally would not talk to. Strike up conversations with parking attendants, stewardesses, commuters, or students. Then go a little further. Volunteer for a phone-a-thon, take an internship in an office as a receptionist, or work in a retail location. The best way to deal with fear of the unknown is simply to jump in and learn to swim. If you immerse yourself in a situation where you'll be forced to do what you're afraid of, you'll learn to do it.

For Al, I offered an internship project which required that he call over three hundred people to update their membership information. At first, I must admit, I wasn't thrilled. He was terrified, and it showed. But within a few hours he was chatting away with members he found interesting and didn't seem to ever want to get off the phone. In one week, eighteen-year-old Al had more "professional telephone" experience than most people have in their mid-twenties.

Recognizing the fear then understanding how to combat it is the best way to deal with it effectively. In most cases, people's fears of speaking to strangers are unfounded and illogical, as with most phobias. Once you can confront your fears you are much more likely to overcome them.

Just in case you have any doubts about the possible advantages of talking to strangers, here are a couple of brief examples. Twenty-seven-year-old Scott Mendelson happened to bump into Donald Trump at a bar in the Trump Plaza one night. "Nice suit" was the best that Scott could come up with at the time, and though he hated himself afterward, his originality did spark a brief conversation with the mogul.

Candy Brush, a professor at Boston University and a well-known expert on women's entrepreneurship, once had a great conversation with a woman she met in the Ladies Room at a conference. The woman turned out to be a reporter from the *Wall Street Journal,* and a few weeks later Candy saw herself quoted as an expert in a *Journal* article the woman wrote.

Sometimes the simplest comment can start a great conversation. Laugh if you like, but commenting on the weather, the service at a restaurant, or someone's tan can be the small talk that relationships are built on. Just think about the last time you spent half of a plane trip talking to the person next to you. How did that conversation start? "I can't believe how late we're leaving," "Do you live here in Dallas?" or maybe, "Can you pass me the air-sick bag?" (Although hopefully not the latter.)

From: Bo Peabody—Tripod
The Start-Up Swallow

2:30 p.m. April 27, 1996—"Hi, Tracy, this is Bo Peabody calling from Tripod. A friend of mine who does work with one of your clients has asked me to contact that client about advertising opportunities with Tripod. I wanted to touch base with you before I go ahead and do that. I look forward to hearing from you."

8:30 a.m. April 30, 1996—"Hi, it's Bo Peabody calling. Again, I just wanted to touch base with you before I contact your client about possible advertising opportunities with Tripod."

5:00 p.m. May 2, 1996—"Hi, it's Bo Peabody calling again. I'd appreciate it if you could call me back regarding contacting your client about advertising opportunities with Tripod."

10:30 a.m. May 5, 1996—"Hi, it's Bo Peabody from Tripod calling again. I realize you are busy but I would appreciate a call back regarding advertising opportunities with your client. Thanks."

3:30 p.m. May 6, 1996—"Hi, Bo Peabody here. I realize you are busy but I've left several messages for you regarding contacting your client about advertising opportunities with Tripod. If I don't hear from you in the next day or so I am going to go ahead and contact your client directly. I look forward to hearing from you."

5:30 p.m. May 6, 1996—"Bo, this is Tracy from Agency 555. I don't appreciate you calling me up and threatening to contact my client directly. We're busy over here and I don't have time for that crap. Who are you anyway?"

"Thanks, Tracy, for calling me back. My name is Bo Peabody and I am from Tripod. We are an Internet-focused media company located in Massachusetts. We have a website and print magazine targeted at young people that a friend of mine thinks might be of interest to one of your clients. I thought it would be right for me to contact you before contacting your client directly."

"I can tell you that our client is not interested in looking at anything right now. But if you want, you can send down a proposal and we'll look at it and call you if we think it makes sense."

This is the toughest spot to be in. This woman is clearly being a snot. And, make no mistake, I am pissed. But where is retaliating going to get me? Nowhere. So, I sit back and take a big start-up swallow and say,

"Ok. That sounds fine. I'll have the proposal out before the end of the day and will look forward to hearing from you. Take care and thanks for getting back to me."

Of course, I never heard from Tracy or anyone at Agency 555. I ended up contacting her client directly and six months later we were doing business with them. A month after that I heard that Tracy had left Agency 555 to take a senior position at another one of her agency's clients. Just out of coincidence, I happened to be friends with the woman who hired her.

Three months later, things were going quite well for Tripod. We had made a lot of progress with building our audience and had attracted many big advertisers. One day, I got a voice mail from Tracy.

From: Bo Peabody—Tripod
The Start-Up Swallow, (Continued)

"Hi, Bo. My boss Sandy asked me to give you a call about us possibly working together to reach young people. She thinks very highly of what Tripod has accomplished. We are launching a new product and are interested in reaching the same audience. I know we got off on the wrong foot and I apologize for that. If you could give me a call back at your convenience I'd really appreciate it."

A few hours later I called Tracy back and we had a nice conversation. I joked about our exchange of six months prior and told her that it was no big deal. Two months later we took an order from her company and have been doing business with them ever since.

Burning bridges is stupid. People appreciate honesty, but getting worked up in an unfriendly way never pays. Industries are so small that you almost always end up running into people over and over again. In the above scenario I could have ended up with no orders or two orders. It was my decision. And because I kept my cool, I ended up with two.

Ben Burgeosis, a Hollywood event planner, starts conversations with everyone he ever sits next to on planes. On one fateful trip he found himself engrossed in a conversation about his work, only to find out that he was speaking to the vice president of Pepsi Co. By the time the plane landed, Ben had landed what would later amount to a $7 million dollar account.

As you can see, there are any number of ways to meet people, as well as any number of possible outcomes to those meetings. If you're just starting out, though, one of the best places to find people to talk to is in industry organizations and associations.

Organizations and Associations

I'm assuming, for the moment at least, that you haven't actually started up your business. Even if you have, though, it wouldn't hurt to learn more about industry organizations and associations.

What kind of organizations you should approach, and who you should meet within those organizations, can depend to some extent on where you are in terms of starting your company. Chances are you'll fall into one of the following categories.

You Haven't Found an Industry *or* an Idea

Haven't yet found "the idea" that will launch you into entrepreneurial bliss? The best strategy for you then would be a broad one—to keep your filters open to a wide range of people and companies.

Start with your local Chamber of Commerce or Junior Chamber (generally, for people under forty). These are located in thousands of cities around the world and serve as the center of each city's business and social community. You will meet all sorts of people, from restaurant owners to local government officers, consultants to retailers. Most chambers are loaded with entrepreneurs who are very accessible, just from their very affiliation with the group. Attend one or two events to see if the organization strikes your fancy. If you can track down the membership director, he or she will make sure that you are introduced to many different people and get a good overview of the chamber's events and activities.

If you can locate a local networking group for entrepreneurs, attend their meetings. Be prepared, though, for a search, because most of these groups are fairly small and hard to locate. For those affiliated with a college or university, look on campus for other chances to meet like-minded people. Many universities and business schools have organizations for entrepreneurial students or events to keep their alumni in touch and in tune with each other as well as their alma mater. These are great opportunities because you are guaranteed to have something in common, and alums love to talk about their college experiences and help fellow graduates (or current students) whenever they can.

If you still need help finding other young entrepreneurs or would like to meet some from other areas of the world, The Young Entrepreneurs Network (310-822-0261/http://www.yenetwork.com) was created for that purpose. (Successful entrepreneurs always know when to plug their own businesses!)

You've Found the Industry But *Still* Need an Idea

Okay, you know that you love the fashion industry, or high tech, or international trade, but you haven't quite figured out what you want to do with your interest. From a networking standpoint, don't worry—you're in a great position. Knowing that you are interested in a specific industry narrows your focus enough to help you start an efficient search for your ideal business, and at the same time opens you up to a whole range of opportunities within that field. Think of it in terms of being an athlete: Would you rather look for athletic gear at a department store or a sporting goods store? There's really no question that the specialty store will offer you many more choices than you know what to do with, and it might even turn you on to some things you may not have considered. And who would you rather talk to anyway, someone at a department store, who might sell baby clothes 300 feet away, or someone at a sporting goods store, who dedicates most of her/his time to that field?

So what now? Where do you find these people with a common interest in your field? In case you didn't know, there's an association and publication for practically every field. Yes, there is even an organization for fly fishermen, as well as a newsletter. So if you are still in doubt about whether support exists for you, don't fret any longer. Organizations, trade associations, and clubs exist to bring people with common interests together and offer them support in a variety of different ways. This is where you need to be.

You've Already *Got* an Idea

Even if you already have a good idea of what you want to do, you still need to be in touch with others in your field. Follow my advice and join groups that support your field. If you can find organizations for people in your exact business, all the better. But do keep yourself in tune with other people in the broader industry. You will never know what trends might be emerging or what opportunities for expansion or diversification might exist for your company if you confine yourself and your contacts to those who only do exactly what you do. Definitely know your specific competitors, but know the vastness of your industry as well—it will keep other doors open, should you ever need them. It will also make you more knowledgeable about your work and will help you appear as if you are more of an expert.

Finding an Organization for Your Industry

Here are some tried and true methods of finding an organization for your industry:

- If asking around doesn't help you find a great club or organization to check out, go to a store that sells equipment, supplies, or services people in your field. Ask the sales people and the managers if they have any suggestions for you. (Hint: The smaller or more specialized the store, the more likely you are to find someone who really lives for the business. The store owner would also be a good shot.)

- Look in the Yellow or White Pages of your phone book under associations.

- Go to a library with a good-sized reference desk. Ask for the *Directory of Directories* and the *Directory of Associations*. (It's a shame how few people know about these resources.) In each, search under your industry heading, narrowing or broadening your search as needed. Here you should find any directories of people in your field and any related associations, organizations, or clubs that may exist.

- Find a school that teaches classes in your field. Regardless of whether it's a trade school, community college, or major university, people in the department will most likely know how to find what you are looking for and may well turn out to be great contacts themselves.

When you find the associations that support your field, you may very well experience that "born again" feeling. The greatest experience is when you first discover that there are hundreds, thousands, or even millions of others with your interests, and a good number of them can be found through an organization or at an expo. If it hasn't already happened to you, you'll understand what I'm talking about when it does.

I had that born again feeling when I first found and attended a conference for the Association of Collegiate Entrepreneurs while I was a sophomore in college. I felt like a kid in a candy store. Hundreds of young entrepreneurs were running around to different seminars, giving speeches, trading business cards, and meeting as many people as they could. It was amazing! I have often called this my "entrepreneurial coming out of the closet," because this was the first time that I finally realized that this is who I am and that I don't have to hide it or be embarrassed about it. I can be proud to be an entrepreneur. And better yet, there are all these people who live the same life as I do (even in college). I then understood the importance of peer support. And that's why you need to find and join organizations for people like you. There is no reason to pursue your entrepreneurial dreams alone.

How to Meet Important People

There are a couple of tricks that even the most well-known people use to meet other hard-to-reach people. Sometimes, you just need a little luck (like sitting next to the right person on an airplane or bumping into someone in a restroom), but most of the time you need to be creative to get an audience with certain people.

Before you start, for your own sake, have a very clear purpose in mind for wanting to meet with them. If you just want the chance to shake their hand and tell them how much you admire them, that's one thing. To ask someone to speak to you as a mentor, business adviser, or industry expert, you must be respectful of their position and their time. If you compromise either, your chances of establishing any type of relationship are slim. Once you have established a purpose for your meeting, run the idea by a few people who you respect, just to clarify your objectives. (Sometimes even the most clearheaded people waste their few precious moments with an admired person on babble, then live to regret it.)

Personal Introductions

A personal introduction, even if from an acquaintance, secretary, or neighbor, is the easiest way to get the time of day from someone who might normally be unreachable. This is particularly true in politics and in the media. When people, because of their jobs or positions, have to live life on the defensive (from fans, the press, or the public), they are constantly dodging unknown people. You are probably one of them—until they have reason to believe otherwise.

Eddie Soleymani, a twenty-seven-year-old entrepreneur in New York, decided that his next venture would involve starting a magazine for college students. After telling everyone he knew about the idea, a friend who worked for *Family PC* magazine offered to help. Though the magazine she worked for had little to do with college students, she had met Keith Clinkscales, the editor and CEO of *Vibe* magazine, one of the top-sellers in the eighteen- to twenty-four-year-old market. She made a quick phone call on Eddie's behalf to *Vibe*. Within five hours of leaving a message for the owner, Eddie had his call returned, and within five days Eddie was meeting with him personally. The two had a lot to talk about. Eddie then turned around and introduced me to Keith, who turned out to be a very approachable and inspiring person. Who would have known? Certainly not the CEO if Eddie's friend hadn't stepped into the picture.

Out of Their Element

Though you might think that arranging a meeting in someone's office is great, remember it is rare that you will have their undivided attention. The phone rings, secretaries pop in, the clock and schedule book are in front of them, problems need attention.

Over the past few years, I've been lucky enough to become friends with the editor-in-chief of *Entrepreneur* magazine. Despite the fact that our "quarterly" lunches usually last about four hours it's virtually impossible to keep Rieva's attention for more than three minutes, until we're in a car or a restaurant. Then her attention turns into advice of gold. So while she often teases me about never finishing my lunch, I'd much rather spend that time pitching every idea and new venture that I can to get her feedback.

Few executives can truly devote their attention to something (or someone) totally unrelated to their company when in their own business environment. Yes, there are exceptions, but just watch. Even the most conscientious hosts cannot help themselves from drifting sometimes. So if you're just looking to create a great bonding situation and not for a wealth of information (in which case being in their office might be best), get your new friend(s) out of the office and into an environment where they can unwind. You never know what might happen.

While in Boston on business for a few days, Jason Gold and Barry Swatzenbarg, founders of Office Perfect, invited me to dinner with some investment bankers that they had been trying to soften up for a few months over the phone. When the bankers arrived at the hotel, it was 7:00 p.m. Usually quite territorial and controlling, the visitors were thrown off base, particularly when they met me. After all, who was I? And why was I there? To be polite, the bankers avoided talking too much business in front of their unexpected company. So we talked small talk over a few drinks. By 9:00 p.m. we had all moved into the hotel lounge and were entrenched in conversation. Laughing, sharing stories, and talking a little business, we practically had to force ourselves to leave at about midnight. Jason and Barry's relationship with the investment bankers was changed forever. The formality vanished from that night on.

One night at a franchise conference, I wandered into a bar with my father and uncle. Gathered in one corner were the owner, publisher, editor, and advertising director of a major business magazine. My father waved to one of the group members, whom he knew, and they waved us all over. Already on their third round of drinks, they insisted that we join them. Long after my father and uncle retired, I stayed up talking with them. And for the two nights after that, I was invited back to join their little "unwinding sessions." Nearly five years later we're all still friends. And when business is on the table, I am offered carte blanche.

In Their Element

If you are going to meet with someone in their office, try to make your appointment at a time when few others will be there. Early evenings, Friday afternoons, and weekends are usually the best time to catch executives at ease in their own, comfortable environments.

After attending the Southern California Entrepreneurship Academy for a year to personally meet the top entrepreneurs in Los Angeles, I came across one amazing young entrepreneur named Paul Feller. His sports marketing company, ProSports International, was fascinating to me, as I had been struggling to put together my own sponsorship packages for a project I was working on. We opted to meet at a great jazz bar and spoke for hours. Another friendship was cemented. Three years later we still get together every time we're in the same city. Aside from being a great friend he is an amazing mentor. His multimedia projects, international offices, relationships with corporate sponsors, and experiences have given me much food for thought and some great ideas.

Letters and Gifts

Don't ever think that you should bribe people with gifts to meet with you (although it *did* help the young entrepreneur played by Charlie Sheen to meet the great Gordon Gecko in the movie *Wall Street*. Remember that great box of cigars?). On the other hand, it never hurts to remember someone's birthday, anniversary, favorite wine, or cigars. If you really want to meet a specific person, read anything you can about them and find some little personal preference that they may have for a hint. Maybe they're big golfers, or travel buffs, or even supporters of a particular nonprofit group. Use your imagination. Anything that is rare, hard to get, or requires a bit of time or creativity works well to get the attention of unsuspecting others. There is no reason for you to spend an excessive amount of money. Sometimes a good book or even an article clipping will do the trick.

Contact Management

Once you start meeting all the people that you always wanted to—and many that you never even anticipated—you will need to start thinking seriously about how to manage your business contacts. Nothing is more foolish than losing touch with great people in business. If you don't have some sort of system down pat (a Rolodex, business card file, address book, or contact management software program), not only will you lose touch, but you'll start to lose friends.

The more organized you are with your business contacts, the more you can impress them with birthday cards, articles of interest, or even random notes or calls to say hello. If you find out that someone has just had a baby, taken a great vacation, or received an award, take the opportunity to write a note.

However, if your business calls for you to meet more individuals than most people meet in a lifetime, it can get overwhelming . . . fast. At first you miss birthdays, then lose contact, then you can start forgetting to follow up on promises or postponed meetings. Those are bad situations. Avoid them, or people will start to avoid you.

Mentors and Advisers

Mentors

If you ask any successful entrepreneurs what their greatest business assets are, or to what they attribute their success, odds are that most will mention something about their mentors. In a simplistic sense, mentors are like parents. (Just don't ask them to help you with your rent or show up uninvited for dinner.) Yes, you can grow up successfully without them (professionally, too), but why would you?

Mentors are like family members with whom you might be very formal or incredibly close. Regardless, they will be there when you need them and even more so when you don't think you do, but do. Mentors will point out your flaws to you because they'd rather do it than have someone else (like clients) realize your shortcomings. (And you thought that job was reserved for your family and significant others.) Just as your parents spent half their time teaching you new things, correcting your mistakes, and guiding you through life, mentors can play a similar role with you and your business.

Speaking of avoiding mistakes, my mentors have helped me avoid quite a few in my life. One of the most significant was my idea to start a company called Video College Tours. While attending a conference for young entrepreneurs in New York City, I found myself enthralled in a breakout session on "guerrilla marketing." The speaker was so inspiring that when he urged us to fearlessly approach the people who could help us with our businesses, I realized that he was the first person I wanted to meet. As it turns out, John Katzman happened to be the president of The Princeton Review. When I told him about my idea for Video College Tours, he showed a genuine interest in helping me. I was stunned. When he told me his story about barely making it out of Princeton after starting his company during his junior year, I began to reconsider my own idea. Not that starting a business was a bad idea, but this—a labor intensive, expensive, venture—wasn't the smartest thing for me to be focusing on at the very beginning of my college career. Of course, John was right. We've stayed friends over the years, and he is always there when I need anything. And as far as opening new opportunities for me, well, how's the chance to write this book for an example?

Mentors are amazing people for many reasons, the first being that they help you because they want to. When you find mentors you should always remember that their support for you is due to their faith in you and your business. That means they probably actually like you. Don't be too shocked—you probably do deserve the attention, most likely for reasons beyond your own comprehension. Think of these people as friends, because that is essentially what they are. If you are still perplexed, look at your business venture as if it were a personal relationship. Whatever help your friends would be inclined to give you in a personal relationship is the same type of help that mentors can give you with your business. If your company never gets off the ground, or fails, your mentors are still there for you, just like friends. Mentors want you to succeed, just as your friends want you to be happy.

Of all of the different ways that mentors can help you succeed, here are a few of the most significant and most common.

BASIC BUSINESS ISSUES

We've all been in situations—probably more often then we'd like to admit—where we didn't really understand what was going on. Maybe it was a job, a class, or filing your tax returns. Somehow you had to quickly learn something that you didn't know. Maybe you hadn't even realized that you didn't know what you needed to. So what happened? Either something happened that forced you to learn what you needed to (before anyone realized that you didn't know what you were doing) or someone who cared about you pointed out the problem and offered some guidance. In the latter case, a mentor stepped into your life.

Most people have a mentor and don't even realize it. The word sounds so formal that many assume that having mentors requires some sort of formal agreement or relationship. Some people think of mentors as they would a business plan. "Yeah, I know I need one, but I just haven't gotten around to it." If this sounds familiar, you've got it all wrong. (See, another one of those situations where you thought you understood but didn't.)

INDUSTRY LESSONS AND KNOW-HOW

Nothing beats mentors where industry lessons and know-how are concerned. If you don't have thirty years to spend gaining experience for your business ventures, why not just learn from someone who's already experienced? Mentors have usually been there and done that, and they are more than happy to share their knowledge with others. Just think about how many people are sick of hearing your business stories. Mentors are as eager as you are to let people know what they've been through. Another thing to keep in mind is that mentors don't have to worry about impressing people the way you do. So where you would rather die than admit to someone in your industry that you have no idea what you are doing, a mentor will often come right out and tell you about the time that he or she was in the same situation.

And as far as becoming an industry insider is concerned, your time will come. But why not get the benefits from others in the meantime? Your mentors may be very well connected in a particular field and thus will know what makes the industry tick. All of these little things that you would normally have to learn on your own can be right at your fingertips, just by consulting your mentors.

PERSONAL INTRODUCTIONS

In business it's not just who you know but who the people you *know* know. Ever hear of the term "six degrees of separation"? How about the idea that "there are only four people between you and anyone you want to meet"? Well, it may be a little more, or a little less, but the idea is that anyone you may possibly need to get to isn't really as far away as you may think. People who we assume are unreachable really have only two or three people standing between them and us. They could be secretaries, best friends, their mentors, their family, or any of dozens of different people who are close to them. You just need to get to one of them.

Here's where mentors come into play again. The higher up your mentors are in your industry, the more likely they are to introduce you to others at the top. And maybe you're not even interested in meeting the industry leaders. Maybe you just need a good lawyer, ten minutes with a publisher, or a friend at an ad agency. Whatever or whomever you need, your mentors should be able to assist you. As long as you have good relationships with them and they trust you, they should have no problem with introducing you to anyone whom they might already know.

DAY-TO-DAY DECISIONS

When you run your own business, each day presents you with situations, options, and challenges that must be dealt with, whether you know the right answers or not. Many of these daily decisions are inconsequential, whereas others could have significant ramifications on your professional reputation or even on your survival. Instead of going solely with your hunches, or basing decisions on a limited amount of information, consult your mentors. It's always good to ask the opinions of a few different people you trust when major issues crop up in your life. Just think, if you ask advice from one adviser of yours who's been in business for thirty years, one for fifteen years, and the other for five, you have fifty years of experience in the industry guiding you.

FEEDBACK AND HONEST ADVICE

If you ask for it, the people who care about and understand your business will give you the advice you are looking for. As an adviser or mentor, it's just part of the territory. If they don't tell you what you are doing wrong, they've defeated their purpose. So be direct about asking for honest advice and take it like an adult when it comes. Nothing can destroy a business venture faster than an ego.

Advisers and the Advisory Board

Doug Mellinger, one of the original founders of the Association of Collegiate Entrepreneurs, built a $10 million dollar company with his mentors. As the director of ACE Doug met some incredible business leaders, and he found an excuse to contact the CEOs from a hundred top high-tech companies. Doug knew that to succeed in his field he had to be aligned with these companies. So he picked up the phone and called each one. After introducing himself and his company, he asked each person if they'd be his mentor. By the time he got through the list he had amassed an advisory board of over twenty of those top executives. With their help Doug's company grew rapidly, and it continues to do so today, earning tens of millions of dollars a year.

There are two reasons to build a board of advisers for your company. The first is to bring together a well-rounded group of people who believe in you and your company enough to counsel you as it grows. By having a strong mix of people with various, yet related, professional backgrounds, you can ensure that your business will always benefit from a variety of opinions, backgrounds, and expertise. An advisory board allows you to build your business in the most ideal and nurturing environment possible. The second reason to assemble a board is for credibility. If you are going to be competing with major corporations—where names and titles are important— you'll be doing your company a big favor by gathering together a board that will support you on paper. Printing the names of your advisory board (if it's impressive) on your stationery or other company literature shows people that you mean business. An advisory board can be as substantive or as cosmetic as you need or want it to be. If your advisors are well respected, those who hold them in high regard will usually give you respect based on your affiliation.

Now don't confuse a board of advisers with a board of directors, because the difference is significant. A board of advisers is an informal group of people who consult with and counsel a business without assuming any legal or financial responsibility. A board of directors, on the other hand, is a legal entity whose members do have some fiscal responsibility and are often given partial ownership (or shares) in return for their participation. Boards of directors are mandatory for corporations, public companies, and non-profits. People who sit on company boards as directors can be liable should the company break the law or become involved in a legal battle. Being on a board of directors is a very serious decision and is not taken lightly.

For your business, unless you are building or running a major corporation, shy away from this in favor of a board of advisers. Your needs as a business owner probably don't warrant this type of commitment at this stage anyway. Advisers will be there for you when you need them. So take this opportunity to prove yourself to them as they help prove your credibility to others. Should you need to assemble a formal board of directors down the line, they will be the first ones at your side.

Now, before you get all stressed trying to figure out who your advisers *should* be, realize that everyone has a different mix of people who they rely on. Some of it is due to conscious decision making and the rest of it is left to chance. You never know who you will bond with or who will immediately be interested in you and your business. It could be the person who cuts your hair, a college professor, or the president of a multimillion dollar corporation.

Advisers should be people who believe in you and your company. They should be people you respect and people who are well respected by the business community. The better known and more experienced your advisers are, the greater your credibility will be. In cases where your ability or experience might be questioned, the experience of your mentors and advisers will be taken into consideration. For this reason, pay close attention to the people your advisory board should impress the most. Who is respected in your field? Are corporate executives, entrepreneurs, or government officials in high esteem in your industry? Create your advisory board with this in mind. After all, enhancing your own credibility is one of the two main reasons to formally build an advisory board.

As so much business is conducted socially (you know—golf courses, country clubs, power lunches, happy hours), your advisers can be very instrumental in getting you into such social situations. (See "How to Meet Important People.")

One last tip: Don't hesitate to have one wild duck who has crazy ideas on your board (as long as they are on your side), Tom Watson, legendary leader of IBM once advised. In this way your company can get the benefit of abstract and extreme views while having the ability to objectively analyze their applicability to your needs.

How to Initiate Relationships with Mentors/Advisers

I always say that when it comes to meeting important people in business, read what they read, go where they go, do the things that they do, and learn about what they already know, or should know. The idea behind this is twofold. First, how are you ever going to get the chance to meet these people if you don't know how to get to them, either formally or socially? Second, how will you say something of interest to them if you don't know what their interests are? If they're experts in a certain area, you should know about it. If they have some consuming hobby or personal mission, such as environmental preservation, your conversation will flow more smoothly if you have this kind of knowledge about them. It also shows that you care enough to have done your research. If you have one of those dazzling personalities, you might shrug off this advice and say that you can meet people on your own. I wouldn't if I were you. Even the most engaging entrepreneurs should build up their arsenal of background information. Finally, you should go to trade shows and conferences where prospective mentors or advisers may be lingering. This will surely help you add a few more to your list.

Okay, so you're at a trade show and have isolated the people you most want to meet. (This, by the way, is one of the first things that you should always do at an event like this—check out the attendance list and make sure you know who is there so you can mentally prepare your intro and plan of attack.) Now what? Do you just march right up to people and start talking? In most cases, yes, but every situation is different. A few months ago I was listening to C. J. Meenan, a teacher for the National Foundation for Teaching Entrepreneurship, teach a lesson about finding mentors, and he told the following story:

Every year while the organization still existed, C. J. would bring his students to the annual ACE (Association of Collegiate Entrepreneurs) conferences so that they could see hundreds of other successful young entrepreneurs. He explained that the ACE conventions had an energy that he had never seen before and, consequently, felt he had to share with his students. Everyone knew that Michael Dell, founder of Dell Computers (and the youngest Fortune 500 company owner in history), would again win the Young Entrepreneur of the Year Award. They also knew that Dell always claimed to not have a business card on him when asked for one. But one day someone caught him handing a card to someone, shortly after telling someone else that he didn't have one.

Now it's a year later, and C. J. and his high school class are planning their annual business card collection contest. The object of the game is to collect business cards, thus meeting as many people as possible. The average entrepreneur's card was worth one point, but if the students were to get a card from one of the top-ten collegiate entrepreneurs it would be worth ten points. The Young Entrepreneur of the Year, Michael Dell, was worth 100 points. Since C. J. knew Dell's reputation for not giving out cards, he offered an additional $100 reward to anyone who could get their hands on one.

At the ACE meeting, Omar, a street-smart, outgoing, and incredibly persistent high school student, declared that he would be getting the card and the $100. But by the time dinner rolled around, no one had been successful. C. J. was convinced that the $100 dollar bill in his pocket would remain there. But just as Michael Dell finished delivering the key note speech and left the room, Omar got up and followed him out the door. C. J. followed to see what Omar was up to. Just as C. J. made it through the door, he saw Michael entering the men's room, with Omar following right behind. About ten minutes passed. Nothing. Then Dell walked out, and C. J. expected a sullen Omar to follow. Omar walked out, not with disappointment on his face, but with a business card in his hand. It turned out that Omar had engaged Dell in a conversation by asking him about his marketing, operational, financing, and sales strategies for Dell Computers. Dell was so stunned to be hearing such questions from a fifteen-year-old that when Omar asked for a card, Dell didn't even hesitate.

Despite losing the hundred dollars, C. J. said that the story was worth it. As it happens, Omar and Dell stayed in touch for years, all because C. J. had posed the challenge and Omar had had the guts to meet it. (By the way, if you ever want to meet one of the best teachers of entrepreneurship in this country, C. J. (Chris) Meenan can be found at The National Foundation for Teaching Entrepreneurship in New York, an organization he helped build from the ground up. After watching him train hundreds of teachers over the years and offer his support to more people than I can count, I'm sure he wouldn't mind hearing from a few more people.)

And You Find Mentors Where?

Let's review: Learn what they learn. Read what they read. Industry publications will give you an idea of what trends and topics are hot, what events people in your field are attending, and will often write about guest speakers or special awards or recognition being given to various people in your community. Your ideal adviser might be one of them.

Once you find out where they are, go where they go. If you know your target frequents a certain restaurant or goes to a particular gym, find an opportunity to casually bump into him or her and introduce yourself. Mention that you hope to run into him or her again one day, then leave your prospective mentor alone, unless you get the chance to chat a bit longer. Don't bug them, though. That can blow your chances of ever getting close enough for a relationship. Here are a few more tips to help you along:

- Catch them alone. At big trade shows speakers are often just as lost as you are. If you sense that your target person is not quite sure where to go or what to do next, offer to help or try to find your way together.

- Find out if they are speaking at any seminars or breakout sessions. (Most likely, if significant in their field, they will only attend trade shows or events if they are organizing them, exhibiting, or speaking at them.) Attend their seminars and maintain eye contact with them as much as possible. Let them know that you are sincerely interested in the material. Speakers will always focus their attention on those who seem the most involved in the discussion.

- Ask questions that are pertinent to their experience and that give you a basis to introduce yourself later.

- Be the last one to leave. A speaker will usually be the last one left in the room. The people who linger after everyone else has asked their questions are usually the ones who have the greatest conversations and opportunities.

- If you are in any situation and you see someone you would like to meet speaking to someone who you know, ask your friend for an introduction. Introductions are much more powerful when the person who introduces you is well respected in your target adviser's eyes.

These are just a few of the tricks I've picked up from attending dozens of business events. To prove to yourself that you are really getting out there and hustling, hold on to the name badges that you get at these events. Hang them up or keep them somewhere visible. As simplistic as it may sound, these little badges can be your own symbol of those times that you ventured out and conquered. Be proud of these because it shows that you are really doing what you need to succeed in your field. If you start to accumulate more name badges than you know what to do with, you've done well. You probably know more (and more people) than you could have ever imagined before you started. Have fun with "the networking thing." If you look at it as a chore you'll probably pass up a lot of great opportunities and people who could become amazing friends and mentors.

PART FOUR

Creating a Professional Image

CHAPTER 10

The Entrepreneurial Image

IMAGE IS EVERYTHING. YOU'VE HEARD IT SAID A MILLION TIMES. WHETHER OR not you believe it, when it comes to your business, this is one cliché that you'd better pay attention to.

As a young entrepreneur, you will find that credibility is going to be your biggest problem. You may argue that contacts, financing, location, and business expertise are more significant obstacles, but doesn't each of these in some way hinge on your credibility? If you can't get through your customer's front door, past your vendor's sales reps, or arrange meetings with prominent people in your field, you're not going to have much of a business. What is it that people do to make these things happen? They present themselves as having the expertise, insight, determination, and potential that, bundled together, shout credibility. This is no easy task for a rookie. So with all of this pressure on you to dazzle intellectually, why distract people with a sloppy personal appearance, poor etiquette, or unattractive promotional material? When you take the time to do something, do it right. Your image is the last thing you should be neglecting. Okay, so you're busy, don't have the time or money, and really feel that your expertise can sell itself. Right? Wrong. Make the time, find the money, be creative, and understand that, in business, knowledge without the proper packaging is close to worthless.

Personal Presentation

Take it upon yourself to learn your industry's language, buzz words, and trends. If you are concerned that you might not sound as professional as you think you should, study those whom you admire most. Watch your role models very carefully, paying close attention to their speech, gestures, and mannerisms. You may even want to take a public speaking class to brush up on or develop your verbal presentation skills. Nationwide programs like Toastmasters are excellent at teaching people the art of effective public speaking.

A verbal impression is usually the first one that you offer people of you and your business, so make sure that what you say is well received. Even if you are just talking to someone on the phone, the tone and speed of your voice, the articulation and eloquence of your words, and the personality that you project can leave a powerful impression on someone you have yet to meet in person. For this reason, you should be very aware of your own verbal presentation and do whatever you can to improve it whenever you have the chance. Here are a few tips to help you out.

On the Phone . . .

RECORD YOUR CONVERSATIONS

Tape record your conversations or have someone you trust listen to a few of your conversations on a speakerphone. It's easy to get so wrapped up in situations and your own thoughts that you neglect paying attention to how well you have communicated with other people. By listening to your conversations afterwards or asking someone else for input, you are likely to find out about habits or problems that you never would have picked up on your own.

PLAN WHAT YOU ARE GOING TO SAY

If you have a call scheduled, particularly with someone of great importance, planning ahead is just about the most important thing you can do, for several reasons:

- You may be drilled with questions that you can't answer.
- You may have one of those really uncomfortable periods of silence and have absolutely nothing of value to fill in the gap.
- The other person may become frustrated because he or she cannot understand the real purpose of your call.
- You may appear unknowledgeable and therefore not serious.

Take a minute before you call someone to jot down a list of things that you want to discuss. That way, you can bring up the reasons that you are calling in the beginning and be sure not to forget anything at the end. You can have your whole conversation planned out before you even pick up the phone, and no one will be the wiser.

TAKE NOTES

Often, people speak so quickly on the phone that many pieces of important information get lost in the process. Sometimes, too, you're just nervous or excited and have a hard time remembering all the details. Taking notes while on the phone is a great habit to get into. You can keep a record of important comments, quotes, names, and perceptions; and you can respond to questions more intelligently by noting possible answers while they are still speaking. Take notes whenever you are speaking on the phone to a client, a prospective client, a disgruntled customer, a credit agency, or a vendor. When you hang up the phone, you will have a much clearer picture about what just happened if you can refer to your conversation notes afterward (you'll also be sure to always remember the person's name).

DON'T EAT

All of those times that you thought you were quietly munching on some grapes, or a Powerbar, or sucking on a Lifesaver while on a call, you weren't fooling anyone. Don't underestimate the sound quality of your phone. (The next time you start slurping on soup or opening candy wrappers while on the phone, just remember the Sprint commercial where you can hear the pin drop.) Eating when you're on the phone can be considered very rude to the person on the other end. If you happen to be caught in the act when the phone rings, don't pick it up until you're done chewing, otherwise your "good afternoon" just may translate into "goob afbermoom." Not exactly the most professional greeting.

In Person (Socially) . . .

BE ANIMATED

People who use body language, such as hand gestures and facial expressions, capture and retain people's attention more easily. If someone is visually animated, they are more interesting to watch and listen to. Fluctuate the tone in your voice while illustrating with your body the messages that you are trying to communicate. This isn't to say you should put on an entire one-person theatrical production or flail around like a marionette gone crazy. Just don't sit there and blend in with the furniture so much that someone comes over and sits on you.

CHOOSE YOUR WORDS CAREFULLY

Being aware of your audience will enable you to articulate your points more effectively. Whether to use big words, complex sentence structures, or slang phrases should be determined by whom you are speaking to. If you are talking to industry experts, use the appropriate terminology, mirroring them in tone. If you are sharing your business concept with a group of students, simplify your points and integrate slang terms that might make them more comfortable. Base your verbal presentation on your audience, but always be sincere.

ENGAGE THE ENTIRE GROUP

If you are speaking to a group of people, whether there are two or twelve, try to involve everyone you can in the conversation, even if just by maintaining eye contact. You can involve people by referring to them, gesturing toward them, or using their names in hypothetical situation stories (for example: "Let's say that Bill and Gena came to my office and I was on the phone with Mike . . . ;" or "Kate, you're an artist, I'm sure that you can understand my concern.") By making everyone feel as if they are a part of the conversation, you'll hold their attention and make them more interested in what you're saying—and they're more likely to walk away feeling good about their encounter with you.

IN CONVERSATION, NEVER DISREGARD ANYONE

Sometimes in trying to quickly or powerfully convey a message to a particular person in a group, it's easy to cease paying attention to others whom your target might be standing with. For example, a few months ago, I was sitting at a conference with a friend of mine who was the president of a major educational organization. A middle-aged man approached us, briefly nodded to me, and launched into a monologue directed at my friend—never mind that he was totally interrupting us—about sports stars who he was trying to get to endorse the organization and the troubles that he was having. As I sat there being completely ignored and entirely boxed out of the conversation, I realized that I had a few personal sports contacts that would make both of their heads spin.

Did he assume that because I was a young woman that I knew nothing about sports? Maybe. Whatever assumption he was working under, he lost out. So you should never ignore or underestimate people (especially because of their appearance). You never know what or who they know and how they might be able to help you.

CHOOSE YOUR ARGUMENTS CAREFULLY

We have all encountered people who we simply don't agree with or don't care for. The more upset they make us, the more inclined we are to disagree or fight back. But before you jump into the verbal boxing ring with someone, consider a few things:

- Will your argument make you look insecure, immature, or arrogant?
- Who are they? Could they know more about this subject than you? If you could suffer from going into battle with them, are you prepared and willing to take the consequences?
- Could you offend someone else around them? Is it appropriate to debate their position in front of their friends, coworkers, or peers? Will you belittle them publicly?
- Do you want people to see you in an aggressive, hostile state?
- Are you going to burn a bridge with someone whom you should stay on good terms with?
- Could it lead to violence? This may seem like a crazy question, but better safe than sorry.

If you find yourself answering "yes" to any of these questions, it would probably be best for you to back off.

ASK QUESTIONS

Most people love to talk about themselves and are more than willing to express their opinions whenever they find an audience. So ask people to tell you about their thoughts, insights, business, day-to-day life, or anything else relevant to the conversation. Asking people questions shows that you are interested in what they have to say.

In Person (Business Encounters) . . .

SILENCE IS GOLDEN

Too many of us, especially when we are young, new, and overeager, spend too much time talking and not enough time listening. It's important to know what you're talking about and show it, but listening is equally important and impressive. You can always add a comment, but you can't take things back once they've fallen off your tongue. Be quiet, hear what's being said, and then add your two cents. Stop and take the time to ask questions and listen to the other person first. You'll be much better equipped to deal with them if you do.

SELL TO THEIR NEEDS

Whenever you find yourself answering the "what do you do?" question, take the opportunity to sell smart. Instead of saying "We have a consulting division that works with companies that are looking to explore different market opportunities or countries," say "We have a consulting division that works with companies like yours, who might want to expand into [insert a logical field] or start exporting your [insert current products] to India, for example. We had a client just recently who [mention someone like them]. . . ."

By putting your examples in their terms, you not only make it easier for them to understand what you do but enable them to quickly understand how you might help them.

USE PEOPLE'S NAMES

After meeting so many people, as we networking fiends do, you tend to forget the names of people you encounter. A great way to re-member people's names and keep their attention is to plug their name into your conversation. "John, what do you think we should do?" or "Susan, didn't you have the same problem last year?" When people hear their own names, they perk up. It's true, try it. One caveat: don't overdo it. You'll end up sounding like a sweepstakes letter from Ed McMahon. Just use the name every now and then when directly addressing someone.

DON'T BE BORING

If a conversation is getting dull, learn to pick up on it quickly, and lighten it up by changing the subject, making a joke, telling a quick story, or just starting to smile. You never want someone to start silently calculating how much longer they have to spend talking to you before leaving looks rude. A close family member of mine has always had a real problem with this one. I won't say who, but she's of the female persuasion and usually referred to with three little let-ters. Okay, it's my mom. I'm not saying that she's boring, just that she doesn't know when a conversation ceases to be a discussion and becomes a one-woman monologue. Her tangents, which are usually about computers—her favorite subject—are legendary in our family.

We all, of course, understand what passion can do to a person. But if you're not family and don't have the good sense to run when she gets going, you could honestly be trapped for hours. Most people just sit there and smile, nodding occasionally out of respect once they've zoned out, and try to plot a way to make it all end. Yes, I know this sounds a bit funny, and it really is, but it loses its humor when you find this kind of thing in a business situation. The worst is when you're at a conference and have a lot of people that you want to meet but get stuck listening to someone who doesn't realize that you're not on the same page as they are.

I'll let you in on another trick I've learned: If you can't stimulate the conversation when your business might depend on it, bring over someone who can. (This works really well at cocktail parties.) We all know people who are dazzling conversationalists. Use these people as reinforcements in case your presentation takes a downward spiral turn.

Don't Overstate Your Case

I learned a valuable lesson from an experience speaking at the Harvard Club in Brussels. Sitting in my hotel lounge later that evening, Steve Mariotti, a close friend and business adviser, and I discussed how well the dinner meeting had gone. I asked him how I had done and he immediately replied, "Very well." A few seconds later, he hesitantly told me that he had noticed one problem: "On two occasions, the first few sentences of your comments were brilliant, but you continued speaking with information that was redundant. You could have had a much greater impact if you made your point, then stopped there." I thought about it for a minute, then realized how right he was.

Think about all the times that people have tried to sell you something. Your most annoying experiences have probably involved people who just would not give up. Maybe this was at an airport where some Hare Krishna was trying to sell you books, or a telecommunications rep was trying to convince you that her company can save you ten more cents a minute. Maybe you even listened for the first few minutes, possibly falling a bit for their big pitches. But they went too far, said too much. Selling yourself out of a deal is very easy to do. The worst part is that you rarely even realize that you are doing it.

I remember one time that I received a call from the director of an organization who thought that we should be working together in some way. He introduced himself, his organization, his idea, then went on . . . and on . . . and on. From the onset of our conversation I had agreed that our causes were both very similar and that we should in fact look into some sort of marketing partnership. But the guy rambled on and on about why he was so important, why his organization was so substantial, and all the media attention he had received—important information, but too much of it. He sold himself right out of a deal with us. I simply did not want to talk (or shall I say listen) to him any longer. To avoid wasting your time or someone else's with a sales pitch, be aware of the following signs:

- After several minutes the other person makes no noise.
- When you stop talking, there is only silence.
- The other person is typing or shuffling papers.
- The other person is having another conversation while you're still talking.
- The person interrupts you frequently to take other calls or do other things.
- The other person doesn't maintain eye contact with you.
- The person looks bored or upset.

If you can remind yourself to be aware of the other person's response to your sales pitch, you will always be a step ahead of the game. Anticipate what the person will do next and listen to what his or her body language is telling you.

Physical Appearance

As with most professions, business has its own set of tools and props. By tools I mean items or equipment that helps you do your job better, while props are sometimes used just to make you look better while doing your job. I am not trying to advocate putting up a big façade for your clients, but rather my aim is to show you how you can look older, larger, and more successful (until you are).

A Nice Suit

In an ideal world, your physical appearance should have little to do with your success in business. But for young entrepreneurs, your appearance does matter. On several occasions I have witnessed more successful entrepreneurs and high-ranking business people passed over in conversations, while better dressed, more presentable people were fawned over. This is not to say that your business knowledge, personality, or intelligence are unimportant, but rather that your appearance can sometimes be equally crucial.

Appearance is most important at the beginning of relationships and when introductions are being made. The old warnings about first impressions hold true—even more so if you're under thirty.

A Briefcase

Even if you have nothing to put in a briefcase, get one. Inside you should always have a notepad, business cards, a pen, and any literature about your business that you may have. I personally get turned off when someone shows up for a meeting without something to write on or with. It's as if they haven't bothered to prepare because they don't expect anything serious or valuable to happen. The fact is that you simply look more serious if you are ready to take notes at a meeting, or offer someone your card or company literature. You are also more likely to close a sale if you can respond to a request for more information immediately. (One bank manager I know says that he always carries new account applications with him in his car.)

Business Publications

It also doesn't hurt to throw into your briefcase a business publication, such as *Entrepreneur, Success,* or *Inc.* If you really want to succeed in business, you must get into the habit of treating your mind like a sponge—use any chance you get to learn about something new. Any random facts or background knowledge you can collect about your business or related industries will no doubt be of use to you at some time or another.

THE WALL STREET JOURNAL

While we're on the topic of business publications, you should get in the habit of reading the be-all and end-all of the whole lot. The *Wall Street Journal* is probably the most highly recognized and respected business publication in the world. Though it can be intimidating to the newer reader and a bit dry to anyone new to business, it is probably one of the best symbols of determination in the business world. Okay, so this will probably remain a prop for a while, but get used to reading it every so often. The articles make excellent conversation topics with other business people, and you'd be amazed at what you might learn.

A Nice Pen

Carrying a nice pen, such as a Mont Blanc or a Cross, implies that you care about appearances and take pride in your work. Does it really mean that you know your stuff? Well, no. But it looks a whole lot better than a chewed up Bic.

A Nice Watch

Similar to a pen, your watch can be a good indication of your personality. For example, if you wear an old Timex or Swatch with a rubber strap, you're telling people that image is not at the top of your list or, worse, that you're just a kid in a nice suit. Avoid wearing anything super casual if you are in the financial, apparel, or marketing business. In these cases, you will be surrounded by people with money and/or a trained eye on image.

Cleanliness

Okay, so this might sound painfully obvious, but it is better to err on the side of over-sensitivity when it comes to cleanliness. I hope that this isn't all news to you, but just in case, here is a checklist of the essentials of personal hygiene:

FOR MEN

- Hair should be clean, brushed, and properly cut (you be the judge of that).
- Don't overuse any styling products that will make your hair appear greasy.
- Nails should be filed short and kept clean.
- Deodorant is *not* optional.
- If you chew tobacco, don't admit it or let anyone see you doing it or catch on by the stains on your hands or beard.
- Cut any visible nose or ear hair.
- Clean your ears.
- Keep the hair on the back of your neck shaved.
- "Monobrows" are not cool.
- If your skin is flaky or white, use a moisturizer (it's not just for women).

FOR WOMEN

- Know when to cut your hair (if it's scraggly, take a hint).
- Keep hairsprays and gels to a minimum.
- Don't wear so much makeup that you could pass for a soap opera star. Use it to enhance your face, not hide it.

- Watch out for lipstick on your teeth.

- Shave (everywhere that's appropriate).

- Nails should be at the very least clean and evenly filed (people do notice if you snack on them until they bleed).

- Use caution with green nail polish or any of those other funky colors (they can cause the wrong kind of attention in some professional situations).

- If you wear sandals or open-toed shoes, toenails should be trimmed, clean, and preferably polished.

- Don't overdo the perfume (put it on a half hour before you leave for an appointment, or spray it in the air and walk through the mist).

Regardless of whether you are a man or a woman, you do need to follow some code of personal maintenance when you're presenting yourself in the business world. If you pride yourself on your aversion to conformity, think of it this way: No one's asking you to surrender your individuality, only to consider your appearance as an admission ticket. If you don't get in, it won't matter how smart or knowledgeable you are—there won't be anybody around to listen. Chris Neimann, a very conservative-looking young entrepreneur, once said, "I'm a rebel on the inside. I don't have to pierce my nose to prove it." Look at people around you in the business environment. Take your cues from the ones who seem to get the most respect and attention. In addition to being bright, they're usually the ones that present themselves the best.

Good Business Etiquette

By now you must have heard about the first-impressions rule a million times. Although it's true, you may not have dealt with many business situations before, if any at all.

To help guide you, here are some general rules about business etiquette:

- Introduce yourself

- Speak clearly

- Be courteous

- Don't bore people

- Never embarrass or insult anyone—even your competition

- Never curse
- Don't lose your temper in public
- Do what you can to make others comfortable
- Never make racial, religious, or gender-sensitive remarks, even in jest

How Old Are You?

If you haven't already noticed, your age can have a serious impact on your success. Though your age can work to both your benefit and detriment, deciphering when to use—and when not to—is a lot like holding an ace in black jack. Consider your "tender" age your wild card. Use it very carefully.

Before I go any further on this topic, you must remember and understand one thing—age need not have anything to do with your credibility in the business world. Your credibility is a reflection of you. With this thought in mind, you must take control of your own situation. If this means dressing, speaking, or acting a certain way to blend in or stand out, do it! But pick your poison wisely. Nothing is worse than standing out in an industry that doesn't tolerate rebellion, like venture capital, corporate finance, or accounting. On the other hand, in some industries it's absolutely essential to stand out. Public speakers, marketers, and comedians can go out of business if they aren't distinctive enough to separate themselves from their competition. Make sure that your strategy is a smart one.

Your age is a delicate subject. Especially when you consider that some industries are just not supportive of younger entrepreneurs. Even though things are changing in our favor in industries such as high technology, not everyone is on the youth band wagon just yet. Keep this in mind as you decide when it is appropriate to bring up your age.

Generally, it's okay to reveal your numbers when you:

- Need help
- Need to impress upon people that you are unique
- Can't afford something and need a good deal on a price
- Are looking for mentors or expert advice
- Need to raise money (not more than a few thousand dollars)
- Want to barter services

- Can get a grant
- Are being interviewed by the media
- Are dealing with much older (successful) business people

This last point needs a little further explaining. Although I generally recommend you not make your age obvious to others in business, there are times when you need help to survive. If you are down and out and all else has failed, showing someone how responsible and determined you are despite your age can often influence someone to give you that little extra help you may need.

These rules are not chiseled into the side of a mountain somewhere. They are just meant as a basic guide. Ultimately, you will have to judge how to handle different situations. The more you deal with others who are older or more experienced than you, the more savvy you'll become about when to use your age in business. At twenty-four, I still run into some situations I'm not quite sure how to handle, despite the fact that I've been running my company since the age of nineteen. Having to make up for or defend your age is just an inevitable consequence of being a young entrepreneur.

May I See Some ID, Please?

Earlier in this chapter I gave you the rundown on how to boost your outer image as a young entrepreneur. If you brushed it off, you might want to reconsider. Putting on that suit may help you avoid some potentially embarrassing situations.

Take, for example, twenty-four-year old Jonathan Kane. Jonathan walked up to a bartender one night with five prospective clients following close behind. Armed with his American Express Corporate Card, Jonathan's goal was to show his guests a great time, find out what his company could do to help them, then hit them up for the big sale. Simple, right? So Jonathan leans over the bar, motions the bartender over and begins rattling off everyone's requests. He drops the corporate card on the table just as he is finishing the order. "... And I'll have a Sam Adams." "May I see some ID, please," was the bartender's response. In shock, Jonathan reached for his wallet, turning red as the men waiting for him began to laugh. This was not the type of bonding experience he had hoped for.

A few months later, Jonathan told me this story and asked what he could have done differently. There were a few key questions I asked Jonathan to help him come up with an answer: What were you wearing? Were you carrying a briefcase or a businesslike bag? Was there anything about your appearance that would make anyone think you were not only too young to drink but too young to do business? After he thought about it, he realized that he didn't really look the part of a serious businessperson. He'd worn a casual button-down shirt with no jacket. He may have been of legal age, but to the bartender, he looked questionable.

If you are just over twenty-one, don't assume the whole world can tell. Do you generally get carded when you go out socially? Then take a hint. You look young. As for alcohol consumption, just use your common sense no matter how far over twenty-one you are. Never get falling down drunk with a business associate. Chances are, after six vodka tonics you're not exactly equipped to be talking about anything, let alone your business venture. Sucking 'em back with the big boys may seem cool for a moment there, but if you lose a business deal because you ended up driving the porcelain bus in the restaurant bathroom, you'll have more than a hangover the next day. You'll have a reputation for being unprofessional.

And what if you're under twenty-one? Don't call attention to your age if you don't have to. You shouldn't ever put yourself, your clients, or the bartender or restaurant owner in an awkward position because you've decided that drinking will make you look older. It won't. Especially when you get carded. Here are a few tips that I've used to skate through those pre-legal years:

- When asked by a waiter if you'd like a drink, it's best to say, "I'll just have a mineral water with a twist of lime." Mineral water is kind of a trendy thing, and the lime twist sounds like you stole it from a favorite mixed drink.

- Never ask for a "virgin" anything, a Jolly Roger, or a Shirley Temple. These drinks make you sound like you're about twelve, even if you sincerely don't feel like drinking alcohol. The same goes for hot chocolate, or chocolate milk, or any kind of milk anything unless it's going in a cup of coffee or tea. You might as well be asking for Ovaltine or Tang.

- I stressed this point before, and I'll stress it again: Dress like you mean it. No jeans, T-shirts, or any casual clothes that make you look more like you should be strolling on campus than leaning on a bar.

Your Image on Paper

Creating your own presentation materials is probably one of the most important things you will do as a small business owner, and even more critical to your success if you are a young entrepreneur. Yes, it is just paper, but when you send someone your business card, your brochure, or a letter, you're sending them a lasting impression of you. Regardless of how big or successful you are, poor presentation materials can make you look anything but good. Conversely, if you are just starting out, your literature can make it look like you're an old pro.

What follows are some important items to start you and your company's image out on the right track.

Logo

Try to be as creative as possible with your logo, as it is the epitome of you and your company. Impress your potential clients with your creativity and they'll wonder what other things you can do to impress them. Avoid generic logos. World maps and globes are a perfect example of logos that have been taken too far. Look for ideas from your industry, product, or service. Hold a brainstorming session with a few friends or employees and write down every image that comes to mind that in any way relates to your business. Look for symbolic images that represent your style, service, or reputation. Take clues and ideas from other businesses in your field. Trade journals or industry publications are likely to have advertising from other companies displaying their logos. See what other organizations have done with their logos to impress you.

Once you have come up with a good idea of what you want, find a graphic artist to add the finishing touches. An excellent place to find great artists at a reasonable price is through schools of art and design. (Usually you just have to call them up and see if they have a career center or job placement board.) They are usually enormously creative, anxious to find freelance work, and almost always less expensive because they are still in school. Expect to pay anywhere from $50 to $500 for a graphic artist to create a logo for you. And if you happen to have a friend who's an artist or can barter something for your logo, you've got it made.

Use your logo on everything you can when you are new (although try to avoid overkill). The more people who see your company name or image, the more likely they will be to think about you and call when they can use your products or services.

Letterhead

When you design your letterhead, make sure it contains all vital contact information (company name, address, phone, fax, e-mail, web site, and board of advisors, if credibility is a big issue). Your logo should also be prominently placed somewhere at the top of your company stationery.

If you really need to save money, you can design letterhead on your computer, then have it professionally photocopied onto high-quality paper. Look for companies like Paper Direct (1-800-A-PAPERS), which offer extensive lines of pre-designed stationery, brochures, and business cards for new and smaller business owners who need to present a professional image but don't have the budget for it. These are not really great ideas for the long term but will do the trick until you can afford to have your letterhead professionally done.

Business Cards

Your business card is like a mini-advertisement. Give away as many as you possibly can and you significantly increase your name recognition, referrals, and, hopefully, sales. Make sure to include all the same contact information that's on your letterhead. Your logo should be displayed prominently, yet not be overpowering. If you wish, you can even add a one-line slogan or business description to add more information on your philosophy or specialties. Many times your company name will not be enough to tell people what you really do. Business cards allow you a very brief but excellent opportunity to advertise your strengths.

Brochures

Brochures are an opportunity for you to shine. For all those times that you can't be face-to-face or don't have the chance to fully explain what you do, a successful brochure can go a long way in selling you and your business. Before you do anything, decide what you need to say in your brochure. Be brief. (White space is a premium when it comes to literature.) Pay close attention to the text, tone, and even font in your brochure. Don't try to say everything, because you can't. And check out your competition's literature to see if there are any industry standards as to how brochures should look.

Create a mock brochure, even if it must be in black and white at first, because most companies at some time or another are asked for more literature. Play around with different sized paper and ways to fold or bind—tri-folds or half-folds are the most common. Keep in mind, though, how you'll be mailing them, because you may require special-sized envelopes, which are usually available through any office supply store and can be spruced up with a nice (glossy) label.

Mailing Labels

Labels are a cheap, easy, yet very impressive way to professionalize your mailings. They can be used on different sized envelopes as well as on postcards, boxes, disk mailers, or even newsletters. Again, labels should include your logo. The more a client or prospect sees your logo, the more impressive you look, and the more opportunities you have to subtly reinforce your name in their mind. Look at glossy labels if you can only afford to use one ink color or if your literature is a little bland looking. Glossy labels usually don't cost too much more than matte (flat finish) but look like you spent a lot more money. (Quick tip: If you plan on using your computer to print your labels, make sure that you have them printed on sheets and not individually cut by your printer.) A great company to buy labels from is NEBS in Massachusetts (1-800-225-9540). They are one of—if not the biggest—label manufacturers in the U.S.

•   When your company is new or small, your logo can do wonders for your company's image. After all, usually only larger companies can afford to have their image on everything. The smaller you are, the less likely you are to have an impressive office, large staff, or even a recognized company. So you should use everything you can to substantiate your company and make you look older, larger, and more successful. When you can send a client a package of information on your company with a logo prominently displayed on your mailing labels, letterhead, brochure, and business card, all neatly packaged in a customized presentation folder, you look tremendous. As a first impression, a package like this can really win clients.

I remember once sending some literature about my company to a lawyer who was organizing a conference for young entrepreneurs. When she told me she was looking for speakers, I offered, mentioning that I had done a lot of public speaking in the past. She was silent for a few moments, but finally said, "Thank you, but I really think we need younger entrepreneurs." I was twenty-one at the time, and when I told her my age she was completely shocked. All she knew about me and my company was that I had sent her a two-color, glossy brochure. At that moment, I knew that the extra money I'd spent on the printing was worth it. If you skimp on your presentation materials—or your personal presentation—you compromise your image. It is as simple as that.

CHAPTER 11

Publicity, Advertising, and the Internet

I F THERE IS ONE THING THAT ENTREPRENEURS ASK ME ABOUT MORE THAN anything, it's how to get media attention. We all know what the media can do for a person, a trend, or a company. Not only did it launch the whole pet rock craze, but also funky nail polish, the health food market, and even the men's boxer phenomenon. You probably have several examples in your own house of products that only came to your attention because you saw them on television or in a magazine. As you well know, the power of the media is incredible.

So what can publicity and advertising do for you? They can help get the word out about your company. They can educate people about your service. They can highlight a need in your consumers' lives. And, most important, they can issue a "call to action" for consumers by promoting your products or services with endorsements, testimonials, and surveys.

Getting recognition for your company can also be personally rewarding. After all of the work you put into building a business, it's a nice validation to have the media pick up on it, or to see your company in an advertisement. When The Young Entrepreneurs Network started to be recognized in the media a few years ago, I was amazed at the response we received. Not only did hundreds of people start calling, e-mailing, and faxing us, but people even began to stop me on the streets after recognizing me from a magazine or television show. I couldn't believe it.

Once, at a franchise conference, I had the former head lawyer for McDonald's approach me out of the blue. "Jennifer, I saw you on CNBC the other week. Thought you were great!" A few weeks later one of the anchors on CNN did the same thing. When friends called, especially ones I hadn't heard from in years, that was particularly amusing. Like when Olga, one of my oldest friends from junior high, called me screaming one day after seeing me in *Elle*. I hadn't heard from her in months. When I was introduced to people at a cocktail party or other event, many started to respond, "Yeah, I've heard of you guys." What an incredible feeling.

If you're wondering what the difference is between publicity and advertising, the answer is simple. Publicity is when a company is written about in the media, while advertising is when a company writes something about itself then pays a fee to have it placed in the media. A really good way to understand the difference is to take a look at a fashion magazine or even a business magazine. You can usually tell an advertisement when you see one. They're the ones with the models, bottles of cologne, hotels, copiers, and promotional messages urging you to buy the product or service. Classified ads are also advertisements and so are those special "bingo" cards that tear or sometimes fall out of the magazines urging you to circle the products and services you are interested in. Sometimes people even disguise their advertisements to look like editorial pages of the magazine. In these cases, the magazine will usually print in small type at the top of the page "This is a paid advertisement"—just so you don't think that it's really an endorsement.

Publicity, or public relations, is different, and much harder to identify, because it can have an invisible effect on what journalists write. Sometimes an article will even be reprinted word-for-word from a press release that a company sent to a magazine, but that's not usually the case. Publicity is when a company promotes itself to the media in the hope that a journalist will write about them. In even a single issue of a magazine, dozens of different press releases could be behind various articles, but readers usually can't tell. Journalists often just use a press release to spark new ideas, then do their own research and interviews to build their own stories.

While I am in no way an expert on PR or advertising, after appearing in front of tens of millions of people in the media, I've learned quite a bit about it. So here's a pretty good guide to getting it for yourself. I'll also talk a little about advertising opportunities, particularly on the Internet.

Publicity

There are two things that are really great about publicity. The first is that it's free. The second is that it's objective. When you advertise, you are making the claims about your company's products and services. Objectivity is really questionable. When a journalist, on the other hand, writes about your product or service, it's his or her job to be objective. For this reason, people take claims about companies in articles more seriously than when they are seen in advertisements.

One of the greatest things about publicity is that it feeds off itself. Once you or your company begin to get recognized in your community or industry, the media will start to come to you. Really. I didn't believe it either, until it happened to me. When my partners and I were starting IDYE (*The International Directory of Young Entrepreneurs*, our on-line directory), we figured that one of our first major tasks was to get some media attention. Why? Because you can't start an internationally recognized business network if no one knows about it. So we set out to get someone, anyone, to write about us, or even mention our company's name somewhere. Our first hit was in an educational newsletter. The second was a mention in a related organization's member mailing. Then the third and most amazing publicity arrived. The week before my twenty-second birthday, *Entrepreneur* magazine ran close to a full-page story on us. We were living large.

From that point on, various other magazines and newsletters began calling us to set up interviews. In the six months that followed, we were subsequently mentioned in two books on youth entrepreneurship, a national radio talk show, two or three college publications, *Home Office Computing, Minority Business Entrepreneur* magazine, and CNN. In less than six months, the big players began to approach us. By May 1996, I had been contacted by *The Wall Street Journal, Success* magazine, *Spin,* MTV, *The Los Angeles Times,* the *New York Post, The Boston Globe,* the *Boston Business Journal,* the BBC, and *Business Week,* as well as a slew of smaller publications and media representatives. Who else will call in the next year, I can't imagine. But let me just remind you of one thing. They came to us. All of them.

So where PR is concerned, get as much as you can, then do your best to handle the demand for information on you and your company.

How to Get Media Attention

As an entrepreneur, dealing with the media will be one of your most potentially profitable activities, but it can also be the most confusing, frustrating, and—sometimes—unrewarding one. The biggest problem that most people have in attracting PR for their business is in simply misunderstanding the very people they need to appeal to.

Journalists are in business, too, and like you, they have pressures, deadlines, idiosyncrasies, and (gasp!) lives. If you think your life is stressful, follow a journalist around for a little while. Showing them that you understand and respect their jobs will give them the incentive that they need to give you the time of day, and sometimes even their friendship. As with any other relationship, to ensure success you must invest the time and effort in understanding what motivates the people you are dealing with, particularly what it is that makes you of value to them. Once you understand these basic subtleties, your business relationships will become more plentiful and profitable. To build the foundation for a favorable relationship with the media, consider the following simple steps.

FIGURE OUT WHY THEY SHOULD WRITE ABOUT YOU?

Come up with a list of story angles that a journalist could use to write an article about you and your business. Decide what makes your story newsworthy.

- Are you unusually young for a business owner in your area/field?

- Have you started a company that is out of the ordinary or provides a new or specialized product or service?

- Are you making a substantial amount of money for someone in your position?

- Are you a student at a local or major university?

- Have you been able to secure high-level clients or corporate support?

- Have you challenged the competitive positions of major corporations?

Then, write down a list of attributes that could be used as "buzz words" or phrases to describe you or your venture. Some examples might include: "woman business owner," "Native American," "cyber-junkie," "virtual corporation," "green" (environmental in nature), "gourmet," "global," "international," etc. If you are doing your homework and reading your industry's trade journals, newsletters, and other publications, you should have no problem finding the industry catch phrases.

BUILD YOUR OWN MEDIA LIST

Next, compile a media list of publications and media sources (newspapers, journals, radio shows, talk shows, news programs) that you believe are most likely to be interested in your story. Collect all of their vital information—complete company name, address, phone, and fax numbers—as well as a suitable contact person, if possible. Be selective. Don't send information to people who clearly do not cover your industry or topic, or share your audience/clients. Journalists are constantly bombarded with unsolicited press kits. Don't waste their time or your money sending them literature on your business, banking on the off-chance that they might make an exception. There are too many publications, journals, organizations, and news stations that will be interested in what you are doing to bother those who don't.

The worst thing you can do is provoke a journalist to request that you don't contact him/her again. One young entrepreneur—we'll call him Todd—e-mailed an unsolicited press release to the editor-in-chief of a major newspaper. A few hours later, the editor e-mailed him back demanding that Todd "remove [his] name from his cyber-junk mailing list."

Ideally, you should read the publications yourself, or scan back issues at a library, to see which journalists specialize in topics related to yours. For business publications, send media kits to the managing editor or senior editor. They are more likely to be the ones personally writing or overseeing feature stories and are usually the best ones to review new story leads. For general interest publications, find the name of one of the editors who cover your field (i.e., the business, entertainment, or fashion editor).

If the names of individual journalists or special editors are not available, you can call the company directly to inquire, or send your literature to the editor-in-chief. (Contact information is available in all publications, usually in a thin column called a "rote box" in the first few pages of a magazine or newspaper.) Never bother the publisher. Remember that in the publishing world the publisher is the business manager of the company, not a journalist. Often publishers are not even located in the same offices as the editorial departments and, thus, are most likely to disregard or misdirect your information.

KNOW WHEN TO PITCH YOUR STORY

Create your own media calendar to help you pre-plan PR campaigns. A good way to start is by studying your company/industry's business cycles. When are your busiest months? If, for example, you provide a career-oriented service for students, your business cycles would peak around May and December—when students are most likely to be hunting for jobs. If you look at some of your media targets around these times, they too are probably keeping tabs on graduating students. This is when you most need them to know who you are.

First, determine whether your media targets have daily, weekly, or monthly editions. The frequency of release, whether you're looking to be on a weekly news program or in an annual special edition, greatly dictates when the best time is to contact your media sources. Say, for example, that you are looking to have an article written on your company in a monthly magazine. Most major monthly magazines have a three-month lead time. On your media calendar, keep track of your "target media months," or months when you would like your information to appear in the press. Then, from each of your target months, move two months backward and note issue-closing months. Then move one more month before and note press release due dates. (Keep in mind that this timetable applies only to monthly publications.) For example:

- December—Target media month (peak business season)
- November
- October—December issue closings
- September—Send press releases/media kits

If you are dealing with a daily or weekly publication, the best times to release information to them is usually a few days or three weeks prior to publication, respectively. For any other distribution cycles, call the publication directly to inquire about their specific issue closings. While you have them on the phone, another good idea is to request a copy of their publishing calendar. This will give you the specific dates that they plan to run special features. See if you can tie your PR into one of these dates. The more information they have for these, the better their feature stories are, and the more of that issue they sell.

Understanding when journalists are most likely to be interested in your story can save you a lot of time and greatly improve your chances of being mentioned or featured in an article.

MAKE YOURSELF INVALUABLE

Be a resource to the media. If a journalist or editor calls you for information on your company, or even your industry, jump. Don't appear too anxious, but give them everything they want, and more—but keep it brief. If they say that they're on a deadline (and they'll tell you), restrict your correspondence to brief faxes, voice mail, or quick calls, should they request that you contact them directly. The more attentive you are to their needs, the more likely they are to keep in contact with you. Every journalist has his or her own group of people they consider sources for various issues. If you can become one of these people, sooner or later you are sure to be rewarded with some great publicity.

FOLLOW-UP

Always follow up with a thank-you letter for any article or interview that you receive. Even if you are interviewed but do not appear in the article (which happens often), follow up and thank them anyway. It's very easy to get frustrated after you have spent a great deal of time gathering or offering information and insight to a media agent and you don't get recognized for it, but it happens. Another important thing to remember is that journalists must disregard the majority of the information that they receive, due to limited editorial space. Journalists also have editors, or bosses, who can be merciless when reviewing a new article. If you thought your English professors preferred their red ink to your writing, ask some journalists about their editors.

KEEP IN TOUCH

Send your media contacts an occasional note or mailing as your company changes, expands, or diversifies, to let them know about the latest news. This is an excellent way for you to stay fresh in their minds and allow them to keep abreast of your progress effortlessly.

Press Kits and Media Contacts

While having to create a press or media kit may bewilder and even scare you, don't get too worried. The whole process isn't as painful as it seems. If a journalist asks you for a press kit and you don't have one, yes, you will panic. And of course you'll promise to send one right over, knowing full well that not only do you not have one but you really don't even have any idea how to put one together. (But that's just another one of those risks you take as an entrepreneur— saying, "Sure, I can take care of that," then thinking, "How do I do that?")

So just in case you are confronted with the inquiring mind of a journalist, or want to launch your own PR campaign for some media exposure, here are the items you need to include:

LITERATURE ON YOUR COMPANY

Here again, the "image is everything" rule applies. In addition to having to impress prospective customers, your literature must be impressive enough to make it through the scrutiny of those who see countless pieces of business literature on a regular basis. Journalists are certainly among those who are regularly bombarded with promotional material. Make sure that yours is up to par. If there is any chance that your information will lead them to question the substance of your business, your credibility as an expert, or whether the subject is worth writing about, your media opportunity can be instantly blown. Any pictures or small product samples that you can add will enhance the presentation and give the journalist more "meat" for a story on you. And be sure to attach a business card.

PRESS RELEASE(S)

A press release is similar to an article about you or your business. The most valuable assistance you can give a journalist, a press release not only pitches a story to them but gives them something they can take excerpts from, or even reprint in full. Journalists rely on press releases for new story ideas because they are short and sweet, get right to the point, offer a story angle for them to pursue, and often "hand them a story on a platter." Press releases make writing an article easier. It is also the most widely accepted way to solicit media attention.

To compose a press release, keep the following tips in mind:

- Offer a contact person and phone number clearly at the top.

- Give your press release a title (something dramatic if you can), but make sure that it is appropriate for the publication(s) you are sending it to.

- Start with a powerful, information-packed beginning (just in case they only read the first paragraph). Don't waste their time by obscuring the point.

- Use personal quotes and statistics whenever possible.

- Mention crowning accomplishments.

- Keep it short. You don't have much more time to convince someone to grant you an interview than with the typical resume.

- Print it on company letterhead, if available.

- Duplicate the writing tone of the publication it is intended for.

As far as deciding how many different press releases to include, a good rule of thumb is probably no more than three. Don't add extra press releases just for the sake of bulking up your press kit either. Only write the second or third press release if the story of your business has a different twist to it and you think the media would find it interesting.

PERSONAL BIOGRAPHY

Personal bios are like resumes for big shots. If someone asks for more information on you or your company, send them a bio first, not a resume. Sending someone a bio makes it look like a lot of people ask for information on you personally (usually for media purposes, or speaking engagements). If it is for media purposes, you might want to even include a professional picture to improve your chances of being included in a bigger article or having your picture published along with the press release.

PRESS ARTICLES

If you or your company have received media attention before, have the articles copied and include them in your press kit. The more you can show that people have taken an interest in writing about you before, the more reason they have to think that you really are newsworthy. If you start to accumulate a few articles for your press kit, organize them by putting the most substantial or impressive pieces first, or if they are all pretty similar, display them in chronological order, working from the present backward.

CLIENT LIST

If you have rustled up a list of some well-known or impressive clients (even if the work you did was unpaid), create a client list to include in all of your promotional material. If you want to be creative, you can even include quotes from some of them endorsing your work. (Just make sure that you check with them first about advertising your relationship.) Client lists are excellent ways to build your credibility and should be used whenever possible.

PHOTOS

If you have some great photos of you, your staff, your products, or any pictures that are lively, unique or descriptive of your business, toss a few into your press kit as well. While you might not want to spend the money to send real photos to everyone, you can take your favorite three or four, arrange them on a page, draw some arrows, add a few quotes and captions, and have them photocopied. Voila! You have a great new press piece.

Advertising

All businesses have to promote themselves to stay in business. The key is to be as creative as you can to optimize every dollar. Advertising offers a pretty wide range of opportunities for businesses these days. You can advertise in magazines, newsletters, on postcards, the radio, the Internet, on billboards, and now even in bathroom stalls. (Yes, it's true. You can find them in some restaurants and clubs.) So how do you get started? First you need a plan, then you need to do your research, then you have to collect bids. Last, you have to create the add and sign the contracts. Let's take a quick run through these steps just to make sure that you know how to get started.

Create a Plan

While there are formal advertising plan formats that you can follow if you really feel you need a formal plan, I'm just going to give you the basics so you know what to do. If you want to find more information on advertising plans you can always get a book on the subject or maybe even find one on the Internet. Another good source is a university with a business or advertising program. You can take a class on advertising or just call up one of the professors and ask where to get a good outline.

When devising a plan, these are the things you need to think about:

- What are my objectives in advertising?
- What do I want to say to potential customers?
- Who specifically am I trying to reach? (your target market)
- What do my target customers read, listen to, and watch. Where do they socialize?
- Where would my advertising be most likely to confront them?
- What is my budget? (Yeah, I know most of us don't have a formal budget for this stuff, though we should.) What can you afford to spend? (That's probably a better question.)

Do Your Research and Collect Bids

You have a couple of options when it comes to doing research. If you have a lot of money to spend, you can always call an ad agency and ask them to make a presentation to you outlining your options. And if that's totally unrealistic, you can make a bunch of phone calls to people you know who know about these things, or just hit the streets with your eyes open. Since I'll assume that you have some idea about what types of advertising vehicles you want to use, find samples of them and look for contact information for the company that handles the advertising. It's often just that simple. If you still can't find the sources you need, make a quick call to your local chapter of The Ad Club and see if they can help you. As you can see, this is where your networking comes in handy.

Your next task is to call the companies up to find out what programs they have and to ask them for more information about the opportunities they offer. They'll tell you about their pricing structure as well as provide you with a lot of statistical information to help you determine how many people will see your ads. Demographic information should also be available to let you know about the average viewer's age, race, income, occupation, etc. Tell them you are in the process of getting bids and collecting information. Let them know that you will call them back as soon as you have all of your options laid out.

Create Your Ad and Sign the Contracts

Once you have all of your quotes and data, take a few days to review it all and make your decision. Talk to other people—particularly your customers—to find out what advertising vehicles they would be most likely to see and respond to.

Then you have to do the toughest part—design your ad or message. Make sure you take the time you need with this, and be sure to bounce the ad off a few people before you submit it. If you can afford to try out a few different approaches or hire someone to create the ad for you, all the better.

All that's left then is to review the company's contract, preferably with your lawyer, then sign on the dotted line. Make sure to read the contract thoroughly and ask any questions that you have. Make your payment, make sure that you see a final "proof" before the ad is mass produced and shipped, and wait for the customers to call. You should, of course, be very selective with your advertising, because you're talking about spending money. (Remember, only publicity is free.) Do your homework before you commit to any kind of advertising to ensure that the money you spend has the best chance of hitting the exact customers that you want to reach. If you are strapped for cash, start out as small as possible. Make sure that you have sales coming in from your smaller ads before you start funneling money into larger ones.

You'll have to bear in mind, too, that there are several different types of ads, including:

CLASSIFIED ADS

Test out a few classified ads in industry trade journals or major area papers. See if you can take ads out in organization or association newsletters. Go right for the most targeted sources to save time and money. Use classified ads when you want to test market a new product for very little money or test a new market for an established product. But to make sure that you are not belittling your company name or product, first study the other classified ads in any publications that you are considering. Do they sound anything like yours? Would your product be the only one of its kind? Would people question why you are only taking out a classified rather than a bigger ad? Ask around. Be aware that classified advertising is not always right for every product and service.

LARGER AD SPACES

Unless you have a lot of money to play with and are absolutely sure that you are spending it in the best possible way, start small. Advertising fees can bankrupt you if you are not careful. Do your research.

Make sure that you are buying into the best advertising opportunity. Look for your competitors' ads. Where are they and how successful are they? Learn from their mistakes.

PROMOTIONAL ITEMS

If you can avoid getting too carried away, investigate the different kinds of promotional items that you can give away to publicize your company name and logo. Coffee mugs, pencils, pads of paper, magnets, and stickers are the most common. Look for things that your clients would really use or keep around. Then make sure that you can afford to spend the money on what you want. Don't talk yourself into spending $3 apiece on something that you have to buy 100 of if you are not sure that you're really going to benefit from the exposure. It's far too easy to get excited about seeing your own company name on Post-it notes or mouse pads. Be careful.

How to Barter Ad Space

Though there's no real rule of thumb for bartering advertising space, it may just be because it's not really done as often as it could be. And before you start designing your ads, realize that this is one of those feats for the amazing talkers, salespeople, and deal-making entrepreneurs that always seem to get whatever they need. Bartering ad space is not impossible, but it takes a lot of luck and creativity. Your first question should be, "What can I do for them?" If you can't find an equivalent or greater value to what you are prepared to do for the media rep, then you might just be wasting your time. The best situations you can create to help you in your quest for free advertising space are as follows:

- Involve the publication or media agency in a project that you are doing that you'd like to promote. Offer to make them a sponsor of your event and show them how their exposure as a supporter would be beneficial to their image, would help you, and wouldn't cost them any money.

- Offer to give them a percentage or commission from all sales or a free copy of your product(s) if they are a small publication. Larger, established publications will not usually bother with requests like this and may be annoyed at your asking.

- Create a cross-marketing opportunity. If you have access to a certain target market or clientele that your media prospect does not, offer to strike a deal to help them reach those clients.

- Another opportunity is to work with a brand-new magazine. As new ones are always being created, you have quite a few opportunities to get into them for little or nothing if you play your cards right. Remember, new magazines rarely get the advertising rates that they first ask for. Most publications even give space away to advertisers in the beginning to attract others later. (This usually involves an agreement to purchase space later, though.)

Whatever kind of deal you try to finagle, keep in mind that magazines make their money off advertising and not subscription sales. Magazines have huge overhead expenses and don't often have the freedom to give away or barter too much. But particularly in newer, smaller publications, the advertising sales department is often made up of one person, who probably isn't being paid too much yet. Often deals can be struck with them, because the publishers have said to them, "Do whatever you can to bring in ads." And they do.

Colby Forman, a twenty-six-year-old entrepreneur from Los Angeles, worked for a while with a new startup publication. As the advertising rep, he spent his days going to local restaurants, bars, and specialty retail shops selling ad space for the new, trendy, local publication. The owner had given Colby a certain range that he could bargain with, offering him a substantial commission on each. Colby was smart. He realized that the advertisers were wealthy and often had great products and services to offer. In many cases, he walked out of stores with great ads (heavily discounted) and his commission in tailored suits. He dined at great restaurants for free and made deals with advertisers that made everyone very happy.

What could you have offered Colby? Think about it. Here's a perfect example of advanced negotiating for entrepreneurs. What can you do for them? Think of that question first whenever you go into any negotiation situation and you'll never be scrambling for a good deal or leaving the other people wondering why they need you.

Unfortunately, very few new business owners, let alone ones our age, have the financial resources to launch any substantial advertising efforts in the beginning. So do your homework, make your decisions wisely, and take a look at some of the following options.

Marketing on the Internet

Regardless of what business you are in today, if you are an entrepreneur who aspires to do great things you must familiarize yourself with the Internet pretty quickly. Odds are you already have a decent grasp of what's possible, particularly if you're reading this book. After all, people our age are driving a significant amount of the growth and development in technology, and most of us were raised with computers, or at least video games. If you are still not using a computer pretty regularly, don't have Internet access, an e-mail address, or your own web site, you have some work to do. If you were a personal friend I'd start embarrassing you into it from this moment forward. Not for a good laugh, but because it really hurts me to see people not taking advantage of all the resources that are available out there. So now that we're all friends, what are you waiting for? Technology has made entrepreneurship so available to people (particularly in their teens and twenties) that ignoring it is as big a sign of cultural ignorance as any I can imagine.

If you're in business, technology can be the greatest advantage you can have against the bigger companies that you'll have to compete with. The Internet has been such a coup for all of us that I like to call it the "Great Equalizer." It's not impossible for us to look like multi-million dollar companies anymore. We can even build companies around web sites and cut our overhead so much that our profit margins can skyrocket. The world is changing fast, and they don't call this the Information Age for nothing.

There are any number of books on marketing on the Internet out there, so I'm not going to go into too much detail here. I'm just going to give you enough information to enable you to start thinking about how you might market yourself, your products, or your services on the Net. There are several ways you can go about it, the most basic of which is e-mail.

E-mail

E-mail is incredible because it allows us to communicate with many more people on a much more frequent basis than ever before. Even more important from a business perspective, it allows people to contact you at virtually no cost to either of you. It also allows us to build relationships with people we might never be able to access normally—like CEOs, editors, and industry leaders, or people we would never have the occasion to meet in person or on the phone.

Setting up an e-mail account for yourself requires no more than a computer with a modem, a software package (often available for free), $20 or so for the monthly fee (as of today), and a phone call to a major Internet provider. With so many companies like Netscape, Earthlink, Microsoft Mail, Eudora, and Hot Mail out there, you should have no trouble setting up your own e-mail account. (If you are a student, or are currently employed by a sizable company, you should probably already have an account through the university or company for free.)

Web Sites

I'm sure you don't need me to tell you how important it is for you to have a presence on the Internet. You can get away with just having an e-mail account for a while, but for most people in business, having a place that people can go at their leisure to learn more about you, without having to contact you directly, is essential today. And just think about all the people who might have been curious about you or your company but never learned about it because you failed to make it simple enough for them to find the information on their own.

You can create a site very simply or very elaborately, either by yourself or by hiring a professional designer. The amount of energy and time you devote to it depends on you, and should be guided by the norms of your industry. Then just make sure that you have the basic information that your customers would be most interested in. This usually includes:

- Company background
- Profiles of the founder(s) & employees
- Product or service description (with fees/prices)
- Pictures of the product or service being performed
- Ordering information
- Client lists
- Helpful tips
- FAQs (Frequently Asked Questions)
- Contact information

Look around you. See what your competitors and peers are doing on-line. What kinds of information are they offering? You'll get a pretty good idea of what is appropriate for your site by checking out others.

On-line Advertising

In the next few pages, I'll try to give you a quick run-through of what you can expect to encounter when you start investigating on-line advertising options. As usual, I'll try to give you the free options whenever I can.

As simplistic as it may sound, your web site and even e-mail address can be incredible advertising tools for you. That's why it's essential that your contact information appear on every e-mail you send out. Providing that information on every e-mail message is just like giving your business card to someone you've just met. Just as you never know where that business card might end up, you never know who else will be directed to your site from that contact information.

After constructing a site that is an effective ad for your company, your second big challenge is positioning your site appropriately on the Internet. Here are a few fundamentals that will ensure your site can be found easily among the millions of others on-line.

SEARCH ENGINES

Registering your web site address is as important as having your business listed in the phone book. People today are used to getting the information they want when they want it. So, if you're not in the places they're most likely to look for a company like yours, you're going to lose them as customers, and that's definitely the last thing you want to happen.

The way people find you on the Net is by using search engines. You probably already use engines like Yahoo, Alta Vista, and Lycos, but there are hundreds of others that web surfers use. You need to have your site listed in as many of these engines as you can. But don't worry—you no longer have to register your site with each one individually (although you can if you have nothing better to do with your time). Sometimes your web developers will even do it for you. If not, and you can afford to spend a few bucks (usually around $100), you can pay a company to register your site on anywhere from 50 to several hundred search engines. You've probably been spammed with junk e-mail advertising some of these companies— one of the most popular of which is called Submit It. You can find them on-line at, wouldn't you know, www.submitit.com.

LINKING

Linking, or hyperlinking, is putting a reference mark on a web site that allows someone to jump to another site by clicking on the reference. You can usually identify a link pretty easily, because the text is usually printed in a different color and is underlined. If you're ever not sure, all you have to do is click on the word and see if it takes you anywhere. If it does, you just have to click on the "back" button and you're back where you started.

People link with other sites for a variety of different reasons. One reason for doing it is that it enables a site to offer additional resources to their visitors. Also, some sites have partnerships or clients that they want their viewers to know about. But ultimately the reason people create links is to increase traffic to their sites. Traffic means people visiting your site, and you want as many people to visit your site as possible. Just to give you a better idea of what I'm talking about, here's an example from our site—www.yenetwork.com—which supports young entrepreneurs.

Since so many people have started calling us for information on all sorts of resources for young entrepreneurs, we figured we'd take advantage of our web site to help these people. So we put together a resource section where people could find brief descriptions of other organizations that worked with young entrepreneurs in specific areas and in different stages of building their businesses. Then we added hyperlinks to each of the organization descriptions so people could just click over to them. The idea behind all this was threefold. First, people wouldn't have to call us directly for references like this. Second, it would hopefully encourage people to come to us first when they had other questions like this in the future (making us a resource they relied on). And third, because it helped us send business to organizations which would, in turn, refer people to us.

Linking is a great form of advertising for your site not only because it's free but because it's so immediate in its delivery. Imagine, for example, that you go into a shoe store and see a pair of shoes that you like only to discover that the store doesn't have them in stock. The salesperson *could* tell you about another store that does have the shoes, and you might eventually get around to visiting the store yourself. On the other hand, if the shoe store had the kind of link that exists on the Internet, it would be the same as the salesperson taking you by the hand and leading you into the shoe store across the street. If someone is visiting a site and they could logically be thinking about your product or service, a link would allow them to get more information on you instantly just by double clicking on your name.

So once you've set up your own site, you should start thinking about other sites that would be appropriate links. Think about businesses with complimentary products or services, organizations for your industry, search engines, directories, or general business-to-business sites. If you spend a little time surfing the web you should be able to come up with a few more creative options.

What you really want, of course, is for other sites to be linked to yours. Depending on how successful other sites are (and who you are), you might be able to barter if you can both benefit from a reciprocal link. Speak to the web master for the site, the company's president, or the marketing director to discuss any relationships. Make sure before you initiate contact that you spend some time looking at the site you want to link with so you'll be able to suggest logical places for a link to your site. Also, make sure that you can clearly and quickly describe how a link to your site would benefit the company.

BANNER ADVERTISING

Banners are those rectangular ads that appear—usually at the top—on popular sites. People pay for these adds on the basis of either impressions or click-throughs. Impressions are the number of people that view a page, and click-throughs refer to the number of people who use the banner as a link and "click through" to the advertiser's site. As you can imagine, there are likely to be many more impressions than click-throughs. The only other thing you really need to know is the pricing term "CPM," which stands for the amount of money that you pay for every 100 impressions. Advertisers usually pay between $30 and $50 per 100 impressions, but the cost can be lower or higher, depending on demand and the uniqueness of the audience.

If you are interested in purchasing banner advertisements for your site, you can contact one of the many advertising agencies that now deal exclusively with Internet advertising. I would recommend contacting them first, rather than individual companies, because the advertising companies can give you a lot more information about what is available and offer you a wider range of advertising options. The only problem, if you go this route, is that you do end up paying the agency a fee for any ads they place for you.

SPONSORSHIPS

Though there aren't really too many hard and fast rules to on-line sponsorships, you do have to be creative to get the best deal possible. Unless you see information about sponsorship opportunities on someone's site, e-mail them or give them a call for more information. If they can't rattle off a list of options or don't seem sure what they can offer, assume that they don't have a standard program and prepare to take control of the conversation. The more you can direct the terms of the agreement, the less time they will spend making up numbers and terms to offer you. If you still feel like you need more direction, ask your target companies about other partnership relationships they have, or contact some people you know who have their own.

Overall, you need to understand that advertising on the Internet is relatively new, and while some standards have been set, there are still a lot of gray areas. Take advantage of those gray areas to create win-win situations for everyone you get involved with on-line.

CHAPTER 12

Your Office

O NE OF THE BIGGEST DECISIONS YOU HAVE TO MAKE WHEN YOU START A NEW business is where you plan on working or operating from. The idea of opening an office or a store is an exciting one, but is it really necessary right now? Yes, you do need an "office"—someplace to work and call your home base. And while it doesn't actually have to be your home, there's also no reason that it can't be. Whatever you decide, you're going to have to at least make people *think* you have an office.

What you really need to do here is to take a close look at what your needs are, what your industry dictates, who your customers are, how much they really care about where you work, and, most importantly, what you can afford. I made a few mistakes myself, so this chapter will give you the benefit of what I've learned in hindsight.

My advice is: Start small. Spend your money (if you have any) carefully. Work where you can be comfortable so you can stay focused and be efficient. Make sure you have the equipment and tools that are essential. And don't look like a home-based business if you don't have to. Trust me. It's okay to do it—just don't broadcast it.

The rest of this chapter will help you make the big decision about where to open your office and what to fill it with. Coupled with the information on staffing in Chapter 7, you should be able to get a pretty good idea of what your start-up costs will be. I'll also give you some great insider tips on what kind of equipment you need, computer systems and software that are essential, and, of the utmost importance, your phone system.

Opening Up Shop

The Choices

Most small companies started by young entrepreneurs do get off the ground from home. There's no shame in that. But we all do our smoke and mirrors acts to hide the fact that our offices are really not what others would expect. And I think we're right in concealing them. Over 14 million people work at home in the U.S. today, and many of them are out of the closet (so to speak). But if you are a young entrepreneur you're probably doing everything you can to look older, larger, and more successful to impress and attract clients and vendors. Your office is one of those big image factors. If your competitors have their own offices you probably should, too (or at least look like you do at first).

There is a lot of debate today among entrepreneurs of all ages who are struggling with the question of whether or not they should work from home. Let's try to first figure out how you make that decision—based on your industry and available resources—then look at what you need to do to make your decision work.

You basically have six choices in deciding where to open your office:

Commercial Space: A retail location (storefront or street level space with big glass walls for window shopping) or a formal office space in a building filled with other offices. These tend to be in areas with other commercial buildings, so it's hard to pull off a home/office here because people don't usually live in commercial buildings.

Executive Office Suites: Commercial office space where a management company will lease an entire floor of a building and sublease it out to entrepreneurs. These buildings are usually located in the best parts of a city, the floor is nicely furnished, and there's an array of shared amenities (such as a mail room, receptionist, copy center, conference rooms, lunch room, etc.). Tenants usually pay rent on a short term basis (three months or so), rent individual offices or a suite of offices, or even pay for something called a "virtual office" program. Virtual office programs offer entrepreneurs offices that they don't ever have to go to. For a few hundred dollars they will collect your mail (thus, you have a great mailing address), take your phone calls (forwarding them to you anywhere you'd like), and even give you limited on-site privileges to use a conference room or office should you need to meet with clients.

Subleased Space: Basically, this is just a portion of a space in a commercial building that another business rents out to you at a reduced price. You usually find subleased space from friends or family who want to help you out, or from other companies which are not using all of their space and want to recoup a bit of the wasted rent. You can sometimes find listings for such space in a newspaper or business journal's classified ads, or from local commercial real estate brokers.

Shared Space: Similar to subleased space, but requiring more of a partnership between you and another company to assume equal (or close to equal) responsibility for an office space.

Home/Apartment: Wherever you live, or your parents live, or the home of someone really close to you who doesn't mind you turning a portion of their living space into an office.

Bedroom/Dorm: This is sometimes your only option when you're a student or teenager. You can work out of a very confined, highly distractible space work, but it could be a challenge. Accept the fact that your bedroom furniture will now double as office furniture and you might have to share your sleeping or entertaining space with office equipment.

Weighing the Pros and Cons

Commercial Space

PROS	CONS
• Very professional looking	• Can be very expensive
• Can be situated in prominent location	• Often have to sign two- to three-year leases
• Have many other businesses as tenants	• May have to personally guarantee
• Great working environment, motivational	• Substantial overhead (renters' insurance, workers' compensation, electricity, security alarms)

Executive Office Suite

PROS

- Lease periods are shorter and more negotiable
- Can rent as little as one office at a time
- Can sign up for "virtual office programs" where they just collect your mail and answer your phones without an office
- Surrounded by many other small business owners
- Great way to project a very professional image
- Makes your company look very big
- Excellent amenities, support staff is on call for you at all times
- Great locations

CONS

- Additional service fees can add up very quickly
- Offices are usually small
- Phone answering system can be impersonal
- Can be very expensive

Subleased Space

PROS

- Can lease premium space for great deals
- Very prestigious looking
- Can usually share receptionist
- Often furnished
- Terms are more flexible
- Background checks are not as rigorous
- Monthly bills much lower

CONS

- Can be hard to find
- Agreements can be very insecure—can lose lease with little notice
- May be claustrophobic, depending on how space is divided
- Hard to establish your own image in office

Shared Space

PROS

- Can get great deals
- Little legal work involved
- Can often barter services to reduce or eliminate rent
- More casual environment
- Can often share equipment and other amenities
- Monthly bills much lower

CONS

- Usually need good contacts or luck to find
- Agreements insecure
- Closely shared spaces can cause problems
- Hard to establish own image in space

Home/Apartment (Your Own)

PROS

- No commute, convenient
- Have more space than could otherwise afford
- No regulations
- Very low monthly costs above and beyond personal expenses
- Great write-off

CONS

- Hard to have clients visit
- Isolation is very lonely
- Hard to motivate yourself to work—many distractions
- Stricter tax laws for operating a business out of a home

Bedroom/Dorm

PROS

- Very convenient
- Rock-bottom expenses

CONS

- Small spaces
- Impossible to have clients visit
- Can be very embarrassing if discovered
- Very difficult to motivate yourself
- Many distractions from others around you

What Do I Really Need?

This is a very important question to ask yourself when deciding where to locate your business. Yes, you probably can work anywhere, but do you really want to? Do you have a choice? Ask yourself the following questions to help you decide where you really should be working and what you do, in fact, really need.

- Does it matter where you work?
- Will you ever have clients over? (e.g., apparel, consulting, manufacturing, publishing)
- Do you require special equipment or require permits for your work? (e.g., food service, manufacturing, health care, cosmetology)
- Will you have employees working at your location? (e.g., interns, independent contractors, clerical workers)
- Who are your clients?
- Does your image affect theirs? (e.g., public relations, event planning, advertising, promotional work, professional management)
- What image do they expect? (e.g., high profile, low key, highly skilled, very professional)
- What image do your competitors have? (e.g., high profile, trendy, conservative, low key)
- What are the most modest spaces your competitors operate from successfully? (e.g., home, garage, shared space, high-rise office building)

Again, if trying to look larger and more substantial than you are is going to hurt anyone, it's going to be you . . . if you start believing it yourself. Just keep your feet on the ground and your head out of the clouds (which, trust me, I know is hard!) and you should be fine.

What Can I Afford?

When it comes to deciding what you can really afford to spend, be so honest with yourself that it is painful. How much money are you *really* making? How much can you honestly say that you can expect to be making? As young entrepreneurs, we get so used to convincing people that we *can* do things that even we're not sure what we can actually do. And, to tell the truth, sometimes we have trouble being completely honest with ourselves. Yes, out of control overhead expenses have sent many businesses to their graves, and unrealistic rental commitments are largely to blame. We all want to look larger than we are, but is it worth risking our businesses?

Equipment and Supplies

Of course, much of what you will need will depend heavily on what business you are in, but most companies today seem to have a lot of trouble coping without a few of the basics. Here's a list of a few of

From: Kenneth Cole— Kenneth Cole Productions

Fourteen years ago, I wanted to open a shoe company with limited money. From experience I knew I had to get in quickly because so often new companies run out of cash flow before they get the chance to conduct business. I also knew it was easier to get credit from factories in Europe who needed the business than from American banks that didn't. So I lined up the factories, went to Europe, designed a collection of shoes, and returned to the States to sell them.

At the time, a shoe company had two options. You could get a room at the Hilton and become 1 of about 1,100 shoe companies selling their goods. This didn't provide the identity or image I felt necessary for a new company, and it cost a lot more money than I had to spend. The other way was to do what the big companies do and get a fancy showroom in midtown Manhattan, not far from the Hilton. More identity, much more money too.

I had an idea. I called a friend in the trucking business and asked to borrow one of his trucks to park in midtown Manhattan. He said sure, but good luck getting permission. I went to the mayor's office, Koch at the time, and asked how one gets permission to park a 40-foot trailer truck in midtown Manhattan. He said one doesn't. The only people the city gives parking permits to are production companies shooting full length motion pictures, and utility companies like Con Ed or AT&T. So that day I went to the stationary store and changed our company letterhead from Kenneth Cole Inc. to Kenneth Cole Productions Inc. and the next day I applied for a permit to shoot a full-length film entitled *The Birth of a Shoe Company*.

With Kenneth Cole Productions painted on the side of the truck, we parked at 1370 6th Avenue, right across from the New York Hilton, the day of the shoe show. We opened for business with a fully furnished 40-foot trailer, a director (sometimes there was film in the camera, sometimes there wasn't), models as actresses, and two of New York's finest, compliments of Mayor Koch, as our doormen. We sold 40 thousand pair of shoes, the entire available production, in two and a half days and we were off and running.

To this day the company is still named Kenneth Cole Productions Inc. and serves as a reminder to the importance of resourcefulness and innovative problem solving.

the most vital pieces of office equipment that you could end up hating yourself down the road for not having.

Computer

Whatever your business, odds are that it could be significantly improved by having a computer. From basic letters to client billing to presentations and fliers, how entrepreneurs today survive without one is a mystery. And especially if you are young and in business, you'd better have e-mail. As a young entrepreneur, computer know-how is supposed to be part of your birthright. (For more information on computers, see "Technology and the Virtual Office" below.)

Laser Printer

While good quality ink jet/bubble jet printers are becoming remarkably inexpensive, if you have a choice, stick to them for color printing and rely on laser jets if you write a lot of letters, prepare presentations, or just communicate with various people in writing. Ink jets still do not compare with the quality black printing of laser jets, and any trained eye will be able to tell the difference. If you are in a business that depends on written communication, opt for a laser printer first, then splurge on color printers for your second round of purchasing.

Fax Machine

The only thing worse than not having e-mail today (or even more catastrophic, a computer) is not having fax capabilities. Anyone with any computer knowledge knows that most new computers are fully equipped with internal fax modems and all of the software that you need to fax your heart out. And while a computer fax does have some limitations (unless you also have a scanner), it will certainly do the trick for you if you can't yet afford to get a real fax machine. Another thing to keep in mind is that real fax machines can photocopy a few pages at a time quite well. Either way you look at it, you never want to be confronted with the question, "Now why can't you just fax it to me???"

Photocopy Machine

All right, it's not really a necessity for all of us, especially when copy centers such as Kinko's are everywhere these days. But if your business really needs one, and you are not conveniently located near a retail copy store, then this is another piece of equipment you may have to start thinking about. Copy machines can be pretty expensive, but they are starting to make some that are on the cheap side (both price and quality-wise—be careful). Machines start as low as $250 for the no-frills versions, and run well into thousands of dollars. Be sure, though, that you're not throwing money away. Some fairly substantial businesses have survived for great periods of time without copiers.

All-in-One System

One of the most beautiful things about technology is that it's always evolving in ways that can make our lives easier. The next time you're flipping through an office catalog or are in an office supply store, take a look at one of the all-in-one office systems. In most cases, these machines function as a laser printer, a fax system, a photocopier, and a scanner all in one. Designed specifically for the small business owner, the all-in-one system, which costs several hundred dollars, can save you a lot of money when you don't have a lot to begin with.

As far as standard office equipment goes, with one exception, these are the basics. Always keep your eyes open for good deals on new, used, or refurbished equipment, demonstration models (at office supply stores), and discontinued models. Even look into leasing. Most important, check the quality. Don't settle for equipment that will make you look unprofessional.

Telephones

Telephones are, of course, that exception. But since there's a lot more to know about setting up a telephone system than you can imagine, I've dedicated a whole section to it.

Telephone Systems

The goal of this section is to teach you how your company can look like it employs ten people even if it's only you and your cat. With a little creativity, you can make your company look pretty substantial with a few phone tricks.

Telephone Lines

Okay, here's the rundown. Residential lines are cheaper than business lines and even offer cheaper calling rates. But without a business line, your company name will not be registered with the phone company as a business. So if you have clients who are likely to look you up, they won't find you if you are registered as a residential customer. Registering as a business also gives you a free listing in the Yellow Pages under any category that you think is appropriate. Many people get a lot of business from ads in the Yellow Pages, so, it's an option to seriously consider. Make two calls to your phone company—one to the residential office, and one to the business office. Ask each of them which calling packages are available, and what the associated fees are for each. Compare the two answers and you are very likely to find great differences in service and price.

If you are not a patient person, you might want to just forget about this section all together, because dealing with the phone company takes a lot of patience, perseverance, and persistence. And then, most of the time, you still don't get what you want. But if you are willing to sweat a little to benefit a great deal, read on.

Voice Mail

This is not optional. A company that does not have an answering system for those times when the phone cannot be answered personally is archaic. Not only does it anger customers looking for information and assistance, but it makes your business look like some fly-by-night operation that could be run out of a van.

If you insist on hanging on to your answering machine, do so at your own risk. Messages get lost, can be retrieved by anyone in the room, and can be disconnected in a power failure. Voice mail, because it is controlled (and housed) at the phone company, will never stop working for you—even through most natural disasters. For as little as three to five dollars a month, the phone company can offer you voice mail service that can answer your phone calls when you're not able to. If you want to get really fancy, or just emphasize that your business is more than a one-person operation, ask for a group or family voice-mail system. This will allow callers to select from one of several different people or departments.

When recording your message, make sure that you are brief (long phone messages drive people crazy). If callers can press the pound (#) key to skip the outgoing message, tell them so near the beginning of your message. (Your regular callers will be most appreciative.) If you don't have a great phone voice, find someone who does and have them record your messages. One struggling young entrepreneur named David had no staff, no office, and no money, but he gave people the impression that he was worth millions. His phone message was left by a very professional sounding British woman who spoke of the company and its "representatives" as if it were a major international corporation. On average, it took clients, and even friends, three to five calls before they realized that there really were no representatives—long enough to get David into the door of some major corporations himself.

If you have any questions about what you should be leaving on your voice mail, just make a bunch of phone calls at night to businesses that you know. Listening to different phone messages will give you a good idea of how you want yours to sound. A good, generic message to leave is:

> "Hello. You have reached The XYZ Company. We are sorry that we are unable to take your call at this time, but we are either on another line or assisting other customers. If you leave your name, company name, phone number, and a message, someone will get back to you as soon as possible."

Always clearly state the name of your company, and apologize for not being able to answer the phone. You could be out working on your tan, or rustling up new clients, but no one has to know. Notice that the message says "we" and not "I." Always refer to your company in the plural. Saying "we" makes it sound like you don't run the company alone.

Call Waiting

Call waiting is not an absolute necessity. With all of the cool phone tricks, it really does seem unprofessional to have your call waiting interrupt your calls. A good way to compromise, by keeping your call waiting and your professional image, is to see if call waiting will enable your voice-mail service to answer calls that you do not accept while on the phone with someone else. What this means is that if you are on the phone with your best friend, and your call waiting beeps, you can put your friend on the other line and check to see if the other call is business. But if you're on a business call and the call waiting beeps, you can ignore it, and your voice mail will pick up the incoming call. Not all phone companies are equipped to do this, so check beforehand, because if they can't your second caller will just get a never-ending ringing. And remember what we said about not having your phone answered?

Ring Mate

If you are starting to get your business moving and are still working from home, you might want to invest another three dollars per month on Ring Mate service. If you are on a tight budget, and unable to spend another $20 a month every time you need a new phone line, Ring Mate may be able to help you. One problem that early-stage young entrepreneurs face is sharing their personal phone with their business phone. This becomes a big problem when you answer your phone all groggy on a Sunday morning and it's a client. Or when your roommate picks up a business call by accident while music is blasting in the background. Or when people that you are trying to impress ask you for your home phone number and it's the same as your business. Ring Mate will solve these problems by allowing you to use a second phone number (in addition to the one you are already paying for) on the same line as the first.

What happens is that the two phone numbers share one phone line, but have different rings so you can identify which phone number is being called. Make the main one your business line if you've already used the number, and make the Ring Mate line your "home." One of the great benefits of Ring Mate is being able to identify which calls are personal and which are professional before you pick up the phone. Then you can adjust your greeting from "Hello" to "Hello, this is John," or "Good afternoon, XYZ Corp."

Fax Switch

Even if you've already gotten a fax machine, you're still going to need a dedicated fax line (another phone line) to answer any incoming faxes. But what if you don't get faxes often enough to justify getting another line? A fax switching box is a great little contraption that allows you to hook up several different pieces of equipment to one line so that they can share phone access. Usually, people hook up their phone, fax, and even modems. What happens is that when a call comes in, whether it's a voice call or a fax, the fax switch can tell the difference, and direct the incoming call to the right machine. It also works in reverse. If you happen to be using your computer's modem and a voice call comes in, instead of being cut off from your data connection, your caller will be sent to voice mail, or will receive a busy signal. For about $300, fax switches are costly, but can make a big difference to a new, growing company.

Technology and the Virtual Office

Who would have thought a few years ago that a nineteen-year-old could run an international corporation from his or her bedroom? Not many. But would you question it today? Probably not. As the computer has single-handedly reshaped the business environment, it has also had a profound effect on how we do business and who is able start one. Regardless of your age, educational background, financial situation, or professional appearance, if you have a decent computer (one with communications capabilities, such as a modem, software, and on-line service), you can do business with almost anyone from virtually anywhere. Undetected, young entrepreneurs everywhere give the appearance of representing and running major corporations, even though the reality might be quite the opposite.

Since the virtual office concept has become an accepted norm in the small business world, mastering it has become critical to the success of young entrepreneurs. Thank goodness, because in most cases new entrepreneurs couldn't afford to build their own businesses any other way. As an entrepreneur that's just starting out, you have a lot of things to consider.

- You need time to test your business concept.

- You have to keep overhead expenses to a minimum.

- An office lease can bankrupt you, tying you into a long-term commitment you may not be able to keep.

- Working from home delays your hiring employees (another major commitment).

- A virtual office forces you to be cost-efficient and creative with your image building.

- The day-to-day masquerade keeps you on your toes.

- The (sometimes) meager experience gives you something to aspire to and look forward to—a real office one day.

With all of these new responsibilities, creating your own virtual office might be one of the smartest things that you can do. Don't be too quick to jump into a commercial office space. Yes, it does look a heck of a lot better, particularly when you are trying to impress clients. But take it from one who has been there, you can get away with it for much longer than you might imagine, and your business will probably survive much longer for your sacrifice. Despite what you might think, it is okay to work at home today. So many older people are already doing it, and flaunting it, that if you have a virtual office you are not alone, so don't fret. Use this time to build your empire. You can still look like a major corporation with a virtual office—you just need to get into the swing of things, pay close attention to detail and have fun doing it.

Software 101

As a business owner, there are four major categories of computer software that you should be concerned with having to make your operations more efficient and your image more impressive. These four categories include word processing, spreadsheets/financial programs, databases, and graphic software. To give you a quick rundown, here's a brief explanation of the basics for each.

WORD PROCESSING

Word processing is the most basic type of software that is essential to any computer user. The easiest way to write letters, create fliers, format mailing labels, and address envelopes, word processing programs provide even the biggest computer novice with the ability to look professional. The most popular programs on the market right now are Microsoft Word and WordPerfect. If you learn nothing else about computers, learn how to use word-processing software.

SPREADSHEETS/FINANCIAL SOFTWARE

If you ever need to work with charts and graphs, create financial statements, or manipulate different sales or cost scenarios, spreadsheets are the absolute best way to do so. Though it does take some time to learn all the tricks (like automatic calculations, linking different documents, and using formulas) it is well worth the time investment. Once you learn to do your finances on a spreadsheet program you will never attempt it with a pencil and paper again. (Microsoft Excel is the most popular, with Lotus 1-2-3 being second on the market.)

Even better than spreadsheets for financial planning, though, is using financial software. Because so many people hate doing their own bookkeeping, software developers have made these programs as user-friendly as anyone could wish them to be. Again, spend a little time learning the program with the tutorials or user guides included, and you will be happy you did. (Keep an eye out for Quicken for simple accounting, and Quickbooks, Peachtree Accounting, or MYOB—Mind Your Own Business for more complex businesses.

DATABASES/CONTACT MANAGEMENT SOFTWARE

Databases are crucial for any business that needs to keep track of customers, vendors, or other business contacts. Basically, any business owner can benefit from tracking the people that they do business with. Database software allows you to maintain an organized file of people's names, contact information, history of your relationship, buying habits, etc. Using database software to manage your business is a critical step toward building a competitive company in any industry. (Look for Dbase or Fox Pro [or even better, the one's listed below] for your database needs.)

And for those who have advanced people-and-information management issues, contact management–software programs are invaluable. Programs like this were originally created to assist sales managers in keeping track of their clients and sales calls. Because they were designed to keep track of the histories of numerous accounts—including phone calls, faxes, meetings, and tasks—contact manager software is of incredible assistance to anyone struggling to maintain control and organization of their work. (ACT!, Goldmine, and Microsoft Access are the top sellers.)

GRAPHIC DESIGN

Depending on your individual needs, it might make sense to have a graphic program that will enable you to spruce up your image should you ever need to create fliers, advertisements, announcements, newsletters, etc. Though they can be very complex to the new user, graphic programs enable anyone with a little patience, time, and an eye for design to become a graphic artist. (Look for Page Maker, ClarisWorks, or QuarkXpress for the more advanced designer.)

While most software packages today come with built-in tutorials, training classes are available everywhere. If you are a student, and your university has an Information Technology Department, odds are they will offer some sort of tutoring or training. If not, look in your local newspaper or yellow pages for classes. You might even call up some of the computer superstores, like CompUSA, which are starting to diversify into classroom training as well.

A Few Cheap and Creative Equipment Solutions

If there are pieces of equipment that you need for your business and still can't afford, be creative:

- Think about places that would have already purchased the equipment that you need but might be looking to upgrade soon. If you have friends in those businesses ask them if they'd be interested in selling their old equipment.

- If you know of a company that is going out of business, ask them, too. When people are in trouble financially they usually want to sell whatever they can for cash.

- Look in the classified section of your newspaper or in one of those "recycler" publications in which people place ads to buy and sell merchandise. Place an ad yourself.

- The Internet is another great place to find used equipment, though it might not be visibly advertised. Check out newsgroups, user groups, and bulletin boards where people in your industry congregate. Leave a message asking to purchase or trade used equipment.

- Scour catalogs or call stores that sell the type of equipment you are looking for. See if they are selling refurbished items, have older models, or can sell their demos.

You can usually get some great deals if you don't mind settling with used equipment until you can afford better. Just ask around and don't be shy about asking people who know where the great deals are. They will appreciate your dilemma and, if they can do so, will usually point you in the direction you need to go.

PART FIVE

Insider Information (Tales from the Trenches)

Coping with Life as an Entrepreneur

WHEN PEOPLE FIRST HEARD THAT I WAS PUTTING SOMETHING IN THIS BOOK about the stresses of being a young entrepreneur, several laughed at the idea, probably because they think of young entrepreneurs' businesses as "hobbies" rather than real live entrepreneurial ventures. I probably shouldn't have been surprised, but the truth is that we have the same issues, and many other unique ones, that older and more experienced business owners do. One of the reasons I wrote this book was to identify the issues that are different for us as young entrepreneurs.

This chapter represents a period of my life during which I was just getting familiar with the lifestyle of an entrepreneur in her twenties. Now, a few years later—after a lot of hard work, sleepless nights, struggle, sweat, tears, and loneliness—I feel that I can finally look back and shed some light on this stage of life for others. As a result, this may be the most important chapter of the book.

I never had anyone sit down and explain these things to me. Nor had I ever really read anything about living the life of a young entrepreneur from someone who had been there. (Thankfully, major business magazines are now starting to run articles dealing with this sort of thing.) Eventually, I just figured these things out on my own.

Again, though, I'm hoping that this book will provide you with enough help so that you don't feel you have to figure it out yourself.

As a young entrepreneur, your life will be different, and it's important that you know how to deal with some of its more challenging aspects before they take you by complete surprise. Rest assured, there are proven ways to deal with people who don't support you, including family and friends. There are also great ways to avoid feeling isolated when you're working for yourself. And balance—something we usually hear much older people with families and high pressure careers talk about—is something that we need to maintain ourselves. A business can take over your life if you're not careful. If I had known in the beginning all of what I'm about to tell you, I probably would have been a lot more successful a lot sooner. I also would have learned the true meaning of balance and happiness much earlier on. This, in a sense, is my gift to you.

So go out there and start the business of your dreams. Just don't forget that you're a person, not a machine. We all work the way we do, trying to accomplish so much at an early age, because we want the freedom and independence to thoroughly enjoy the second half of our lives. But you have to be smart about the sacrifices you make and never lose sight of what is most important to you.

Welcome to the Entrepreneurial Life

Don't Give Up on Yourself

I can't tell you how many times people rolled their eyes when I used to talk about my entrepreneurial plans. They might as well have said to me, "What now, Jennifer?" or "Why don't you just go get a job?" As far as I'm concerned, people always seemed to be more skeptical than supportive. And I know that this situation is true for most young entrepreneurs. After all, many of us pursue our first big ventures while we are in school, and how do our families respond to that? "Why are we paying all of this money for your education if you refuse to focus on it?"

In the beginning, roadblocks seem to be everywhere. No matter how hard you try, how hard you work, or how enthusiastic you are about your concept, there will always be people trying to convince you to do something else. Sometimes the temptation is enough to make you want to give up. Life would be a lot easier if you just acted like any normal person your age. Why should you continue to put yourself through this? Because you are different, and you should be proud of that. Success does not come easy—the faster you learn to deal with that, the faster you can break through to the other side.

People often ask me how I got the idea to start the Young Entrepreneurs Network. After I confess that it was really my original partners, Benjamin Kyan and David Meadows, who identified the opportunity, I tell people that it was this—the struggle of the young entrepreneur—that made me want to do something to help. In 1991, I first learned about ACE—the Association of Collegiate Entrepreneurs. Until I attended my first ACE conference in New York, I had never realized that so many other young entrepreneurs existed. It was one of the most amazing experiences of my life. All of a sudden I was surrounded by others whose goals, ambitions, thoughts, dreams, and lifestyles were just like mine.

Giving up on yourself is pretty easy when your business ideas seem to be going nowhere; but failure is just the first step to understanding what you need to do to succeed. As Henry Ford once said, "Failure is the opportunity to start over more intelligently." Without a few of those early businesses that never went anywhere, I sincerely don't believe I would have known what to do to finally succeed. And about the roadblocks, well, learning to stomach and maneuver around them taught me how to deal with the much greater setbacks that are inevitable in the course of doing business. But as the entrepreneurs in my family have taught me, when something goes wrong—whatever it is—you just pick yourself up and move on. Your entrepreneurial career will prove this if you give it the chance.

Welcome to Your New Older Life

Relating to people twice your age better than people your own age is a strange thing to happen to someone in her twenties or, even worse, teens. It makes perfect sense that we become friends with people our own age in school, because we share our life's activities with them. But as you've noticed, people mature and discover who they really are, and who they want to be, at different times. If you decided to start your own business before any of your friends had the idea or could even comprehend what you were talking about, there's a good chance that you turned to older people for advice and support. This is perfectly natural. The only problem is that you set yourself apart at a time when being different could mean social suicide.

My mentors often joke that I'm twenty-six going on forty-five, and sometimes I believe it. In many ways I *have* taken on the professional responsibilities of someone much older. My friends are a different story. It's a terrible thing to lose touch with some of your closest friends because you simply can't relate to their lives anymore. But on the other hand, when you devote all of your energy to building your dream, look at what you can accomplish while you are still so young? I sometimes think about what life will be like when I'm well into middle-age. Will I have the same stresses that that age brings, or will it be easier because I started my professional life so much earlier? I am banking on the latter.

Why Am I Doing This?

It's 3:00 a.m. on Saturday. You are at your office. You're beginning to nod off, despite the fourth cup of coffee you finished about an hour ago. You check your voice mail, as you usually do a dozen times throughout the day (including Sundays). Nothing. Listening to your saved messages (of which there are usually about twelve), you remember the invitation that you received for dinner . . . seven hours ago. You hang up, stand up, and try to stretch your legs. You notice another pile of letters, documents, and bills hidden behind the door that you had totally forgotten about. "I'm never going to get this all done before Monday's meeting."

Normally you would have just wandered back into the office on Sunday, but your mother insisted that you come celebrate your sister's birthday . . . a four-hour drive in weekend traffic. "What can I bring with me?" you think. "I'll work a little bit before dinner . . . no, they'll kill me. I haven't even told them that I have to drive the same night. I wish that it was just Monday already. Weekends are too stressful." *Why am I doing this?* you ask yourself.

When you own your own business, you inevitably end up working harder than you've ever worked for anyone in your life. The personal vows you once made to use your professional freedom to allow you to do the things that you never before had time for are nothing but a distant memory. You now work harder, longer hours; have more stress, less of a life; and probably take a smaller salary then ever before. "Why am I doing this to myself" is a question that entrepreneurs often ask themselves. But despite your daydreams of working 9 to 5, taking two-week paid vacations, and not really caring about much more than your own job, you wouldn't trade being the boss for anything in the world. You love it too much. You think.

When you have those "Why am I doing this" moments, it's important to have peers to talk to. Not just your family, not just your friends, but other young entrepreneurs who are probably also at *their* offices on Saturday night. Any motivation and words of encouragement you may receive from your loved ones is great, but ultimately not very valuable. In most cases they really have no idea what you are going through. So for your best friend to tell you that everything is going to work out sometimes just doesn't do the trick. They're trying to make you feel better the only way they know how, but what you need are people who *really* understand.

If you haven't done so already, start to build your own network of friends who are immediate peers. Seek out people in your industry or related fields. Find people who can not only give you excellent professional advice but who can be there to lend an ear when you're just about ready to give up. Go ahead, neglect your other needs (which you probably already do). But attend to this one first.

On the Couch: How a Psychiatrist Defines the Entrepreneurial Personality

According to Manhattan psychiatrist Joanna Polenz, the entrepreneurial character is marked by three functions: risk-taking, innovation, and, to a lesser degree, managing. Other qualities regularly attributed to the entrepreneurial personality have been high achievement, motivation (the strong desire to excel), and a need for autonomy, power, and independence. Personal relationships, as in family and friends, are important, but rarely occupy the No. 1 position in an entrepreneur's heart.

Polenz says that even though few studies exist on the personality profile of an entrepreneur, evidence suggests the following:

- Entrepreneurs are more likely to come from ethnic, religious, or other minority groups. The experience of feeling different seems to have an important influence on an entrepreneur. If the family of the entrepreneur itself does not seem to fit into the established order of things, their offspring may have little choice but to create a new niche for themselves in society.

- Some studies see entrepreneurs as "anxious individuals who are inner directed," meaning they possess an internal focus of control as opposed to bowing to external forces.

- Other studies suggest that the fathers of many entrepreneurs were self-employed. Familiarity with self-employment seems to increase the chances of creating one's own business.

- Entrepreneurs frequently describe having an absent (or emotionally not present) father, and a very overbearing, controlling mother.

- Some entrepreneurial personalities truly cannot function in a structured work situation and, in fact, appear to be allergic to authority. "This is a smaller subgroup of entrepreneurs, but for them, having control is vital to them. They react like caged animals when forced into a regimented environment," says Polenz.

It's your immediate peers who will teach you how to best deal with all of the other elements anyway. You are the driving force of your company. If you're not operating at optimum levels, no one and nothing else will either.

Don't Be Afraid of Failure

People ask me about failure all the time. *What happens when a young entrepreneur fails in his or her business venture? Is it more devastating for them? Don't most businesses fail anyway?* Let's get the record straight here. One of the biggest reasons for you to start a business when you are younger is that failure doesn't mean the same thing to us as it does to those who are two to three times our age. They can think of our ventures as hobbies if they want, but we have to look at every business we start as a learning experience. If a business doesn't work out, we're young enough to start again without the situation tearing apart our lives. In most cases, we don't start out with commercial office space, formal investors, full-time employees, and tremendous debt. And there's a definite upside to that: If we had all those things and still failed, our losses would be much greater.

Also keep in mind that we, as young entrepreneurs, tend to start multiple business ventures in our teens and twenties. The more experience you have at running your own business, the more likely you are not to be out hunting for a job upon graduation. That's not so bad, is it? So you start three different businesses and close down two because you weren't making any money, or because you just got bored with them. That's okay. People give us a lot more leeway at our age and are usually quite impressed that we've gotten out there and taken such bold steps.

The truth is that failure only becomes a big deal if you borrow a lot of money, build up a lot of overhead, hire a big full-time staff, or end up leaving customers with unfulfilled orders. That's another great reason to start multiple businesses—we learn more, and take on more responsibility gradually, learning along the way. It's kind of like our own subconscious, built-in entrepreneurial defense mechanism.

But if you are in a failing business and things are starting to get pretty tough, just think about the things that I've been telling you from the beginning. Make sure that you stay in close contact with your advisors and mentors. Let the people closest to you know that you need help and/or support. Be creative in finding solutions. Try to cut down your overhead and start thinking like a true bootstrapper. Maintain enough balance in your life to stay healthy and focused. And keep going, if you believe in what you are doing. You can always change the course that you have chosen and alter your business model, services, or product offerings. Try taking a few days off, getting completely away from the business and stress, and try to find different solutions to your problems. And finally, don't forget why you started this whole thing in the first place. If it no longer seems worth it to you, take a hint and do something about it.

If your business fails, what's the worst that can happen? You've made incredible contacts and gotten a lot of business experience. People will have a whole different level of respect for you now. You're definitely more employable and should command higher salaries and better benefits. You have the rest of your life to start again. And you know what to do differently the next time.

This isn't to say that the answer to what to do about failure is easy or simple, because it's not. But it is something we live with as entrepreneurs. And remember, the ones who are left standing at the end are the ones who really win. Even if your business isn't left on its feet, make sure that you always are.

Dealing with Those Who Don't Support You

Your Family

One of the most unfortunate—and most common—situations that young entrepreneurs face is a family that's not supportive. While your friendships can be replaced, however reluctantly, your family can not. Living with (literally or not) parents or siblings who do not understand, or simply refuse to support your entrepreneurial aspirations, can often be the breaking point for many early-stage entrepreneurs. Here are some questions to ask yourself:

- What is their real reason for not supporting you?
- Are they unclear about what you are doing?
- Have they been saving money for the past twenty years to send you to medical school?
- Have they failed at an entrepreneurial attempt themselves?
- Do they know others who have?
- Do they doubt your ability, due to age, lack of experience, or preconceived notions about what they think you can or can't do?

It is very important to put your own feelings aside for a moment and look at your situation objectively. Once you understand the underlying reasons, face the pessimists directly with a loving confrontation or a plea for understanding. If all else fails, beg.

Once you understand your family's motivations, the next thing to do is launch your own family PR campaign. No, this is not a joke. Anyone who has ever been in this horrible situation knows how difficult these circumstances can be. Hopefully, the following suggestions will help you overcome any bad family vibes that you may be receiving.

- Bring your success stories home with you. Send your family copies of client letters that praise your work. Show them a customer's check for payment. Share any articles about your company from the media with them. Tack them up on the refrigerator or bulletin board—somewhere visible to everyone in the house.

- Let them know how happy your business makes you. Seeing their children happy and actively pursuing goals will usually make any parent happy.

- Discuss your endeavor with their friends who understand business, have children who are not enterprising, or just simply like you. Once they show interest and understanding for you and your business venture, mention that you wish your parents felt the same way. (This works just as well on other relatives, too.) They'll feel so badly for you that they might just take up the issue with your family themselves. Let other people put a little pressure on your family to cut you some slack and show you the respect you deserve for what you are doing. Unfortunately, friends or respected peers are often more likely to recognize your achievements publicly than your family is. Despite how close you might be, it's not uncommon for people to need outside opinions to really open up their perspective—particularly about their own children.

- Be sure to avoid neglecting family responsibilities because of your business, whether they involve visiting your grandparents, family gatherings, or religious practices. Be your own person, your own boss—but do your best to show your family that they still hold an important place in your life.

- Find the most nurturing and supportive person in your family— your mother, father, uncle, grandmother—whoever is most sympathetic to your overall happiness. The more people you get on your side, the better.

- Collect a few stories about people like you who created successful companies. Whether it is the corner grocer or one of the entrepreneurial giants, know their stories well, particularly the vital facts: How old they were when they started, their experience, their family's support (or lack of), their resources, and current success markers (sales, employees, clients, etc.). A good place to find amazing stories is Napoleon Hill's book *Think and Grow Rich*. (You can also check the sidebars throughout this book for some inspirational stories and advice from entrepreneurs who made it big).

- Avoid sharing business problems or frustrations with them. If they really aren't supportive of your venture, your mishaps will only fuel their desire to intervene further, or proclaim that they "told you so."

- Show them that you have researched your business and have a clear understanding of your options, environment, and chances of success. If you are uncertain about your chances, be honest with them and tell them that despite your own doubts you feel that the experience will be well worth any potential failure. After all, the best way entrepreneurs learn about business is by being in business.

- Be someone that not only they, but you yourself, can be proud of.

Your Friends

If you don't already intuitively know this, it's probably time that you faced this issue straight on. Who your friends are does matter. Not because of money, status, or profession, but because of motivation and momentum. Did you ever notice that some of your closest childhood friends slowly drifted away? It's because you outgrew each other. When you are growing up, for a while, your life is quite structured. You tend to bond with people you go to school with, live next to, and share hobbies and interests with. Then you get older and feel the need to pursue your own interests independently. You chose to become an entrepreneur, while your friends decided to go to medical school, wait tables at a club, or maybe take off around the world to postpone entering the "real world."

As an entrepreneur, even very subtle influences from others can be quite harmful to your progress. Look at the people you surround yourself with. Are they people that you respect? Do they motivate, stimulate, or teach you? Do they discourage you, slow you down, or get jealous about your successes? If they are uncomfortable with your lifestyle, fight you on your choices, and influence you to make decisions that you later regret, you need to take a serious step back.

The wrong influences for an entrepreneur don't necessarily have to be obviously "negative" to be counterproductive. Maybe you have friends who just don't support what you do by not realizing how important your business is to you. Of course, the first thing you should do is try to make them understand. But if that fails, there are a few things you can do to keep yourself on track:

- Remove, avoid, or limit negative or counter-productive influences from your life.

- Don't discuss business with people who don't care or don't want to understand.

- Surround yourself with people you admire and who motivate you.

- Read about other entrepreneurs who excite you.

- Accept the fact that you're different.

We talked previously about finding immediate peers or other young business owners whom you can befriend. This advice cannot be stressed enough. I'm not advocating that you ditch all your friends, but just that you try to be very aware of the influences around you and do your best to fix or get rid of anything that's negative or counterproductive to your endeavors. You've worked very hard to get where you are. Don't let anything or anyone chip away at your success or pride in it.

Balancing Your Life (AKA: How to Have One)

Though I'm probably the last one in the world who should be writing this, I will say that I've gotten plenty of advice on the subject. For some reason this issue always seems to come up with friends, taxi drivers, business associates, even with the guy who makes sandwiches across the street from my office at lunch. When I asked around and started observing other young entrepreneurs, in many cases I discovered that they had the same problem. When your business is your life, what is there left to balance? Okay, I know that there is more to it than that, so here's my shot at trying to under-stand what's going wrong in our lives.

Whose Life Is It Anyway?

If you too are a workaholic and absolutely obsessed with the success of your business, you've probably sacrificed a few things along the way. Maybe you've gained a little weight or are starting to look a bit emaciated from not eating regularly. Maybe you don't go out much anymore because your friends stopped calling to ask. How is your family taking all of this? Have you seen them lately? And how happy are you? Really. Take this little quiz* then reassess whether your life needs a little balancing:

- Do you get more excited about your work than about your family or other things?

- Are there times when you can charge through your work and other times when you can't get anything done?

- Do you take your work to bed with you? On weekends? On vacation?

- Is work the activity you like to do best and talk about most?

- Do you work more than forty hours a week?

- Do you turn all your hobbies into money-making ventures?

- Do you take complete responsibility for the outcome of your work efforts?

- Have your family or friends given up expecting you on time?

- Do you take on extra work because you are concerned that it won't otherwise get done unless you do it?

- Do you underestimate how long a project will take and then rush to complete it?

- Do you believe that it is okay to work long hours if you love what you are doing?

- Do you get impatient with people who have other priorities besides work?

*Source: Bryan Robinson, Ph.D., nationally recognized author and lec-turer, and regular contributor to *Psychology Today, The New Age Journal,* and PBS.

- Are you afraid that if you don't work hard you will lose clients or be a failure?

- Is the future a constant worry for you even when things are going very well?

- Are you competitive about everything, including play?

- Do you get irritated when people ask you to stop doing your work in order to do something else?

- Have your long hours hurt your family or other relationships?

- Do you think about your work while driving, falling asleep, or when others are talking?

- Do you work or read during meals?

- Do you believe that more money will solve the other problems in your life?

If you answered "yes" to three or more of these questions, you are considered to be a compulsive overworker, or well on your way. If you answered "no" to about three questions, by the standards of other young entrepreneurs, you are actually quite normal. But you still need help. We all do, I think.

What do you really like to do besides work? What kind of things are important to you? If you feel as though you've lost touch with the rest of the world, and even life in general, it's time to reevaluate your life. No one is going to tell you, especially here, to neglect or give up your business. But you really need to remember why you started your company in the first place.

Was it for freedom from working for someone else? That's a common answer. You're probably also thinking about the freedom to do the things that you want and love to do. But odds are, work wasn't one of them when you started. I'm not asking you to make a drastic change in your lifestyle, because that would be pretty unrealistic. (And you've probably made New Year's resolutions about balancing your life too many times already.) What you need to do is start adding other elements to your days piece by piece.

Start by taking your mom out for brunch next Sunday. Then next week, maybe go play basketball or tennis with some good friends. Take it one week at a time. Eat lunch outside one day when it's sunny, instead of at your desk. If you plan one new, non-work related activity each week, you can start to make some progress without in-flicting any pain on yourself or your business. As soon as you're ready, move your extracurricular activities up to a few times a week, then once a day. Do something for yourself everyday. Go home and take a bath. Read something that has nothing to do with your business. Hey, this is your life. You deserve to live it the way you'd like to. Start to take care of yourself now so in thirty years you don't wind up with a heart condition, an ulcer, even more stress, and even less of a life than you have now. It's no joke: You may be well on your way. You started your business while you were still very young to avoid all of that. Don't forget it. You may say that there's nothing else that you'd rather be doing, and I believe you. Just make sure that your life includes some things other than your work.

Why Staying Healthy Is So Important to Your Business

As if you haven't been given this lecture more times than you can stomach, here it comes one more time. In the simplest terms possible, if you can't function because you're sick, worn out, or in the midst of a breakdown, your business won't either. The image of your business being paralyzed is probably more gut wrenching than the worst illness you can imagine contracting. But think about it for a minute. This is not another friend here telling you to slow down and take care of yourself, this is a direct peer of yours talking—from experience. To help you avoid your own physical, mental, or emotional breakdown, allow me to share mine with you.

I learned my first lesson about personal neglect when I was a freshman in college. As usual, I had a dozen different projects going on—most of which I was creating or in charge of myself. I went out occasionally, worked constantly, slept erratically, and ate horribly. That November, just before Thanksgiving break and midterms, I snapped. I was sitting in a microeconomics class during a review for the exam. I had physically gone to every class, but as I sat there listening to the review I realized that none of the material being discussed was at all familiar. I sat there with a blank stare asking myself "How did this happen?" Just a few months ago I had graduated from high school with honors and a 3.7 GPA. This was not normal. I walked out of the class and right into the career center to find one of my closest friends on the faculty. The minute I saw Bob, I became hysterical. I must have cried in his office for ten minutes before I could get a word out. Even then, I probably wasn't too coherent.

When I finally made it home, to Los Angeles, I walked through the front door of my house only to hear "What happened to you?" as the first words out of my terrified mother's mouth. I was ghost white. That month I had my first emotional, physical, psychological, and academic breakdowns—all at the same time. Back at home,

I slept for the first twenty-three hours, then through most of the rest of my vacation. I was an absolute mess.

I know many other young entrepreneurs who have experienced similar episodes. Conna Craig, the young founder of The Institute for Children, a nonprofit organization for foster children, worked for 362 days one year and contracted pneumonia because of it. To her horror, Conna was hospitalized then laid up in bed for over six weeks while her organization was forced to struggle without her for that time.

Basically, to prevent this from happening to you, you must do two things:

- Become aware of your body's needs and attend to them as much as possible.

- If you start to breakdown in any way, do something about it immediately.

Believe me, it's a lot easier to cure a little depression than a full breakdown. If for no other reason, take care of yourself for the sake of your business. You really are not doing it any good by sticking it out at your own expense. If you can't function, neither will your company.

Health Horror—This Could Happen to You!

If you are concerned that you may be ignoring your own downward spiral, take a look at the following chart. According to the *Physician's Book of Symptoms and Cures,* here are a few of the most common ailments that afflict entrepreneurs and how they can start.

CAUSE	EFFECT
Stress	• Anxiety
	• High blood pressure
	• Asthma
	• Colitis
	• Insomnia
	• Depression
	• Moodiness
Sleep Deprivation	• Fatigue
	• Fainting

- Flu
- Shaking
- Lack of coordination and attention span
- Dizziness

Lack of Proper Nutrition

- Fatigue
- Fainting
- Disorientation
- Nausea
- Cold
- Flu
- Pneumonia
- Cold sores
- Headaches
- Migraines
- Dramatic weight gain or loss

Lack of Exercise

- Muscle stiffness and knots
- Excess tension in neck and shoulders
- Physical weakness
- Fatigue
- Reduced range of movement
- Lower back pain
- Increased tendency to pull muscles
- Weight gain

Sounds like fun, doesn't it? Does that recurring pain in your back or that splitting headache make any more sense to you now? It really doesn't have to come down to this. You don't deserve it, and neither does your business.

If all this talk of neglecting your health is beginning to concern you, there's a great book you should read called *Overdoing It—How to Slow Down And Take Care of Yourself* by Bryan Robinson, Ph.D. In it, he talks about compulsive overworking and how abusive worka-holic habits can be to a person. One part that is particularly inter-esting is a comparison it makes of the symptoms of work addiction.

PHYSICAL SYMPTOMS	BEHAVIORAL SYMPTOMS
Headaches	Temper outbursts
Fatigue	Restlessness
Allergies	Insomnia
Indigestion	Difficulty relaxing
Stomach aches	Hyperactivity
Ulcers	Irritability & Impatience
Chest pain	Forgetfulness
Shortness of breath	Difficulty concentrating
Nervous tics	Boredom
Dizziness	Mood swings (from euphoria to depression)

Now that your mother isn't here anymore to take care of all of these nasty symptoms you can contract from your work, start thinking about doing some damage control yourself. You don't need these horrible consequences to influence you. After all, you probably have come across plenty of your own. So do what you can while you can. You never know when your next chance will be to relax, recuperate, or even eat like a normal person. Speaking of which . . .

How Not to Starve When You're Broke

If I had a cornflake for every dollar that I've spent on phone bills, I'd be overweight. Instead, I was a business bulimic. When my monthly bills were low, which was rare, I overate. When I couldn't figure out where to get the money to pay my bills, I starved. I know what it's like not to have the money for food. The irony in counting change to eat when you're wearing a four hundred dollar suit is just too twisted.

Just for the record, my family never neglected me financially. Most of the time I was just too embarrassed to tell them that I had run through my money for the month by the eighteenth. From the nineteenth on, life seemed to always get rough. But after living through temporary poverty a few too many times, I learned a few tricks.

MAKE LOTS OF FRIENDS

Remind your friends of all the times that you had extra money and invited them all over for dinner. And if you've never done it, you might want to keep in mind the following phrase: One good turn deserves another. In other words, if you're good to your friends, they'll be good to you. And when you most need them you won't feel so bad about inviting yourself over for dinner.

ENJOY HAPPY HOURS

With a little investigating you should be able to find a few bars that offer free hors d'oeuvres during their "happy hours," usually between 3:00 and 6:00 p.m. during weekdays. (Just remember to order at least one or two drinks so you don't look suspicious and risk being thrown out.) If you can't find free hors d'oeuvres, don't worry. Most places usually have very cheap appetizers—like quesadillas, tacos, or baby cheeseburgers—for a dollar or so. When you find these places, eat up!

STOCK UP ON FOOD WHEN YOU CAN

There's no excuse not to buy an extra box or so of cereal, a couple of jars of pasta sauce, or a freezer full of chicken cutlets while you still can. You will surely use them up eventually, and thank God you kept them in storage. And, as Doug Mellinger (founder of PRT Corp., a $10 million dollar company by the time he was thirty) always said, "You can always go back to living on macaroni and cheese." I still keep a few boxes stashed away for emergencies.

ONE WORD: PASTA

Pasta is probably one of the cheapest, most filling, high-energy foods you can buy. At two bags for a dollar, at times it may be the smartest physiological and financial decision you can make.

GO HOME

If you live close to any family members, starving should give you a good enough incentive to finally pay them a visit. They'll be able to tell if you've been eating or not. (After all, aren't they always the first to comment on how much weight you've put on or how you're getting too thin?) And they'll probably send you back to where you came from with a good stock of leftovers and all of the canned goods you can carry.

Overall, the best thing to do is to plan ahead and stash away some money for these rainy days. Yeah, sure. That's what my father told me every time he bailed me out. I'm still having trouble getting that advice to stick in my brain. But logically, it makes a hell of a lot of sense. Particularly when you're savoring your last pretzel crumb.

Conclusion

TO LEAVE YOU WITH SOME BRIEF WORDS OF WISDOM FROM MY SHORT, YET robust ten-year career as an entrepreneur, I would have to stress these five points. These things, in my opinion, are the most important things that you can do *right now* to improve your chances of success in your own business—whether that time is now or sometime later.

Start Now

There is no better time to start working on your career. Regardless of how young or old you are, if owning a business looks like it's in your cards, take advantage of any extra time you have on your hands to start laying the foundation for a solid business venture. Start reading, researching, and learning more, go out and meet more people, attend business expos and seminars, and start to immerse yourself in the world of entrepreneurship. This book should have given you plenty of things to keep you busy until your company picks up the slack. Don't wait any longer.

Surround Yourself with the Right People

While you can't chose the environment you are raised in, you can choose the environment you live in as an adult. This doesn't necessarily mean moving to any place in particular or singling out specific people to target socially. What it does mean is that you should surround yourself with people who are inspirational, insightful, and supportive of you and your business ventures. This advice cannot be stressed enough! Everyone needs a little push now and then, and entrepreneurs are no exception. Yes, we do tend to be incredibly motivated on our own, but life as a business owner can be tough—and you need to know that your immediate environment will be well suited to the task of comforting and nurturing you during even your toughest times. Your environment will have a serious effect on your ability to succeed in business. So make it the best one possible.

Give Yourself Every Possible Advantage

Along the way to building your empire, you will undoubtedly encounter many opportunities to expand your knowledge, expertise, and perspective. Don't shrug too many of these off because you're "just too busy." Make the time to do the things that will count in the long run. Volunteering for charitable activities is a perfect example. While everyone knows they should be doing something for people less fortunate, few take the time to really do something about it. One important thing that most people fail to realize is that volunteer opportunities are everywhere and come in countless forms. The odds are very good that you can even find a worthwhile cause that coincides with your business, field, expertise, or personal interest. I personally feel that it's every person's—and every company's—responsibility to improve their environment in any way that they can. Take advantage of opportunities like this to do something for others, while increasing awareness for you and your business in the community. Get an extra degree. Attend special seminars. Treat yourself and your business each as a package. Every little thing you can do to improve your quality, content, and image will add up and make you stand out in the long run.

Become an Expert

I've probably said it a million times before, but by now you should understand how vital this is to your credibility in business. The more you know about your field, the more likely people will be to give you the respect that you deserve (particularly when you "look a little young" to know what you're really talking about). Establishing yourself as an expert makes everyone around you more confident about working with you—whether they're your clients, vendors, investors, the media, or even your own employees.

Don't Give Up

You've chosen entrepreneurship as your path, so stick it out. You can always go back to the corporate world if you get too overwhelmed . . . but few return once they've left. No one said it would be easy, but in business only the strong survive. Perseverance is the best measure of this. Through good times and bad you must be able to keep going. If you lose a client, there is always another. If your business should fail, there are always other opportunities. If you run out of money, there is always the section on "How Not to Starve When You're Broke." (It's there for a reason.)

If you really want to, you can find as many reasons as you need to quit your job as the boss and let someone else take over the position. Caving in says that you probably aren't cut out for this type of thing. But if you know better in your heart, have surrounded yourself with the right people, are in the right environment, and have spent the time doing what you need to, you should squeak by just fine. Every entrepreneur in the world has his or her share of war stories. Going through rough times, and living to tell about them, will give you something to be proud of for the rest of your life.

As a young entrepreneur, it is very easy to feel alone. You are very different from others and should be proud of that. Being an entrepreneur means that you will have a personal role in shaping the economy, the job market, the business environment, and the course of your own life. Not many people can say that for themselves.

Take your responsibilities—and your destiny—seriously, and make good things come of them. Entrepreneurs can use their abilities to be very self-serving, or they can use their skills and good fortune to improve their communities and help others achieve their goals. As a part

The Young Entrepreneur's 10 Commandments

1. Choose your area of interest carefully, taking into consideration your greatest talents, weaknesses, and current resources.

2. Become an expert on your industry.

3. Know who the industry leaders are, learn about them and their successes, and meet them personally whenever possible.

4. Find a market niche.

5. Create an impressive professional image for both your business and yourself.

6. Make a name for yourself.

7. Assemble an informal board of advisers.

8. Create a client list.

9. Get your company media attention.

10. Always under-promise and over-deliver.

©1995 Jennifer Kushell, The Young Entrepreneurs Network.

of this "new generation of entrepreneurs," I hope you'll choose the latter. Our reputation is banking on it. This is your world now. With millions of young people today pursuing entrepreneurship, your peers are all around you. So take a closer look. You're not alone anymore.

Resource Guide

Business Associations

Adizes Institute
(310) 471-9677
820 Moraga Drive
Los Angeles, CA 90049

American Association of Fund-Raising Counsels
(212) 354-5799
25 W. 43rd St., Suite 820
New York, NY 10036

American Payroll Association
(212) 686-2030
30 E. 33rd St., 5th Floor
New York, NY 10016

American Small Business Association
(703) 522-2292
(800) 272-2911
1800 N. Kent St., Suite 910
Arlington, VA 22209

Business Council for International Understanding
(212) 490-0460
420 Lexington Ave., Suite 1620
New York, NY 10170

Club Managers Association of America
(703) 739-9500
1733 King St.
Alexandria, VA 22314

Council of Better Business Bureaus Inc.
(703) 276-0100
4200 Wilson Blvd., Suite 800
Arlington, VA 22203

Council of Consulting Organizations
(212) 697-9693
521 Fifth Ave., 35th Floor
New York, NY 10175

Future Business Leaders of America—Phi Beta Lambda Inc.
(703) 860-3334
1912 Association Dr.
Reston, VA 22091

General Federation of Women's Clubs
(202) 347-3168
1734 N. St., NW
Washington, DC 20036

Information Industry Association
(202) 639-8262
New Jersey Ave., NW, Suite 800
Washington, DC 20001

International Association of Business Communicators
(415) 433-3400
1 Hallidie Plaza, Suite 600
San Francisco, CA 94102

International Council for Small Business
(314) 658-3896
3674 Lindell Blvd.
St. Louis, MO 63108

International Trademark Association
(212) 768-9887
1133 Avenue of the Americas
New York, NY 10036

National Association for the Cottage Industry
(312) 472-8116
P.O. Box 14850
Chicago, IL 60606

National Association of Private Enterprise
(817) 428-4236
2121 Precinct Line Rd.
Hurst, TX 76054

National Association for the Self-Employed
(817) 577-0888
(800) 232-6273
2121 Precinct Line Rd., Suite 201
Hurst, TX 76054

National Association of Small Business Investment Companies
(703) 683-1601
1199 N Fairfax St., Suite 200
Alexandria, VA 22314

National Federation of Independent Business
(202) 554-9000
600 Maryland Ave. SW, Suite 700
Washington, DC 20024

National Small Business United
(202) 293-8830
1155 15th St. NW, Suite 710
Washington, DC 20005

Small Business Legislative Council
(202) 639-8500
1156 15th St., NW, Suite 510
Washington, DC 20005

U.S. Council for International Business
(212) 354-4480
1212 Avenue of the Americas, 21st Floor
New York, NY 10036

Youth for Understanding International Exchange
(202) 966-6800
(800) 424-3691
3501 Newark St. NW
Washington, DC 20016

Government Resources

ACE—Active Corps of Executives
(202) 653-6768
Small Business Administration
1441 L St., NW
Washington, DC 20416

Administrative Office of the U.S. Courts
(202) 273-3007
1 Columbus Circle, NE
Washington, DC 20002

Bureau of the Census
(301) 763-4051
Public Information Office
Department of Commerce
Washington, DC 20233

Business Liaison Office
(202) 377-3176
14th St.
Washington, DC 20230

Business Tax Assistance
(800) 424-1040

Bureau of International Labor Affairs
(202) 219-6043
200 Constitution Ave.
Washington, DC 20210

Congressional Research Service
(202) 707-5700
101 Independence Ave., LM 213, SE
Washington, DC 20540

Copyright Office
(202) 707-3000
101 Independence Ave., SE
Washington, DC 20559

Department of Labor
(202) 219-7316
200 Constitution Ave., NW
Washington, DC 20210

Economic Development Administration (EDA)
(202) 377-5113

Environmental Protection Agency (EPA)
(800) 368-5888

Export-Import Bank of the U.S.
(202) 566-8990
811 Vermont Ave., NW
Washington, DC 20571

Federal Emergency Management Agency (FEMA)
(202) 646-4600
500 C St., SW
Federal Center Plaza
Washington, DC 20472

International Trade Administration (ITA)
(202) 377-3808

Interstate Commerce Commission
(202) 275-7597

Internal Revenue Service (IRS)
(202) 622-5164
1111 Constitution Ave., NW
Washington, DC 20224

Legal Services Corp.
(202) 336-8800
750 First St., NE
Washington, DC 20002

Minority Business Development Agency (MBDA)
(202) 482-4547
14th St.
Washington, DC 20230

Neighborhood Reinvestment Corp.
(202) 376-3734
1325 G St., NW
Washington, DC 20005

Office of Exporter Credits and Guarantees
(800) 424-5201

Office of Innovation Research and Technology
(202) 653-6458

Office of the Small Business Ombudsman
401 M St., SW (A-149C)
Washington, DC 20460

Office of Small and Disadvantaged Business Utilities
(202) 482-4547
400 7th St., SW, Room 9410
Washington, DC 20590

Office of Public Assistance
12th St. & Constitution Ave.
Washington, DC 20423

Patent and Trademark Office
(703) 308-4357
Crystal Park
Arlington, VA 22202

Small Business Administration (SBA)
(202) 205-6600
409 3rd St., SW
Washington, DC 20416

SBA FIELD OFFICES:

Region I
(617) 451-2030
155 Federal St., 9th Floor
Boston, MA 02110

Region II
(212) 264-1450
26 Federal Plaza, Room 3100
New York, NY 10278

Region III
(610) 962-3700
475 Allendale Rd., Suite 201
King of Prussia, PA 19406

Region IV
(404) 347-4999
1375 Peachtree St., NE
Atlanta, GA 30367

Region V
(312) 353-5000
300 S. Riverside Plaza, Suite 1975
Chicago, IL 60606

Region VI
(214) 767-7643
8625 King George Dr.,
 Building C
Dallas, TX 75235

Region VII
(816) 426-3316
911 Walnut St., 13th Floor
Kansas City, MO 64106

Region VIII
(303) 294-7186
633 17th St., 7th Floor
Denver, CO 80202

Region IX
(415) 744-6402
71 Stevenson St., 20th Floor
San Francisco, CA 94105

Region X
(206) 553-5676
2615 4th Ave., Suite 440
Seattle, WA 98121

**Small Business Administration
Office of Women's Business
Ownership**
(202) 205-6675
409 3rd St., SW, 6th Floor
Washington, DC

**Small Business Center of the
Chamber of Commerce**
(202) 659-6000

1615 H St., NW
Washington, DC 20062

**Service Core of Retired
Executives (SCORE)**
(202) 653-6768

**Tax Forms & Publications Div.
(IRS)**
(202) 622-5200
1111 Constitution Ave., NW
Washington, DC 20224

Tax Payer Ombudsman
(202) 622-6100
1111 Constitution Ave., NW
Washington, DC 20224

Tax Payer Services Div. (IRS)
(202) 622-4220
1111 Constitution Ave., NW
Washington, DC 20224

U.S. Department of Commerce
(202) 377-3176
14th St.
Washington, DC 20230

U.S. Patent Model Foundation
(703) 684-1836
510 King St., Suite 420
Alexandria, VA 22314

**U.S. Trade & Development
Agency**
(703) 875-4357
1621 N. Kent St.
Arlington, VA 22209

U.S. Claims Court
(202) 219-9697
717 Madison Pl., NW
Washington, DC 20005

U.S. Court of International Trade
(212) 264-2814
1 Federal Plaza
New York, NY 10007

U.S. Tax Court
(202) 606-8754
400 2nd St, NW
Washington, DC 20217

Young Entrepreneurs

An Income of Her Own (AIOHO)
(805) 687-0983
P.O. Box 987
Santa Barbara, CA 93102
Programs: Holds business plan competitions (Due December)

Camp Lemonade Stand
(410) 617-2694
(410) 617-5133 (Fax)
Loyola College
Professional Development
4501 N. Charles St.
Baltimore, MD 21210
Age Range: 7–10

Children's Financial Network (CFN)
70 Tower Hill Rd.
Mountain Lakes, NJ 07046
Products: Books and materials on teaching young people about money, banking, and business

Cities in Schools
(703) 519-8999
(703) 519-7213 (Fax)
1199 N. Fairfax St., #300
Alexandria, VA 22314-1436

Area Served: Nationwide
Age Range: Kindergarten–12th graders
Focus: Teaches business basics to students
Programs: Entrepreneurial training program

Center on Education and Training for Entrepreneurship
(800) 848-4815
(614) 292-1260 (Fax)
Ohio State University
Columbus, OH
Programs: Conferences for young entrepreneurs

Commission for Education Foundation
(213) 892-1402
(213) 892-1582 (Fax)
208 W. 8th St., Suite 602
Los Angeles, CA 90014
Area Served: Los Angeles
Ages: 15–18
Programs: Life skills

Distributive Clubs of America
(703) 860-5000
(703) 860-4013 (Fax)
1908 Association Dr.
Reston, VA 20191
Area Served: National
Age Range: High school and college
Focus: Teaches students entrepreneurship, marketing, and management
Programs: Participate in local, state, and national competitions

Dream Builders, Inc.
(516) 348-2381
Long Island, NY
Focus: Creates educational
coalitions to teach
entrepreneurship in schools

EDGE University
(800) 879-3343
474 W. 238th St., Suite 4B
Riverdale, NY 10463
Area Served: National
Programs: Trains educators
in entrepreneurial teaching
techniques; Entrepreneur
camps

**Entrepreneur Boot Camp
for Teens**
(414) 472-2018
University of Wisconsin,
Whitewater
1018 Carlson
Whitewater, WI 53910
Age Range: 12–16
Focus: Teaches entrepreneurship
and business writing skills
Programs: Residential summer
camp

**Free Enterprise Fund
for Children**
P.O. Box 7665
Newport Beach, CA 92658
Focus: Offers grants to help
young people start their own
businesses

**Future Business Leaders of
America (FBLA)**
(800) 325-2946
(703) 758-0749 (Fax)

Phi Beta Lambda Inc.
1912 Association Dr.
Reston, VA 20191
Area Served: U.S. and Europe
Age Range: Secondary–College
age
Focus: Teaches students
economics and business
basics
Programs: Leadership training
programs

**Future Business Leaders
of America (FBLA)**
(209) 443-5187
3132 Fairmont
Fresno, CA 93726

I Have A Dream
(713) 523-7326
P.O. Box 541183
Houston, TX 77025
Area Served: Houston
Age Range: Children 3rd
grade–High school
Programs: Houston Tree Kids
Project

**Institute for Youth
Entrepreneurship**
(212) 369-3900
(212) 369-5361 (Fax)
E-mail: iyeed@aol.com
310 Lenox Ave.
New York, NY 10027
Area Served: New York
Age Range: 12–16
Programs: Develops
community programs to
help students begin and
run businesses

Inventors Workshop International
(805) 962-5722
7332 Mason Ave.
Canoga Park, CA 91306
Focus: "Creativity in America '95" for young inventors
Programs: 4-day conference & expo at Universal Studios, Hollywood, CA (Oct. 26–29)

Johnson & Wales University (College of Business)
(800) 343-2565
(401) 598-1142 (Fax)
8 Abbott Park Pl.
Providence, RI 02903
Programs: Outstanding High School Entrepreneur Contest—$250,000 in scholarships

Junior Achievement (JA)
(719) 540-8000
(719) 540-6299 (Fax)
E-mail: ETaylor@ja.org
Web Site: http://www.ja.org
One Education Way
Colorado Springs, CO 80906
Area Served: 194 domestic affiliates and nearly 100 countries
Range: Kindergarten–12th grade
Focus: To educate and inspire students to value free enterprise and business economics
Programs: Elementary school program (K–6), middle grades program, high school program

Keepers Holiday Gift Shops
(414) 233-2372
(414) 424-3478 (Fax)
Cooperative Educational Service Agency
No. 6, P.O. Box 2568
2300 State Rd., 44
Oshkosh, WI 54903
Area Served: Wisconsin
Age Range: High school
Focus: Helps students open stores before Christmas

Leading Education Equation (LEE)
(914) 331-3978
(914) 331-3978 (Fax)
11 Esopus Ave.
Kingston, NY 12401
Focus: Teaches business, job, video, and computer skills
Programs: Career training and college preparation programs

Lemonade Kids/Businesship International
(305) 455-8869 (Fax)
One Alhambra Plaza, Suite 1400
Coral Gables, FL 33134

National Association of Classroom Educators in Business Education
(317) 478-3261
(317) 478-3265 (Fax)
Lincoln High School
Cambridge City, IN 47327

National 4-H Council
(301) 961-2800
(301) 961-2894 (Fax)

7100 Connecticut Ave.
Chevy Chase, MD 20815
Area Served: National
Age Range: All
Programs: Sponsors state and
national entrepreneurship
conferences for young people

National Foundation for Teaching Entrepreneurship (NFTE)
(617) 239-4458
(617) 239-5231 (Fax)
NFTE—Babson Partnership
Babson College
Babson Park, MA 02157
Area Served: Inter-city Boston
Age Range: 14–20
Focus: Award program for NFTE
graduates
Programs: Eight business grants
and one Young Entrepreneur
Scholarship to Babson College
awarded

National Foundation for Teaching Entrepreneurship (NFTE)
(617) 232-3333
120 Wall Street
New York, NY 10005
Area: US., London, and
Scotland
Age Range: Teenagers and
preteens
Programs: Mini MBA program,
in-school and out of school
programs

North Dakota Marketplace for Youth
HCO5, Box 107
Mandan, ND 58554

Programs: Annual conference
and trade show for young
entrepreneurs

North Dakota State University
(701) 221-6865
(701) 221-6868 (Fax)
E-mail: ktweeten@ndfuext
.nodak.edu
514 East Thayer Ave.
Bismarck, ND 58501
Area Served: None specified
Age Range: Grades 5–8
Programs: Be Your Own Boss
youth entrepreneurship
curriculum (10 weeks of
lessons)

Oklahoma Department of Vocational & Technical Education
(800) 654-4502
(405) 743-5154 (Fax)
1500 West Seventh Ave.
Stillwater, OK 74074
Area Served: U.S. and all other
countries
Age Range: Grades 6–8
Programs: Curriculum for
teaching marketing and
entrepreneurship

Oklahoma REAL Enterprises, Inc.
P.O. Box 100
Forgan, OK 73938
Focus: Pilot program to teach
entrepreneurship to rural
students
Programs: Uses interactive
television to reach students at
four campuses

One to One of Greater Boston
(617) 695-2430
(617) 695-2435 (Fax)
105 Chauncy St., Suite 300
Boston, MA 02111
Area Served: All greater Boston
Age Range: 12–23
Focus: Works with at-risk youth
to help them succeed in
business/life
Programs: Entrepreneur
Program (Pathway)

**Overcoming Obstacles Center
for Entrepreneurship**
(213) 892-1402
(213) 892-1582 (Fax)
208 W. Eighth St., #602
Los Angeles, CA 90014
Area Served: Los Angeles, Kansas
City, Indianapolis, Atlanta,
and Phoenix
Age Range: 15–18
Focus: Life skills for teenagers
Programs: Offers business loans
for teenagers

Project HOPE + E
(316) 636-1266
(316) 636-1288 (Fax)
PO. Box 782050
Wichita, KS 67278
Area Served: Kansas
Age Range: 5th grade students

St. Louis University
(314) 977-3896
(314) 977-3627 (Fax)
E-mail: bowersk@sluvca.slu.edu
St. Louis, MO 63108
Area Served: U.S.

Age Range: Grades K–12
Programs: Tots to Teen
entrepreneur conferences,
next in '96 Products:
"Resource for Internet"

**The Education Cooperative
(TEC)**
(617) 237-3028
(617) 431-0490 (Fax)
160 Grove St.
Wellesley, MA 02181
Area Served: Massachusetts
Age Range: 3–22
Programs: Special need classes,
School-to-work initiative

**The Entrepreneurial
Development Institute (TEDI)**
(202) 822-8334
(202) 822-5090 (Fax)
E-mail: tedidc@aol.com
Web Site: http://www.tedi.org
2025 I St., NW, Suite 11
Washington, DC 20006
Area Served: 18 U.S. cities
Age Range: 7–21
Focus: Teaches at-risk kids
business basics
Programs: Entrepreneurial
training

**The Meyerhoff Business
Alliance**
(612) 781-6819
(612) 781-0109 (Fax)
2105 Central Ave., NE
Minneapolis, MN 55418
Area Served: Minneapolis
Age Range: Junior and senior
undergraduates

Focus: Helping students learn hands-on how businesses are run
Programs: Provides 9-month paid internships in minority-run businesses

Tomorrow's Entrepreneurs Today
(213) 964-1883
P.O. Box 47442
Los Angeles, CA 90047

University of Illinois
(312) 737-1178
(312) 776-2148 (Fax)
Chicago, IL 60609
Programs: Holds youth entrepreneurship symposiums

USC Business Expansion Network
(213) 743-1726
(213) 746-4587 (Fax)
3375 S. Hoover, Suite A
Los Angeles, CA 90007
Area Served: Los Angeles
Age Range: High school
Programs: Wants to start venture fund for young entrepreneurs

Virginia Cooperative Extension Service
Virginia State University
P.O. Box 9081
Petersburg, VA 23806
Products: Mind Your Own Business Leader's Guide for teaching youth entrepreneurship

West Yellowhead Future Business Development Center
(403) 865-1224
(403) 865-1227 (Fax)
E-mail: wycsdc@ycs.ab.ca
221 Pembina Ave
Hinton, AB, Canada T7V 2B3
Area Served: West Yellowhead Region
Age Range: Elementary and secondary school
Programs: Offers workshops where students create a joint company

Young Entrepreneur Program—University Community Outreach Program
(610) 668-5330
(610) 668-5331 (Fax)
Wharton School of Business
401 City Ave., #204
Bala Cynwyd, PA 19004
Area Served: Wharton School of Business, Pennsylvania; Columbia U., New York; and UC-Berkeley, CA
Age Range: Grades 9–12
Focus: Teaches business development and loan acquisition to inner-city youth
Programs: Pairs students with MBA students

Youth Empowerment & Self-Sufficiency
(609) 342-8277
(609) 963-8110 (Fax)
Education Training & Enterprise Center Inc.

313 Market St.
Camden, NJ 08102
Area Served: Nationwide
Age Range: Grades 6–High
school
Focus: Teaches entrepreneurial
curriculum
Products: Market Street Journal
Program: Training along
curriculum

**Youth Entrepreneur Program
Inc.**
(614) 299-6003
600 Shoemaker Plaza, #2
Columbus, OH 43201
Age Range: Ages 15–23
Focus: Personal development
Programs: Internship program
matches students with
business owners 20 hrs. per
week

College/University
Programs

**Association of Collegiate
Entrepreneurs (ACE)**
Young Business Owners (YBO)
(416) 204-1771
(416) 204-1793 (Fax)
Web Site:
http://www.Hookup.net/
~aeecan
20 Queen St. West, Suite 316
Toronto, Ontario, Canada
M5H3R3
Area Served: University
campuses
Age Range: 18–25
Programs: Chapter-based
education

Canadian Youth Foundation
(613) 231-6474
(613) 231-6497 (Fax)
E-mail: cys@cyberplus.ca
Web Site: http://www.cyberplus
.ca/~cys
215 Cooper St., 3rd Fl.
Toronto, Ontario, Canada
K2P0G2
Area Served: National
Age Range: 15–29
Programs: Research-based

Global Education Partnership
(617) 661-4009
8 Peabody Terrace, Suite 21
Cambridge, MA 02138
Area Served: Africa and U.S.
Focus: Helping U.S. businesses
do business with African
countries

Portland Community College
Small Business Development
Center
(503) 978-5080
(503) 222-2570 (Fax)
Montgomery Park, Suite 499
2701 NW Vaughn St.
Portland, OR 97210
Area Served: Portland metro area
Age Range: Ages 11–15
Focus: Teaches entrepreneurship,
finance, leadership, and
general business skills
Programs: One-week day camp

**Southern California Entre-
preneurship Academy (SCEA)**
(310) 544-4959
(310) 590-8514 (Fax)

Area Served: Southern California
Members/Students: 30/semester,
300 alums
Age Range: 18–30
Focus: Offers young
entrepreneurs introduction to
entrepreneurial corporations
and their founders
Programs: Two semester
programs, each running
approximately 10–12 weeks

For Entrepreneurs

American Entrepreneurs Association (AEA)
(714) 261-2325
(714) 755-4211 (Fax)
P.O. Box 57050
2392 Morse Ave.
Irvine, CA 92714
Area Served: National
Programs: Membership

Center for Entrepreneurial Management (CEM)
(212) 633-0060
(212) 633-0063 (Fax)
E-mail: ceoclub@bway.net
Web Site: http://www.ceoclubs
.org
180 Varick St., Penthouse,
17th Floor
New York, NY 10014
Area Served: International
Age Range: Open
Programs: Membership program
for CEOs

Center for Family Business
(216) 442-0800
(216) 442-0178 (Fax)

P.O. Box 24219
Cleveland, OH 44124
Area Served: National
Age Range: All
Programs: Planning management
for family company

Young Entrepreneurs Network
(310) 822-0261
(310) 822-0361 (Fax)
Web Site: http://www
.yenetwork.com
4712 Admiralty Way, Suite 530
Marina del Rey, CA 90292
Area Served: International (40+
countries)
Members: 300
Age Range: Early teens to early
thirties
Focus: To offer young
entrepreneurs access to the
resources most vital to their
early and long-term success
Products: Visions (a quarterly
mini-magazine) and *The Young
Entrepreneur's Resource Guide*

Invention Marketing Institute
818-246-6540
345 Cypress St.
Glendale, CA 91204

Inventors Clubs of America
(707) 938-5089
P.O. Box 450261
Atlanta, GA 30345

Kauffman Foundation
(816) 932-1000
(816) 932-1430 (Fax)

4900 Oak
Kansas City, MO 64112
Area Served: Kansas area
Age Range: Kindergarten–8th
grade
Focus: Teaches economics and
entrepreneurship
Programs: Mother & Daughter
Entrepreneurs in Teams;
Entrepreneur-Prep Institutes

Let's Talk Business
(212) 742-1553
E-mail: larry@LTBN.com
Web Site: http://www.ltbn.com
54 W. 39th St., 12th Floor
New York, NY 10018
Area Served: National
Age Range: All
Focus: Radio talk show and
entrepreneurial and small
business support

**Minnesota Extension Service
Distribution Center**
University of Minnesota
1420 Eckles Ave.
St. Paul, MN 55108
Focus: Personal assessment,
community assessment, and
business plan writing
Products: Y.E.S. curriculum
guides for teaching youth
entrepreneurship

**National Association For
Business Organizations**
(301) 466-8070
P.O. Box 30149
Baltimore, MD 21270

**National Association for
the Cottage Industry**
(312) 472-8116
P.O. Box 14850
Chicago, IL 60614

**National Association for
the Self-Employed (NASE)**
(800) 232-6273
(817) 428-4210 (Fax)
2121 Precinct Rd.
Hurst, TX 76054

**National Association of Home-
Based Businesses**
(301) 466-8070
P.O. Box 30220
Baltimore, MD 21270

**National Association of Private
Enterprise (NAPE)**
(817) 870-1971 (Fax)
P.O. Box 470397
Ft. Worth, TX 76147

**National Business Incubation
Association (NBIA)**
(614) 593-4331
(614) 593-1996 (Fax)
Web Site: http://www.NBIA
.org
20 East Circle Dr., Suite 190
Athens, OH 45701
Area Served: International
Age Range: All
Programs: Trade Association

**National Foundation of
Independent Business (NFIB)**
(202) 554-9000
(202) 554-0496 (Fax)

600 Maryland Ave., SW,
Suite 700
Washington, DC 20024
Area Served: National
Programs: Young Entrepreneur
Awards—Education
Foundation

Network
(216) 442-5600
(216) 449-3227 (Fax)
5420 Mayfield Rd., Suite 205
Lyndhurst, OH 44124
Area Served: National and
London
Age Range: 23–81

**Shad Valley Canadian Centre
for Creative Technology**
(519) 884-8844
(519) 884-8191 (Fax)
Web Site:
http://www.naviss.com/shad
8 Young St. East
Waterloo, Ontario, Canada N2J
2L3
Age Range: 11th and 12th
graders
Focus: Teaches
entrepreneurship, technology,
and science
Programs: 4-week summer
residential program for
accelerated students

**Small Business Assistance
Center**
(508) 756-3513
(508) 792-3872 (Fax)
554 Main St.
Worcester, MA 01615

Area Served: East Coast
Small Business Foundation of
America
(617) 350-5096
20 Park Plaza, Suite 438
Boston, MA 02116

**Small Business Legislative
Council**
(202) 639-8500
(202) 296-5333 (Fax)
1156 15 Street NW, Suite 1510
Washington, DC 20005
Area Served: Washington area
Ages Range: All

The Entrepreneur Network
(313) 663-8000
1683 Plymouth Rd.
Ann Arbor, MI 48105
Area Served: Great Lakes region
Age Range: Teenagers to
grandparents
Programs: Offers counseling
and advice on running a small
business
Products: Newsletter—$10/year

The Entrepreneur's Source
(203) 575-0085
Waterbury, CT
Focus: Helps people assess
entrepreneurial traits, sets up
in franchises

**United States Junior Chambers
of Commerce (USJCOC)**
(918) 584-2481
(918) 584-4422 (Fax)
Web Site: http://www/sggc.org/
usggc/

P.O. Box 7
4 West 21st St.
Tulsa, OK 74121
Area Served: National
Age Range: 21–39
Programs: Volunteer Senior
 Organization

World Entrepreneurs Society (WES)
(713) 496-4696
(713) 496-6393 (Fax)
14421 Misty Meadow
Houston, TX 77079
Area Served: International
Age Range: 18+
Focus: Non-profit
 organization—promotes
 entrepreneurship and business
 development

Young Entrepreneurs Organization (YEO)
(703) 527-4500
(703) 527-1274 (Fax)
Web Site: http://www.yeo.org
1010 N. Glebe Rd., #625
Arlington, VA 22201
Area Served: International
Age Range: Up to age 35
Focus: Young business owners
 with sales over $1 million
Programs: Entrepreneur
 forums, programs, and
 conferences
Products: Networking Directory

Young Entrepreneurs Spirit (YES)
(506) 386-4259
229 Wedgewood Ave.

Riverview, New Brunswick,
 Canada E1B 2E1
Focus: Women & Minorities

American Business Women's Association (ABWA)
(816) 361-6621
(816) 361-4991 (Fax)
9100 Ward Parkway
P.O. Box 8728
Kansas City, MO 64114
Area Served: National
Age Range: All

Association of African American Women Business Owners
(301) 565-0258
Brasman Research
814 Thayer Ave., Suite 202A
Silver Spring, MD 20910

Brothers for Progress
(718) 622-0805
692 DeGraw St.
Brooklyn, NY 11217

Hispanic Organization of Professionals & Executives
(301) 598-2535
87 Catoctin Court
Silver Spring, MD 20906

Leading Education Equation (LEE)
(914) 331-3978
11 Esopus Ave.
Kingston, NY 12401
Focus: Teaches business, job,
 video, and computer skills
Programs: Career training and
 college preparation programs

National Association of Black Women Entrepreneurs
(810) 356-3686
P.O. Box 1375
Detroit, MI 48231

National Education Center for Women in Business
(800) 632-9248
(412) 834-7131 (Fax)
E-mail: necweb@setonhill.edu
Seton Hall College
Greensburg, PA 15601
Age Range: Girls/10–19
Focus: Teaches entrepreneurship and leadership with computer-simulated programs
Programs: Camp Entrepreneur Scholarship Program (Summer Camp)

National Foundation for Women Business Owners
1377 K St., NW, Suite 637
Washington, DC 20005

National Minority Business Council (NMBC)
(212) 573-2385
(212) 573-4462 (Fax)
235 East 42nd St.
New York, NY 10017
Area Served: NY
Age Range: All

The International Alliance of Executives and Professional Women
(410) 472-4221
8600 LaSalle Rd., Suite 308
Baltimore, MD 21204

US Hispanic Chamber of Commerce
(202) 842-1212
1030 15th St., NW, Suite 206
Washington, DC 20005

General Business Organizations

Business Professionals of America
(614) 895-7277
(614) 895-1165 (Fax)
5454 Cleveland Ave.
Columbus, OH 43231
Area Served: National
Members/Students: 45,000
Age Range: High school students
Focus: Professional organization that advocates entrepreneurship as a career option
Programs: In-school classes

Center for Innovation & Business Development
(701) 777-3122
(701) 777-2339 (Fax)
P.O. Box 8372
University Station
Grand Forks, ND 58202
Area Served: North Dakota
Age Range: All
Products: Publishes guides for writing business and marketing plans

Center for International Private Enterprise
(202) 463-5901
(202) 887-3447 (Fax)

Web Site: http://www.CIPE.org
1615 H St., NW
Washington, DC 20062
Area Served: International
Age Range: All

**International Franchise
Association (IFA) Educational
Foundation, Inc.**
(202) 628-8000
(202) 628-0812 (Fax)
1350 New York Ave., NW,
 Suite 900
Washington, DC 20005
Area Served: International
Age Range: All

**National Business Association
(NBA)**
(800) 456-0440
(214) 960-9149 (Fax)
5151 Beltline Rd., Suite 1150
Dallas, TX 75240
Area Served: National
Members/Students: 30,000
Age Range: All ages
Focus: Helps entrepreneurs
 obtain services and products
 at discounted rates
Programs: Provides discounts
 on insurance, car rentals,
 travel, etc.

National Business League
(202) 829-5900
4324 Georgia Ave., N.W.
Washington, DC 20011
Focus: Encourages minority-
 owned businesses

**National Small Business
Benefits Assoc. (NSBBA)**
(217) 965-3470
2244 N. Grand Ave. E
Springfield, IL 62702

**National Small Business United
(NSBU)**
(800) 345-6728
(202) 872-8543 (Fax)
1156 15th St., NW, Suite 1100
Washington, DC 20005
Area Served: National

**New York Office of Economic
Development**
(212) 306-8643
(212) 306-8644 (Fax)
11 Park Pl., Room 801
New York, NY 10007
Area Served: New York City
Age Range: 14–21
Focus: Helps inner-city youth
 build businesses and obtain
 financing
Programs: Career Readiness
 Entrepreneurial Workshop

**Small Business Advancement
National Center**
(501) 450-5300
(501) 450-5360 (Fax)
University of Central Arkansas
UCA P.O. Box 5018
Conway, AR 72035
Age Range: High school
Programs: One-day youth
 entrepreneurship seminars
 and one-week summer camp

Index

accountants
  for incorporation, 73
  for professional advice, 73–75
Adizes, Ichak, 92–98
administrator, 94
advertising, 164, 172–176
  ad design, 174
  advertising plans, 172–173
  bartering for ad space, 175–176
  bids on, 173
  classified ads, 174
  on the Internet, 178–182
  promotional items, 175
  researching, 173
advertising plan, 59
advice, from mentors, 136
advisers, 73–75, 119, 136–138
  initiating relationships with,
    138–140
advisory boards, 136–138
affiliation, with credible partners,
  13–14
age issues, 156–158
  and alcohol, 158
  and credibility, 156
alcohol consumption, and business in-
  teractions, 158
all-in-one office equipment systems,
  191
Alumni Relations offices, 12

angels, 117
An Income of Her Own, 25
apparel industry, business trends in,
  35
Apple Computers, 9
Association of Collegiate Entrepreneurs, 136
associations, business, 126–129
  lists of, 223–225, 235–240
AT&T, 50

bad credit, recovering from, 76–78
balancing your life, 210–218
bank financing, 117–118
banner advertising, 181
Barsamian, Michelle, 43
bartering, for ad space, 175–176
Big 6 firms, 73–74
board of directors, 70
  versus board of advisers, 137
body language, 147
bottom line, 61
bribes, 132
briefcases, and image, 153
brochures, 160–161
Brush, Candy, 124
Burgeosis, Ben, 126
business associations, 126–129,
  223–225, 235–240
Business Buyer's Guide, 50

business cards, 160
business concept/venture
  foundation for, 219
  knowledge of industry, 44–46
  learning by working, 49
  legally establishing, 67–73
  legal structure of, 56
  personal interests and, 40–41, 43
  researching, 41–42
business credit, 75–78
business encounters, 149–151
  enlivening the conversation,
    150–151
  listening, importance of, 149–150
  names, using, 150
  selling business or service during, 150
business etiquette, 155–156
business ideas
  searching for, 127–128
  selecting one, 36–43
business knowledge, 16, 112–113
business law, 79
business plan, 51–63
  appendices, 62–63
  business background in, 56
  business description, 55–56
  complexity of, 52
  executive summary, 55
  financial information in, 50–62
  gathering information for, 54
  legal structure description, 56
  and level of financing, 52–53
  management plan, 57–59
  market description, 56–57
  marketing and advertising plan, 59
  operations plan, 59
  outline for, 54–55
  personal introductory statement,
    55–56
  product/service description, 56
  resource books on, 63–64
  sales and distribution description,
    59–60
business publications, 153
business relationships, 123–141
  advisers and advisory boards,
    136–140
  meeting people, 126–133
  mentors, 133–136, 138–141
business schools, entrepreneur courses
  at, 24, 25
Business to Business Directory, 50
business trends, 34–36

call waiting, 193
Camp Lemonade Stand, 25
capital
  and C-Corporations, 70
  raising, 33–34, 111–121
Carney, Frank, 4
case studies, usefulness of, 48
cash shortages, disguising, 115–116
C-Corporations, 70
Chambers of Commerce, 127
classified ads, 174
cleanliness, importance of, 154–155
client list, for press kit, 172
Clinkscales, Keith, 130
clubs, 128
COGS (cost of goods sold), 61
Cole, Kenneth, 189
colleges and universities
  contacting, for potential interns, 105
  organizations for entrepreneurial
    students, 127
commercial office space, 184, 185
commissions, 59
communication, between partners, 88
community or student leaders, credi-
    bility of, 14
company literature
  in press kit, 170
  professional image of, 159–162
compensation, description of, 57–59
competition
  knowledge of, 45–48
  sharing business with, 46
  working for, 49
computers, 190
conflict, within management team,
    95–96
consultants, 86
contact management, 132–133
  software for, 196–197
Corporate Lifecycles: How and Why Cor-
    porations Grow and Die and What to
    Do About It (Adizes), 92
corporate career path, 6–9
corporations, 69–72
  hierarchical structure of, 7
costs
  estimating, 114–116
  fixed, 61
  hidden, 55
  of overhead, 61
  start-up, 24, 114–116
  variable, 61

Coupland, Doug, 21
cover letters, evaluating, 107
Covey, Steven, 44
Craig, Conna, 214
creativity, 94, 189
credibility, 145
    and advisory boards, 137–138
    and age, 156
    building, 13–14, 220
    and client lists, 172
credit, 76–78
customer satisfaction, goal of, 47–48

databases, 196–197
day-to-day decisions, guidance for, 136
DBA Statement, 68
Dear, Larry, 35
debt financing, 117
decision-making process, 36–43
    in PAEI system, 96–98
Dell, Michael, 4, 139–140
DeLuca, Fred, 5
DePaul University, 25
Directory of Associations, The, 47, 129
Directory of Directories, The, 47, 129
Disney, Walt, 9
distribution companies, 35–36
distribution system, description of,
    59–60
Domino's Pizza, 94
Drucker, Peter, 91–92

EBIT (earnings before income tax), 61
EDGE/Kids Way, 25
Eisenberg, Michael and Jonathan, 35
e-mail, 177–178
emotional strength, of young entrepre-
    neurs, 11
employees
    biographies of, 57
    compensation of, 57
    costs of hiring, 100
    hiring, 109–110
    tax filing for, 80
    turnover of, and interns, 103
employment, corporate versus self-
    employment, 6–9
entertainment industry, business
    trends in, 34–35
enthusiasm, controlling, 31–32
entrepreneurial personality traits, 205
entrepreneurial training programs,
    24–25

entrepreneurs, young
    advantages of, 9–12
    disadvantages of, 12–21
    educational resources for, 24–25
    health of, 213–218
    lifestyle of, 38–40, 201–218
    list of, 228–235
    personal resources of, 26–27
    role in PAEI system, 94
    10 commandments of, 221
entrepreneurship
    choosing, 5–6
    environmental factors of, 23–25,
        219–220
    study of, 24–25
environment, for entrepreneurs,
    23–25, 219–220
equipment, office, 189–191
equity financing, 117
executive office suites, 184–186
expenses, estimating, 114–116
experience, of young entrepreneurs,
    15–16
expertise, developing, 42–43, 220

failure
    exposure to, 9
    importance of, 203, 206–207
families, unsupportive, 207–209
fax machines, 190
    switches for, 194
fear of unknown, dealing with, 124
feedback
    on job performance, 108
    from mentors, 136
Feller, Paul, 132
financial information, description of,
    60–62
financial loss, 10
financial projections, 113
financial security, and entrepreneur-
    ship, 23
financial software, 196
financing a business, 111–121
    amount needed, determination of,
        114–116
    with angels, 117
    with banks, 117–118
    business plans for, 52–53
    equity or debt, 116–117
    from organizations, 120–121
    SBA loans, 118–119
    with venture capitalists, 119–120

fixed costs, 61
focus, maintaining, 32
food, guaranteeing supply of, 216–218
Forman, Colby, 176
freedom, and entrepreneurship, 7, 212
friends
    maintaining contact with, 203–204
    unsupportive, 209–210

Gately and Associates, 74–75
Gates, Bill, 32
Generation X stigma, 21–22
gifts, for business contacts, 132
goal setting, 41, 44
Gold, Jason, 131
government agencies, 225–228
graphic artists, locating, 159
graphic design software, 197
gross profit, 61
guidance, from mentors, 134–135
Guild, Adam, 36–37

Harris, Lynton, 18
Harvard Business School, case studies
    from, 48
health issues, and entrepreneurship,
    213–218
Hewlett, John, 9
Hewlett Packard, 9
high technology industry, business
    trends in, 34
home businesses, 24, 185, 187
hyperlinking, 179–181

ideas
    generation of, 31–32
    separating good from bad, 32–34
image, 115, 145–162
    and age, 156–158
    business etiquette, 155–156
    and office location, 184
    on paper, 159–162
    personal presentation, 146–152
    physical appearance, 152–156
imitation of competitors, 46
income statement, 60
incorporation, on-line, 72–73
independent contractors, 86, 108–109
    taxes on, 80
industry, chosen
    history of, 45
    study of, 41–42, 46–49, 113
    technical knowledge of, 45
    trends in, 45

industry experts
    as mentors, 135
    rapport with, 45–46
industry organizations, 126–129
    locating, 128–129
industry publications, 48
informational interviews, 12
inquiries, for credit, 77
Institute for Children, The, 214
integrator, 94–95
International Directory of Young En-
    trepreneurs, The, 23, 165
international students, as interns,
    103–104
international trade, business trends in,
    36
Internet
    advertising on, 178–182
    e-mail, 177–178
    marketing on, 176–177
    networking on, 24
    researching industries on, 41
    search engines, 179
    Web sites, 178
interns, 101–108
    advantages of, 103–104
    competence of, 102–103
    feedback for, 108
    goals of, 102
    interviewing, 105–107
    job titles for, 107
    locating, 104–105
    responsibilities for, 108
    retaining, 107–108
interviewing, strategies for, 105–107
investors, and business plan, 51–53
Investors Workshop International, 25
IRS (Internal Revenue Service), 79
isolation, of young entrepreneurs, 17–19

job descriptions, 58
    for interns, 104
job market, 6
job security, 7
Jobs, Steve, 9, 19
job titles, 107
Johnson O'Conner Research Center, 37
Junior Achievement, 25
Junior Chambers of Commerce, 127

Kane, Jonathan, 157–158
Kao, Al, 123–124
Katzman, John, 133–134
Kauffman Foundation, The, 23

Kay, Mary, 32
Kenneth Cole Productions, 189
KIDZ IN BIZ, 25
Kinko's, 4
Kirshenbaum, Richard, 6
Kraft, Peter, 93
K.T.'s Kitchen, 1
Kyan, Benjamin, 203

laser printers, 190
lawyers
    for incorporation, 72–73
    for partnership agreements, 90
    for professional advice, 73–75
leadership skills, 19–20
learning environment, establishment
    of, 96
legal structure of business, 56, 68–72
letterhead, 160
letters, to establish contact, 132
Lexis/Nexus system, 41
liability, and business structure, 68–70
lifecycles, of corporations, 92
Limited Liability Company (LLC), 71
lines of credit, 118
linking, 179–181
Link—The College Magazine, 93
loans
    from banks, 117–118
    from SBA, 118–119
logo, 159–160
loneliness, of young entrepreneurs,
    17–19

mailing labels, 161–162
management plan, 57–59
management team, 91–98
    conflict within, 95–96
    decision-making process of, 96–98
    interaction among members, 96–97
    PAEI method, 93–95
    purpose of, 96
Mariotti, Steve, 25, 151
marketing, on the Internet, 176–182
marketing description, 56–57
marketing plan, 59
market segmentation grid, 56–57
market surveys, 48–49
maturity, of young entrepreneurs,
    14–15, 203–204
Meadows, David, 203
media
    attention of, 163–164, 166–169
    power of, 163

media calendar, 168–169
media contacts, establishing and main-
    taining, 167–172
media kits, 167, 170–172
media list, 167–168
Meenan, C. J., 139
meeting people, 129–133, 138–140
    contact management, 132–133
    in their element, 132
    out of their element, 130–132
    personal introductions, 130
    via letters and gifts, 132
Mellinger, Doug, 12, 13, 15, 136, 217
Mendelson, Scott, 124
mentors, 133–136
    finding one, 140–141
    initiating relationship with, 138–140
minority business owners, loans for, 119
minority/stockholder relationship, 86
Mohajer, Dineh, 4
motivation of young entrepreneurs,
    20–21, 40, 204–206, 219–220
multilevel marketing, business trends
    in, 35–36

*National Directory of Addresses and
    Phone Numbers, The*, 50
National Foundation for Teaching En-
    trepreneurship (NFTE), 25, 139–140
National Shopper's Guide, The, 50
NEBS, 161
negotiating, strategies for, 176
Neimann, Chris, 155
net profit, 61
networking, 12, 133. See business rela-
    tionships
    electronically, 24
non-competition agreements, 49
    in partnership agreements, 89–90
non-profit corporation, 71, 73
NYNEX, 50

obsession, 31
offering circulars, 52
Office Perfect, 131
office space, 183–198
    equipment and supplies for,
        189–191, 197–198
    location of, 184–189
    telephone system for, 191–194
    virtual offices, 194–197
One to One, 25
operating costs, estimating, 114–116
Orfalea, Paul, 4

organizations, funding from, 120–121
originality, 33
*Overdoing It—How to Slow Down and
Take Care of Yourself* (Robinson),
215
overeagerness, 17
overhead expenses, 61
and staffing, 100
overworking, 211–212

Pacific Bell, 50
Packard, David, 9
PAEI system, 93–95
Paper Direct, 160
partnership agreement, 69, 89–90
partnerships, 69, 72
advantages of, 83–84
breaking up, 90
considerations of, 86–88
disadvantages of, 84–85
options for, 85–86
partnership agreement for, 69, 89–90
Peabody, Bo, 125–126
Pearlman, Ron, 96
peers, network of, 204–206
pens, and image, 153–154
performer, 94
perseverance, 15, 221
personal biography, in press kit, 171
personal guarantee, for loans, 118
personal hygiene, and business image,
154–155
personal income tax, 80
personal interests, 32–33
business opportunities with, 40–41,
43
personal introductions, 130, 135–136
personal meetings
animation for, 147–148
arguments, appropriateness of, 149
conversation skills for, 148–149
personal presentation, 146–152
phone conversations
etiquette for, 147
planning for, 146–147
recording, 78, 146
taking notes from, 147
photocopy machine, 190–191
photographs, in press kit, 172
physical appearance, 152–155
and age, 158
physical strength, of young entrepreneurs, 11

Pizza Hut, 4
Polenz, Joanna, 205
presentation materials, 159–162
president/vice president relationship,
86
press articles, in press kit, 171
press kits, 170–172
press releases, 170–171
product description, in business plan,
56
professional advisers, 73–75
venture capitalists as, 119
profit before tax, 61
profit or loss from business report, 80
promotional items, 175
ProSports International, 132
publicity, 164–172
public relations, 164–172
public speaking skills, 146
pyramid companies, 35–36

record keeping, 78
Reddenbacher, Orville, 32
resources, 12, 49–50
personal inventory of, 26–27
respect, mutual, within management
team, 96
resumes, evaluating, 107
revenues, 61
Ring Mate service, 193–194
risk taking, 10
rounds of financing, 70

sales, 59–61
Schain, Devin, 55
S-Corporations, 71
search engines, 179
Seitz, Don, 5–6
self-employment, 6–9. *See also* entrepreneurship
self-employment tax, 80
services, description of, 56
*Seven Habits of Highly Effective People,
The* (Covey), 44
shared office space, 185, 187
shareholders, 70
skeptics, dealing with, 202–203,
207–210
Small Business Association (SBA)
field offices of, 226–227
loans from, 118–119
tax advice from, 79
Small Business Success, 50

Smart Resource Center, 50
Sock and Roll, 5–6
software, 196–197
sole proprietorships, 68–69, 72
Soleymani, Eddie, 130
Southern California Entrepreneurship
    Association, 132
Sozzi, Ray, 13–14
sponsorships, on-line, 181–182
spreadsheets, 115, 196
staffing, 99–110
    costs of employees, 100
    employees, 109–110
    independent contractors, 108–109
    interns, 101–108
start-up costs
    estimating, 114–116
    and virtual storefronts, 24
strangers, speaking to, 123–124
strategic planning, 44
Student Advantage, 14
subleased office space, 185, 186
Submit It, 179
Subway, 5
supplies, office, 159–162, 189–191
surveys, of target market, 48–49
Swatzenbarg, Barry, 131

Taggeris, Kathy, 5, 11
Taxes, 61, 79–81
    and C-Corporations, 70–71
    and non-profit corporations, 71
technical knowledge, 45
technology, and entrepreneurship, 23
technology industry, business trends
    in, 34
telecommuters, 24
telephone systems, 191–194
    business versus personal lines,
        191–192
    call waiting, 193
    fax line/switches, 194
    Ring Mate, 193–194
    voice mail, 192–193
textbook, customized, 41–42
Think and Grow Rich (Hill), 209
TK MAB, 35
Toastmasters, 146
trade associations, 128
trade journals, 48

trade shows, 139
trends in businesses, 34–36, 45
Tripod, 125–126
Turner, Ted, 33–34, 96

Uddo, Eleanor, 75
universities
    contacting for potential interns,
        105
    organizations for entrepreneurial
        students at, 127
University of Arizona, 25
University of California Los Angeles
    (UCLA), 25
University of Pennsylvania (Wharton
    School of Business), 25
University of Southern California
    (USC), 25

variable costs, 61
venture capitalists (VCs), 119–120
    and business plans, 52
venture networks, 52–53
verbal presentation, 146–151
    at business encounters, 149–151
    phone conversations, 146–147
    redundancy, avoiding, 151–152
    social interactions, 147–149
Video College Tours, 133–134
virtual offices, 24, 184–185, 194–197
vision, 33
voice mail, 192–193
volunteer opportunities, 220

Wall Street Journal, 153
Walsh, Kimberly, 10
Watson, Tom, 138
web sites, 178
    positioning of, 179–182
Wolfgang Puck's Gourmet Pizza, 5
word processing, 196
women, SBA loans for, 119
working from home, 24, 184–187
Wozniac, Steve, 9
wristwatches, and image, 154

Young Entrepreneurs Network, The,
    127
    media focus on, 163–164
    Web site of, 19

About the Author

Jennifer Kushell is the president and founder of the Young Entrepreneurs Network, a support organization and on-line community for young entrepreneurs from over forty countries. Jennifer started her entrepreneurial career at the age of thirteen, and by the time she was eighteen had begun teaching classes in entrepreneurship. To date, Jennifer has received several national awards, including the Young Entrepreneur of the Year Award from the U.S. Association of Small Business and Entrepreneurship, and from the National Federation of Independent Business. In addition, she heads a thriving consulting practice, continues to teach, write, and lecture, and sits on the advisory boards of the National Foundation for Teaching Entrepreneurship and the National Mentoring Coalition.

At the age of twenty-six, Jennifer is regarded as one of the leading experts in youth entrepreneurship and has been called the "guru" of her generation's entrepreneurship movement by *U.S. News and World Report*. She and her company have also been featured on CNN, CNNfn, CNBC, and Fox News, and have appeared in such publications as the *Wall Street Journal, Business Week, Elle, Entrepreneur, Success* and the *Los Angeles Times*. Jennifer's professional goal is to create "the number-one resource for young entrepreneurs" and to make the Young Entrepreneurs Network the first place people turn to for help in starting their earliest ventures. Her personal goal is simply to make life easier for the millions of young entrepreneurs who struggled the way she did because they lacked the resources so vital to their success.

Jennifer Kushell
The Young Entrepreneurs Network
4712 Admiralty Way, Suite 530
Marina del Rey, CA 90292
(310) 822-0261
(310) 822-0361 (Fax)
www.youngandsuccessful.com

WHERE DO I GO FROM HERE?

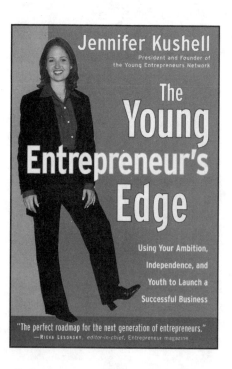

"The perfect roadmap for the next generation of entrepreneurs."
—RIEVA LESONSKY, *editor-in-chief*, Entrepreneur *magazine*

Available at bookstores everywhere.